IRAQ

IRAQ

A Tribute to Britain's Fallen Heroes

MARK NICOL

MAINSTREAM
PUBLISHING

EDINBURGH AND LONDON

First published in Great Britain in 2008 by
MAINSTREAM PUBLISHING COMPANY
(EDINBURGH) LTD
7 Albany Street
Edinburgh EH1 3UG

ISBN 9781845964078

A catalogue record for this book is available
from the British Library

Typeset in Caslon and Requiem

Printed in Great Britain by
Clays Ltd, St Ives plc

Acknowledgements

B oard of Inquiry reports, testimonies of service personnel, both to me and as witnesses before coroner's inquests, Ministry of Defence documents, media reports and my own investigations provide the basis for this account. I have sought both to pay tribute and to give readers a flavour of life in Iraq, as experienced by deceased and surviving military personnel. I have interviewed in excess of 100 veterans of Operation Telic and spent hundreds of hours in the company of those who lost sons and daughters, brothers and sisters, and husbands and wives on this operation. I thank them for their time and their honesty. I have also visited Basra and Maysan.

More personally, thanks go to my family, friends, Jonathan Mantle, Andrew Lownie and, at Mainstream Publishing, Bill Campbell and Paul Murphy.

Contents

Fear no more the heat of the sun,
Nor the furious winter's rages;
Thou thy worldly task hast done,
Home art gone, and ta'en thy wages;
Golden lads and girls all must,
As chimney-sweepers come to dust.

'Song' from *Cymbeline*
by William Shakespeare

Introduction

This was a war of choice, not necessity, and one which exposed our foreign policy as shackled to that of the United States. While a most bloody dictator was removed, his much vaunted weapons of mass destruction proved mythical. Perhaps the British people will never trust their government again.

To date, this choice has cost 176 British service personnel their lives. Let us remember their lives as lost, not wasted – that they answered the call of duty undaunted and achieved much against near impossible odds.

Mistakes were made in the post-invasion period, and the death of Baha Mousa in British custody was an unforgivable episode. However, neither it nor other isolated incidents of abuse of Iraqi civilians should shroud the incredible work done by British troops to reconstruct a region so deprived by Saddam Hussein.

Iraq is moving gradually towards political stability. The southern city of Basra, where so many British soldiers died, is spoken of as a future 'new Dubai', while across central Iraq al-Qaeda and foreign fighters have been forced out of villages and towns. Critics said Iraqis would never take to democracy, yet millions have participated in provincial and national elections. At the risk of becoming a hostage to tragic fortune, their country no longer appears in imminent danger of fragmentation along religious fault lines or of descent into anarchy. All those who served on Operation Telic contributed to this improved situation, which one hopes will benefit Britain in the long term.

To paraphrase Dr Johnson, we live in an era when no longer do men think meanly of themselves for not having been a soldier. Let us not live in an era when the sacrifices of those who fight and die in our name are forgotten, or their memories tarnished by political controversy. Hence, this book is dedicated to those British soldiers, sailors, airmen and airwomen who lost their lives in Iraq. I will make a donation to the service charity Help For Heroes from any royalties accruing from this book.

Mark Nicol
London, August 2008

2003

21 March 2003

Northern Kuwait

Colour Sergeant John Cecil, Lance Bombardier Llywelyn Evans, Captain Philip Guy, Marine Sholto Hedenskog, Sergeant Les Hehir, Operator Mechanic Ian Seymour, Warrant Officer Class 2 Mark Stratford, Major Jason Ward

'I am genuinely very well. I really want both of you to know that. I am not putting up a brave face. All is good here.'

Major Jason Ward, 3 Commando Brigade

After two months in the desert, Major Ward wrote home that he missed baked beans. To the officer, they tasted like caviar, and he asked his parents to post some tins. As he prepared for the helicopter-borne assault of the al-Faw Peninsula – The Royal Marines' opening gambit of the campaign – he also stressed how proud he was at the prospect of leading his troops. 'Wardie' wanted the job done so that he could devote his summer to sailing. As his letters mentioned, he and the quartermaster were running a book on the date of their return to Devon. He stood to win 50 bottles of champagne if that day was 5 May 2003.

The 34 year old was doubtless a little nervous about what lay ahead. There had also been a change of plan. The original idea had been for British forces to enter Iraq from the north through the Kurdish region of Turkey. Under public pressure, the moderate Islamic government of Turkey had withdrawn its offer of support and passage through its territory. The USA and UK had been forced into a last-minute change of tack.

The perceived wisdom ran that the peninsula's key installations were heavily mined and its oil and gas terminals primed for sabotage. The goal was to secure these before fleeing Iraqi troops poured a fortune's worth of crude oil into the Gulf and set the wells alight – thick black smoke would be hazardous for the coalition force's pilots. Like chief of the defence staff, Admiral Sir Michael Boyce, Major Ward considered the actions on which he was about to embark just and lawful: he had told his family that the mission was the right thing to do.

One of Major Ward's close colleagues was distracted by events at home. Captain Philip Guy hoped to return to North Yorkshire for the birth of his second child. His wife Helen was heavily pregnant.

Before his pre-war Oval Office address, President Bush 'fist-pumped' the air and shouted, 'I feel good!' US naval officer Faris Farwell quoted his commander-in-chief's words moments before he achieved the notoriety of firing the opening salvo of the war: 'We will not falter. We will not tire. We will not fail. Following 9/11, gentlemen and ladies, you have not faltered or tired, and we will not fail. God bless the USS *Bunker Hill*. God bless America.'

At 0515 on 20 March 2003, Captain Farwell reached to his left to turn a key. When a tiny green light came on, he gave the final order: 'Batteries release'. His fellow sailors danced in celebration as a $600,000 Tomahawk missile rose up over the slate-grey Persian Gulf in a low arc and sped north.

While the insertion of 40 Commando, Royal Marines, was tasked to 845 Royal Naval Air Squadron, the transportation of 42 Commando was entrusted to the United States Marine Corps. Planning for both lifts began on 12 February 2003 and was followed by two day and two night exercises in northern Kuwait. An assessment of ground conditions and enemy movements was based upon intelligence provided by 849 Royal Naval Air Squadron. Final mission briefings began on 19 March 2003. At 1230 the following day, Major Ward and Captain Guy were flown by a US Sea Knight from Ali al-Saleem Airbase to Pick-up Zone Swallow.

The twin-rotor Sea Knight was the workhorse of the American fleet, a flying bus designed more than 40 years previously and used in Vietnam. In 2002, all 291 Sea Knights had been grounded after a crack was discovered in a rotor blade. Late on 21 March 2003, restless Royal Marines passed the time by squeezing additional personal equipment, ammunition and weaponry into bergens and slapping camouflage cream onto their faces. The steam of their breath was visible as they queued to emplane pilot Captain Aubin's aircraft. The significance of the mission would not be lost on Major Ward and Captain Guy. Their comrades already ashore needed a screen to protect their flank. The plan was for the Sea Knights to land at multiple landing zones while US Cobra gunships provided air support.

Lance Bombardier Llewelyn Evans and Sapper Lee Evans belonged to 29 Commando Regiment, Royal Engineers. When Captain Aubin's helicopter reached its weight capacity, the brothers from Llandudno, North Wales, were separated and Sapper Evans directed towards another helicopter with fewer passengers aboard.

Meanwhile, back at Aubin's helicopter, Royal Marines Warrant Officer Mark Stratford and Colour Sergeant John Cecil counted almost four decades' service to the corps between them, while Marine Sholto Hedenskog, from Cape Town, South Africa, had won his green beret in November 2000. According to his family, Sergeant Cecil, who grew up in Tyne and Wear, never forgot his North East roots and remained a proud Geordie. Known to colleagues as 'Sonic', Marine Hedenskog was fulfilling a lifelong dream. His mother and father thought it remarkable how he laughed in the face of danger and how relaxed he was as he prepared for war. Sergeant Hehir, a 34 year old from Poole, Dorset, was a married father of two boys. Operator Mechanic Seymour, a 29 year old from Deeping St Nicholas, Lincolnshire, had fought back from a serious knee injury to be passed fit for deployment. The eight shouldered huge packs as they clambered inside the humid cargo hold, and shortly afterwards Aubin – call-sign Dash 3 – was cleared for take-off. Buffeted by strong winds, his helicopter began transition lift.

When a technical problem forced one of the US Huey helicopters carrying the mission commanders to return to base, the operation was delayed. Nerves were frayed. As Captain Aubin flew towards Turning Point Buffalo, a plot of airspace six miles south of the Iraqi border, without warning or pre-emptive distress signs his helicopter dipped violently then plummeted hundreds of feet, hit the ground and burst into flames. The moment was captured by a Fox News crew travelling in the same formation.

Captain Aubin's mother, Nancy Chamberlain, watched the footage shortly afterwards at home in Winslow, Maine. Although she was unaware that her son was aboard, she later said that the pictures had given her a bad feeling. While a US investigation suggested that her son suffered a fatal 'spatial disorientation', which led directly to the crash, a Royal Marines board of inquiry blamed technical failure. In what would become routine practice, the US military withheld classified information from Oxford coroner Andrew Walker. His conclusions were based upon the redacted report also given to next of kin, material that failed to substantiate a case against the pilot. Walker said, 'The aircraft was flying at low altitude in straight, level flight when a runaway [a mechanical fault] in both the differential air speed hold actuators [components within the helicopter] caused the aircraft to lose control and strike the ground.' No black box recorder was recovered.

The death of eight 3 Commando Brigade remains the second-largest single loss of British life in Iraq. Stonehouse Barracks, Plymouth, became the focus for grief, with a bottle of Newcastle Brown Ale placed alongside the bouquets. A note written by Sergeant Cecil's widow Wendy read, 'Dear John, I love you so much. This drink is on me (makes a change). Thinking of you always. Lots of love, Wendy.'

His daughter Paige added, 'I love you so much, and I am missing you. I wish you were here, and I wish you'd come back to me. I don't want to go to school.'

Sergeant Cecil's mother, Ann Nichol, said that it was not just her son who was lost, but one of the country's sons. Major Ward's family said that he was the 'epitome of a Royal Marine', a man respected and revered by those who knew him. He revelled in his job and would not have swapped his place on board the fated helicopter with anyone. They said in a family statement, 'He always cared for the man in the uniform rather than his rank. He was always prepared to say if he thought things were wrong, sometimes at personal cost. We will miss him terribly. Once again, he had volunteered for active service in a far-flung corner of the globe, where in his selfless style he did his part for Queen and country. We've received condolences from every continent. The message is the same: Jason was a truly amazing man, an inspirational leader, dedicated professional and a best friend.'

Captain Guy was described as a loving husband and a man as honest as he was brave. All he had wanted was to be a good husband and a good father. Two weeks after the crash, Helen gave birth to Emily Catherine Guy at Airedale Hospital, Skipton, a sister to their young son Henry. Captain Guy's funeral took place in the church where they had been married three years earlier. Locals lined the streets in silence as a party of Royal Marines carried his coffin, draped in a Union Jack, shoulder-high. His friend Captain Daniel Hughes told mourners, 'Phil's legacy is all around: in his wife and children, in his family and friends, in the people who he worked with. He touched a great many lives, and all those he touched will remember him with fondness. Phil was the best kind of friend a person could ask for: dependable, generous, funny, and as a husband and a dad he was hugely loving and compassionate. I will miss him, as I know we all will, but I am confident that his memory will be kept strong and will keep him close to us.'

The families of Warrant Officer Stratford, Lance Bombardier Evans and Marine Hedenskog were proud that their sons, brothers and nephews had died heroes. As the first fatalities of Operation Telic, their deaths were not tainted by the bitterness and anger that marked the passing of so many who died later. They had perished serving a brigade they loved and for a cause in which they believed. Lance Bombardier Evans's father Gordon said, 'On behalf of my whole family, I wish to say that we are all devastated by the loss of our son. While we are deeply saddened, we are, and always will be, proud of him. We would like to thank all of the family, friends and local people for their flowers and messages of support. These have given us great strength.'

Marine Hedenskog's uncle Bruce added, 'He loved the adventure. This was his goal, and he achieved it. He told us he knew what he was doing and he understood the consequences. If something should happen, we were to remember that it was his dream to be a Royal Marine. It is tragic and senseless, but who can make head nor tail of war? He was so happy in what he was doing and so proud. At least he died in the place he wanted to be.'

Operator Mechanic Seymour lived with his wife Lainne and son Beck, whose note attached to a floral tribute laid in his honour read, 'Daddy, I love you loads. So does Mummy. We will miss you always. Lots of love from your baby bear and Tinkerbell.'

His father-in-law Geoffrey Granville, from Plymouth, said, 'He was a fine lad. All we know is that we've lost a son-in-law. He was just great. We miss him already. He was a guy who was full of life. He was a brilliant son-in-law. His son Beck was the be-all and end-all to Ian. He was very proud when he got his green beret. He was a great guy. I am proud of him.'

Sergeant Hehir was survived by a wife and two sons. His widow Sharon said, 'This is the worst blow imaginable. In addition to being an outstanding and highly regarded soldier, Les was an extremely loving and devoted husband, father and son. The loss we feel is really too much to bear. We lived for each other and our two wonderful boys.'

❖ ❖ ❖

Recrimination came at their inquests four years later, by which time the justification for the war had been the subject of fervent protests. The eight were killed during the first twenty-four hours of operations inside Iraq. As military spokespersons stressed, the peninsula and the port of Umm Qasr were captured with minimal resistance and at a lesser human cost than anticipated.

22 March 2003

Persian Gulf

Lieutenant Philip Green, Lieutenant Antony King,
Lieutenant Marc Lawrence, Lieutenant Philip West,
Lieutenant James Williams, Lieutenant Andrew Wilson

HMS *Ark Royal* led the British naval fleet. The fifth vessel
to carry the name of Sir Walter Raleigh's 55-gun ship, the
latest incarnation served as a mobile airstrip and command-and-
control centre. Helicopters including the Sea King Airborne
Surveillance Mk7s of 849 Squadron replaced fixed-wing aircraft
aboard the 20,000-ton carrier, while the absence of an air or sea
threat permitted Captain Alan Massey to continue peacetime
sleep arrangements for his 800 crew. Tiredness led to mistakes,
as he stressed: 'Safety is a huge priority for us, otherwise you
lose aircraft, you lose crews and you fail the mission.'

In the Pacific from 1943 to 1945, 849 Squadron had served
in an early warning and surveillance capacity to counter the
kamikaze threat and resumed its role from 1952 to 1978. The
decision to stand down the squadron left the fleet exposed in the
South Atlantic four years on. The sinking of the HMS *Sheffield*
during the Falklands War prompted the immediate conversion
of two naval helicopters to carry Thorn EMI Searchwater long-
range radar systems – a task completed in just 90 days. Eight
helicopters were subsequently kitted out for reconnaissance
and surveillance, while the squadron found a home at RNAS
Culdrose, Cornwall. By 2003, 849 Squadron's Sea King Mk7s
were equipped with an updated version of Searchwater, capable
of long-range detection of surface and air targets, and the
squadron were commended for their ability to integrate with
amphibious forces during three full-scale exercises off the coasts
of Cyprus, Bahrain and the North Arabian Gulf.

The squadron's pilots were among the Royal Navy's best.
Lieutenant Andrew Wilson, from Exeter, had joined the
squadron in 2000, and his 'powerful personality' and 'humorous
devilment' left its mark on those with whom he flew. He was

married to Sarah. Grammar-school boy Lieutenant Philip Green, from Caythorpe, Lincolnshire, had begun flying with Oxford University Air Squadron, while Lieutenant Antony King, from Somerset, had joined the Royal Navy aged 19 and trained as a Sea King observer. This was his second Gulf War. Lieutenant King met his wife Sarah when he was just four years old. The childhood sweethearts married at their parish church in 1994. In spite of his impending promotion to lieutenant commander, this was to be Lieutenant King's last operational tour, as he wanted to spend more time with his wife and their children, David, five, and Molly, four. For his efforts to enhance surveillance-gathering effectiveness, Lieutenant King had already been recommended to receive a Mention in Dispatches.

As a child, Lieutenant Marc Lawrence, from Westgate-on-Sea, Kent, was more interested in playing the euphonium than joining the Royal Navy. He toured Poland, Czechoslovakia and Germany with the Thanet Youth Concert Band before helicopters distracted him. Lieutenant James Williams had joined 849 Squadron two months before the war began.

Pilots and navigators from 849 Squadron were arranged into seven permanent crews. In the first seventy-two hours of land operations, the crews were required to fly three-hour sorties, including a thirty-minute airborne handover time. Each flew at least once a day, with three crews flying two daily sorties. A typical routine consisted of eight hours on watch – including three hours in the air – followed by ten hours of undisturbed rest.

At around 0400 on 22 March 2003, *Red Rat 34*, piloted by Lieutenant Wilson and crewed by Lieutenant Lawrence and Lieutenant West, began its return flight to HMS Ark Royal after a successful surveillance sortie. It was intended that *Red Rat 35*, piloted by Lieutenant Green and crewed by Lieutenant King, Lieutenant Williams and Lieutenant Thomas Adams, a US Navy officer, would relieve *Red Rat 34* over the operational area to ensure seamless coverage. However, a 'NO GO' technical problem discovered during routine pre-flight checks grounded *Red Rat 35* for 22 minutes. *Red Rat 35* took off from HMS *Ark Royal* as *Red Rat 34* was on its approach – no inbound or outbound flying lanes were in force in the ship's vicinity.

The morning was hazy, with little cloud cover over a low sea state and a 78 per cent moon. The flat sea blended imperceptibly into the sky, obscuring the natural horizon and producing a potentially disorientating effect. Neither pilot was equipped with night-vision aids, while HMS *Ark Royal* was operating on 'reduced and deceptive' wartime lighting. *Red Rat 34* and *Red Rat 35* also apparently put their radars in standby mode; later, a defect was suspected.

Lieutenant Alistair Dale was the duty air traffic controller aboard HMS *Ark Royal* as *Red Rat 35* was dispatched and *Red Rat 34* inbound. An inquest, delayed for four years, heard a conversation between the pilots and the mother ship: 'We are ready to return to mother,' radioed Lieutenant Wilson.

Lieutenant Dale identified *Red Rat 34* on his radar screen as *Red Rat 35* confirmed its take-off. As the Sea King Mk7s closed to two and a half nautical miles of each other, Lieutenant Dale warned each crew: 'Playmate twelve o'clock and two and a half miles.'

'Visual,' responded *Red Rat 34*.

'Visual,' responded *Red Rat 35*.

Lieutenant Dale knew that his radar screen often presented a distorted picture of events: aircraft that appeared locked on a collision course according to his display passed one another at a safe distance. So, on this occasion, he remained calm, in spite of the red flashing lights. He estimated the pilots had one minute of flying time in which to execute a simple and quick corrective manoeuvre.

Lieutenant Dale watched as the flashing shapes continued to close. When Lieutenant Wilson radioed again, it was said that he sounded anxious: 'This is *Red Rat 34*. Where my playmate is now, please?'

At 0425, the lookout aboard HMS *Ark Royal* reported 'a huge ball of orange fire' dropping two hundred feet above sea level, five miles off ship. The destroyer HMS *Liverpool* dispatched a rescue party, but when Lynx pilot Lieutenant Mark Campbell scanned the waters, all he saw was debris. The minesweeper HMS *Brocklesby* and the USS *Dextrous* joined the search for survivors and attempts to salvage the aircraft, black box flight recorders and weapon systems. Enemy action was ruled out, and Royal Navy spokespersons dismissed suggestions of mechanical failure. Captain Massey said that his ship's safety and maintenance procedures were of the 'highest standards', while pilots who flew the fated helicopters in the previous 24 hours said that they had seemed in good working order. As the two Sea King Mk7s represented 50 per cent of the surveillance flight, the crash dealt a weighty blow to the UK intelligence-gathering effort.

Divers pulled all but one of the dead from the water. The failure to recover Lieutenant Lawrence's body for 73 days compounded his family's grief, which hardened to anger with the passing of time. When his mother and father, Ann and George, wrote to Tony Blair, he responded with a two-page handwritten letter, insisting that US and British forces would find definitive proof of Saddam Hussein's chemical and biological arsenal. Blair also acknowledged their son's sacrifice, which he hoped would be recognised in the future 'as being made to defeat the criminal threat to our security in the modern world'.

When Lieutenant Lawrence's former music teacher, Keith Woodger, watched television footage of a memorial service aboard HMS *Ark Royal* and saw an empty chair with an upturned euphonium resting upon it, he broke down in tears. Lieutenant Lawrence was a 'wonderful lad and a talented musician', said Mr Woodger, who set about planning a concert at Chatham House in his honour. Lieutenant Lawrence had been planning to marry his fiancée Elaine Cleaver in 2004 and settle in Cornwall. She said that he had stolen her heart when they first met.

Lieutenant Philip West had also intended to marry. Nicky was a nurse at Treliske Hospital, Cornwall. They had been converting a barn together before his deployment.

After the accidental loss of fourteen British service personnel in two days, forces chiefs needed to strike a balance between mourning and focusing on mission-critical tasks. Group Captain Al Lockwood stressed, 'Sadly, last night something was not quite right, and we are looking to find out what that was as quickly as possible. There is a sense of deep shock and extremely deep sadness. We knew these people. They were our friends, our colleagues, our chums. They were extremely good professionals, and they were thoroughly nice people. There is an enormous sense of loss here. On the other hand, there is also a sense that there is a job to be done. There is a mission out here. It is important. We have to continue to support The Royal Marines ashore.'

The Board of Inquiry report highlighted equipment failures and poor procedures. The Ministry of Defence was urged to fit night-vision aids and identification lights to the Sea King Mk7s. As *Red Rat 34* had peered through the semi-darkness, its pilot and crew mistook a passing Lynx for *Red Rat 35*. Crews routinely switched off their frontal identification lights, as they dazzled or blinded other pilots sharing their airspace. The board noted:

> The conspicuity [*sic*] of each aircraft was significantly degraded from some angles. Thus in trying to maximise their ability to see out of their cockpit each crew was at the same time ensuring that their aircraft was more difficult to see from the most dangerous direction – directly ahead.

An officer on deck told how he witnessed the helicopters for 15 to 20 seconds prior to impact. One of the Sea King Mk7s, probably *Red Rat 34*, appeared to descend towards the other. Other eye witnesses said it was difficult to judge the depth and distance between them. They assumed there was sufficient space for each to pass. The inquiry noted the two helicopters were on 'opposing tracks but not identical heights, moving directly towards each other, impacting forcibly'. Each was found to have had at least one anti-collision light on. Magnetic tapes that recorded the last conversations of both crews were recovered damaged from the sea bed. The board continued:

> Partial voice traces remain which continue until approximately 50 seconds before the collision. Much voice information – over 50 per cent in the final two minutes – is destroyed. At this point the exact sequence of events is thus only a matter of opinion and it is this that prevents the board from arriving at a positive cause of the collision. The fact that the aircraft collided is confirmed by the wreckage, with the tail rotor blade from XV704 found embedded within the tail cone of XV650. The aspect of the initial collision is supported by an initial assessment of

the wreckage that suggested a 'port to port' contact. Due to the speed and momentum of the aircraft, particularly XV650 carrying 3,800 lb of fuel, it is impossible to assess the trajectory of the airframes after the initial impact.

The board suggested that the pilots suffered a breakdown of situational awareness while almost certainly using predominantly visual cues to guide their perception of events. The board said that this was 'mistaken', as:

> the human operator frequently fails to appreciate that when the quality of the visual clues is inadequate, he is unable to build a reliable picture. The failure to recognise the need for such a paradigm shift from visual to other cues was the most significant factor accounting for the aircrews' failure to initiate avoiding action.

Appearing as a witness at the coroner's hearing in 2007, Rear Admiral Massey said that he put 'absolute faith' in the testimony of Lieutenant Commander Dale, which, in the absence of black box recorders and a 'live' set-up in the operations room aboard HMS *Ark Royal*, took on greater significance: 'I never had any doubt whatsoever about the competence of my tactical air control officers and my air control officers.'

When Richard Benson, QC, representing the family of Lieutenant Green, suggested that Lieutenant Commander Dale had been 'morally and lawfully' obliged to intervene further in the final minute before impact, Rear Admiral Massey countered by saying, 'Only if the air controller has reason to disbelieve either of the air captains who have told him they have visual with each other. There was no need, prima facie, for the two aircraft to fly into each other – it could have been avoided. All I know is that the aircraft flew into each other. We can't for the life of us fathom what it was.'

Lieutenant Commander Dale said, 'Messages from both helicopters – one taking off and the other about to land on the carrier – indicated that the pilots could see each other. I could see both aircraft on the radar. The next thing was a visual lookout watch recording an explosion in the sky.'

Sir Richard Curtis, Oxfordshire assistant deputy coroner, ruled the collision an accident and offered no single explanation as to its occurrence. Sir Richard apologised to the families that it had taken four years to bring an inquiry into their deaths, a delay he described as 'quite, quite unacceptable'.

23 March 2003

Iraq–Kuwait border

Flight Lieutenant Kevin Main, Flight Lieutenant David Williams

Flight Lieutenant Kevin Main had achieved a lifelong ambition when he joined the 'Dambusters' squadron. He was in no hurry to leave, declining the offer of a prestigious pilot-training role that came his way before Operation Telic. As a Tornado GR4 pilot in 9 Squadron, Royal Air Force, he knew he would be among the first to fly hostile sorties. He intended to put thousands of hours of flying time on Operation Resinate South – the nine-year mission to police UN-imposed 'no-fly zones' – to best use. He was also awaiting promotion to the rank of squadron leader.

Flight Lieutenant David Williams, Flight Lieutenant Main's navigator and a father of two, had swapped RAF Markham, Norfolk, for Kuwait and joined 1,200 Royal Air Force personnel at Ali al-Saleem Airbase, half a minute's flying time from the border. Operation Telic provided an opportunity to improve on The Royal Air Force's showing in Kosovo, when its pilots were hampered by unsophisticated weaponry, bad weather and the US insistence upon bombing from above 15,000 feet. When allied raids cost 500 Kosovan civilians their lives, there were calls for pilots to be prosecuted for war crimes.

As the waiting game ended in Kuwait, joking and banter ceased and dinners were eaten in tense silence. The Royal Air Force was busy in the first 24 hours of the air offensive, with Tornados and Harriers flying more than 100 sorties, attacking command-

and-control facilities and missile sites with a new generation of precision-guided weapons. When Wing Commander Derek Watson led 9 Squadron's assault on Baghdad on 21 March 2003, he saw a city ablaze, with explosions occurring every few seconds. He watched as one by one his Air Launched Anti-Radiation Missiles dropped away and fired off. His payload spent, he returned to base two and a half hours later.

As Flight Lieutenant Main taxied along the runway the following evening, the tailfin of his Tornado was resplendent with a lightning flash, the angry face of a lynx and a bat – his squadron logos. Beneath his wings were Air Launched Anti-Radiation Missiles and Paveway laser-guided bombs. With a thunderous roar and his afterburners producing rocket-like flumes of flame, Flight ZG710 was airborne and Baghdad-bound. He delivered his payload successfully before rendezvousing with his team leader. Wing Commander Watson led the formation back towards Ali al-Saleem. Beginning their descent from 23,000 feet and at an estimated flight speed of Mach 0.8 (over 800 feet per second), their Tornados reduced altitude rapidly.

Following a grenade attack on a US base in Kuwait the previous evening, nerves were fraught among crews of US anti-aircraft batteries sited on the border. A dot appeared on a radar screen at one battery location. In the absence of an Identification Friend or Foe signal, a computer program suggested that the dot was an anti-radiation missile closing in on its location. When the dot met all the flight profile classification criteria, the software advised its human users to launch a surface-to-air missile. As such batteries operated autonomously, without radio communications with senior commanders, the crew was unable to confirm when friendly aircraft were using the airspace it was tasked to defend. The clock ticked down – 60 seconds for a female lieutenant to decide whether to intercept or let the dot pass. Its altitude was recorded at 17,000 feet and descending fast. At 0248 on 23 March 2003, a Patriot missile was released from its launch pad and flew skywards.

Wing Commander Watson observed a warhead speeding towards him at three times the speed of sound. Executing emergency procedures, he released chaff and radioed a warning. Flight Lieutenant Main might have received the message, but there was no time for him to respond or eject to safety. He and Flight Lieutenant Williams died instantly as their Tornado disintegrated in a ball of flames, shockingly bright against the night sky. The battery officer realised her mistake when other monitoring locations belatedly reported that the dot was 'friendly'. Had she delayed the decision to engage, Main and Williams's aircraft would most likely have been automatically reclassified by the computer when their flight path changed – she might also have allowed an Iraqi rocket to strike a Coalition Forces base.

Royal Air Force ground crews waited on the flight line at Ali al-Saleem in anticipation of two incoming Tornados. Wing Commander Watson's duly landed, followed quickly by another Tornado. Its pilot had jettisoned his fuel tanks and dashed to the nearest allied airstrip. Moments later, Main and Williams's hangar crew reported flight ZG710 missing.

The telephone rang in Group Captain Simon Dobb's office. The Royal Air Force detachment commander received a horrifying sketch of events. He was now missing two very good men, experienced Tornado aircrew, courageous and excellent at their jobs. Their loss would be a huge blow. Although it was inconceivable that they might have survived, the men were formally listed as missing. An investigation began. When the crash site in north-west Kuwait was sealed off, two bodies were recovered.

Group Captain Dobb was visibly disturbed and angry. 'They were not lost in combat but on returning from a mission,' he told the media pointedly.

The US officer in charge of Patriot batteries was ordered to Ali al-Saleem to make peace. Colonel Tim Glaeser apologised and requested that Flight Lieutenant Main and Flight Lieutenant Williams's families receive his condolences. Group Captain Dobb demanded 'cast-iron guarantees' that there would be no repeat – before he could dispatch his crews, he wanted to provide a personal, categorical assurance that they were in no danger of another 'inadvertent engagement'. Colonel Glaeser received the message loud and clear. Tornado missions continued without interruption.

William Farish, the US ambassador to Britain, described the loss as 'absolutely terrible', while chairman of the US Joint Chiefs of Staff, General Richard Myers, said there could be 'no excuses'. Privately, US military commanders pointed to the failure of the Tornado's Identification Friend or Foe system, which, unbeknown to Flight Lieutenant Main and Flight Lieutenant Williams, was disabled as they flew to their deaths. A transponder power failure, possibly caused by something as simple as a blown fuse, meant that the warning light intended to signal its disablement had failed to illuminate.

Colin Main said that nothing could replace his son and that his family was completely overwhelmed by the kind thoughts and sympathy received from across the world: 'I will treasure the words for as long as I live.'

The crew was repatriated along with eight of the Sea Knight and Sea King accident victims into Brize Norton, Oxfordshire. When Flight 22073 landed at 12 noon on Saturday, 29 March 2003, flags flew at half mast, and the stoles of the military clergy flapped in the breeze. As The Royal Marines band struck up Handel's 'Dead March', the coffins, draped in Union Jacks, were carried shoulder high down the ramp of the giant Royal Air Force C-17. Flight Lieutenant Main and Flight Lieutenant Williams were the last to emerge from the aircraft after Captain Philip Guy, Warrant Officer Mark Stratford, Major Jason Ward, Marine Sholto Hedenskog, Sergeant John Cecil, Lance Bombardier Llewelyn Evans, Sergeant Les Hehir and Operator Mechanic Ian Seymour. This was the day the war came home. When the band stopped playing, the families filed sombrely into the terminal building.

A US Army report acknowledged that the breadth of the criteria used by the computer programme caused it to mistake an incoming aircraft, friendly or otherwise, for an Anti-Radiation Missile. No attempt was made prior to the invasion to tighten the criteria or make it specific to the local threat. The female battery officer told investigators, 'I can look back and say that I might have maybe waited longer. Maybe I could have done differently. I have made the decision I have made, and I have to live with that.'

She was asked, 'Did you believe you were engaging an aircraft that night?'

'No, I did not. I thought I was engaging an ARM [Anti-Radiation Missile].'

'Did you have the authority to engage an ARM?'

'Yes. If it's something that is threatening you, it's self-defence.'

More startling claims were made by a CBS radio journalist embedded with the Patriot missile battery. Robert Riggs said that soldiers admitted Patriots were identifying friendly aircraft as enemy tactical ballistic missiles on a regular basis. He described the scenario as 'like a bad science-fiction movie in which the computer starts creating false targets. And you have the operators of the system wondering is this a figment of the computer's imagination or is this real? They were seeing what were called spurious targets identified as incoming tactical ballistic missiles. Sometimes they did not exist at all in time and space. Other times, they were identifying friendly US aircraft as incoming tactical ballistic missiles.'

Theodore Postol, professor of science, technology and national security at the Massachusetts Institute of Technology, said that the Patriot fire unit did not have its data recorder operational during the shoot-down of the Tornado. This 'basically meant that there was no reliable information about what the Patriot operators saw and how they responded. It is not even clear to me that the Identification Friend or Foe of the Tornado failed, as we do not have recorded data from the Patriot and therefore must remain uncertain that the Tornado was properly interrogated as was claimed at the time. That the Tornado was misclassified as an Anti-Radiation Missile raises very serious and basic additional questions.'

CBS News obtained material that made reference to another 'false firing' incident 12 hours before the Tornado was downed. On that occasion, a Patriot battery 'auto engaged' a spurious target. A fortnight later, a Patriot battery shot down a US Navy F-18 over Karbala after mistaking the aircraft for an enemy missile, killing the pilot, Lieutenant Nathan White. US Brigadier General Howard Bromberg, the officer commanding air defence, suggested that the overcrowding of Patriot batteries on the border might have caused interference on the radar screen, leading to accidents and misidentifications.

While a US board of inquiry exonerated the battery operators, Oxford coroner Andrew Walker highlighted failures in their training. Though 'fully trained' from the US perspective, their preparation had focused upon the recognition of generic threats, with too little attention paid to the identification of false alarms or threats specific to their environment. Walker said, 'It is very hard when considering an inquest such as this, where these tragic deaths were entirely avoidable. How best can I deal with that? I can't, other than to say this should not have happened. You sense the panic. They [the battery crew] clearly felt they were in danger and didn't have the training to look at it any other way. You've got a team of people trained to do one task, but they have no appreciation of other things that might stray into their area. That seems to come back time and time again as the main issue – having a battery working on its own. There were glaring failures to identify friendly aircraft in a potentially dangerous area. We don't have the [American] witnesses, because they would not come to the coroner's court to give evidence, so we don't know whether this was a failure in the Patriot software system. We are not privy to that part of the inquiry.'

Colin Main bore no ill will towards the American military personnel involved. He said, 'We feel exactly the same about his death, and we discussed it with David Williams's family, and we are in agreement that if they had to go at the age they did, they died the way they would have wanted to – flying. However, it was disappointing that no one from America was there at the inquest.'

❖ ❖ ❖

The main land, as opposed to the amphibious or heli-borne, offensive began at 0300 on 21 March 2003, with 1 (UK) Armoured Division and 16 Air Assault Brigade leading, 7 Armoured Brigade providing flank protection and 102 Logistics Brigade supporting. Once inside Iraq, the desire to secure Basra without a full-scale assault dictated the pace of operations. Major General Robin Brims, the general officer in command of British troops, intended to enter Iraq's second city at a time of his and not the Saddam loyalists' choosing. While Basra's position at the mouth of the Shatt al-Arab waterway leading to the Gulf had given this once flourishing city great strategic value as a port and trading hub, the prominence of the Shias there and in the surrounding provinces moulded the region's cultural identity.

23 March 2003

Az Zubayr

Sapper Luke Allsopp, Staff Sergeant Simon Cullingworth

> 'The commitment to military action of service personnel
> is always the gravest step that any government can
> undertake.'
>
> Defence Secretary Geoff Hoon MP

Staff Sergeant Simon Cullingworth and Sapper Luke Allsopp were fully qualified bomb-disposal experts based at Carver Barracks, Wimbish, Essex. Staff Sergeant Cullingworth, a soldier for 17 years, was tipped as a regimental sergeant major in waiting, and the 36 year old's professionalism won him the respect of those with whom he served, including the commanding officer of 33 EOD Regiment, Royal Engineers, Lieutenant Colonel Anthony Troulan. Staff Sergeant Cullingworth's marriage to Allison produced two boys, aged nine and three. Sapper Allsopp's slight build gave rise to his nickname 'Muscles'. The 24-year-old divorcee and father of one had served in Kosovo and Cyprus before deployment to the Gulf.

On 23 March 2003, the pair were chosen to join a team of demolitions specialists to clear a site designated as a UK communications facility. When Lieutenant Colonel William Hay signed off a route to the location through the outskirts of Az Zubayr, there was some trepidation among his officers. They described the environment as 'extremely confusing'. This was also the company's first large-scale road move in battle conditions.

Some vehicles took a wrong turn and drove into the heart of Az Zubayr. Gunmen opened fire with AK-47s and rocket-propelled grenades. Rounds and rockets fizzed over the bonnets of the Land Rovers.

'Keep up, keep up!' Staff Sergeant Cullingworth had urged over his radio, as an inquest heard. His men looked to him for leadership and guidance, none more so than Lance Corporal Marcus Clarke, the driver in the vehicle immediately behind him. Without a map, he was entirely dependent upon his sergeant to guide him to their destination.

As British vehicles began to concertina, gunmen advanced and fired at close range. A missile slammed into Staff Sergeant Cullingworth and Sapper Allsopp's Land Rover, setting it ablaze and enveloping Lance Corporal Clarke's vehicle in thick black smoke. He and his passenger, Lance Corporal Philip Law, were blinded and unsure of the direction in which they were supposed to travel. A rocket struck their Land Rover, spinning them through 180 degrees and into another hail of bullets. They jumped clear of the wagon minus their personal weapons, which were on fire. As they sprinted towards a wall, Lance Corporal Clarke was shot in the shoulder.

'Clarkey, Clarkey, come back and get me!' Cullingworth sounded anxious when his voice was heard on the company radio. He and Sapper Allsopp were trapped as a mob attempted to tip over their Land Rover. There was little Lance Corporal Clarke or Lance Corporal Law could do to help. Cullingworth and Allsopp were stripped of their helmets, body armour and weapons as Ba'ath Party officials escorted them to a 'military intelligence facility'. When the soldiers were reported missing in action, Lieutenant Colonel Hay ordered Royal Engineers and Black Watch soldiers to fight through the streets to the crash site. They found an empty, smouldering Land Rover and hundreds of spent bullet casings.

The unarmed Sapper Allsopp, whose ordeal was captured on video, was subsequently shot several times and seen lying on the ground gasping for breath. With the camera recording his desperate fight for life, he was administered morphine by Staff Sergeant Cullingworth, who was also wounded and gave himself the drug. It was suggested by a Ba'ath Party official interviewed by The Royal Military Police that the fatal shots to both men took the form of a summary execution. Staff Sergeant Cullingworth was shot at least five times and Sapper Allsopp ten times with rifles and pistols. Staff Sergeant Cullingworth died a few days after his promotion to the rank of sergeant major. At the time of his death, the post was unannounced.

The video was smuggled to the television station Al Jazeera, based in Doha, Qatar, and screened across the world. Tony Blair condemned the broadcast as a disgraceful breach of Geneva Conventions. Royal Marines fighting at Umm Qasr were angry, with Lance Corporal James Blanchard expressing the popular view: 'It is disgusting. We are dealing with Iraqi prisoners of war every day. We treat them by the rule book – we are firm but fair. We see this and think, what's the point?'

The bodies were discovered by a British search party three weeks after their deaths and moved to Kuwait for forensic analysis. Formal post-mortems were conducted at John Radcliffe Hospital, Oxford. According to eye witnesses, the dead men had been lifted onto a pick-up truck and taken to the outskirts of the city. Sixteen-year-old Iraqi Sahab Ahmed told The Royal Military Police that he witnessed a group of Ba'ath Party officials unload the bodies and bury them in the desert.

Staff Sergeant Cullingworth and Sapper Allsopp were laid to rest in the same English country churchyard, with each soldier receiving full military honours. Their coffins were draped in Union Jacks and carried into All Saints Church, Wimbish, by their comrades.

The BBC justified its decision to show stills from the Al Jazeera footage on the grounds of public interest. While calls to the corporation were divided evenly between those who supported and those who opposed the broadcast, Sapper Allsopp's sister Nina labelled the broadcaster 'heartless and callous beyond belief'. Her formal complaint against the BBC was upheld. The footage was at odds with the version of events as described by an army officer who visited her at home. He had told her that her brother had died instantly in battle, a fate that had been a little easier to stomach.

Staff Sergeant Cullingworth's funeral was attended by more than two hundred and fifty mourners, including his wife and two sons. The service with full military honours included a 12-gun salute. An annual football match between Braintree Town and The Royal Engineers is played in Staff Sergeant Cullingworth's honour.

Major Alec Campbell said, 'I would have expected him to have become regimental sergeant major – he was of that calibre. He was meticulous in the way he ran his troop. He was thoroughly reliable, the sort of man who is the backbone of the British Army.'

Lieutenant Colonel Anthony Troulan, Staff Sergeant Cullingworth's commanding officer, added, 'Simon Cullingworth was an extremely experienced soldier who was respected by his troops. He was in line for promotion, and his dedication to duty and professionalism won him the admiration of everyone with whom he served.'

At the inquest, the soldiers' commanders admitted that the pair were ordered into a town that British forces were warned to avoid. Coroner Andrew Walker suggested that if the town was as dangerous as intelligence reports suggested, British soldiers should have formed a physical barrier to its entry. Walker told Captain Eastough, who oversaw the route, 'It is difficult to understand how this convoy made its way into an area which was highly risky without encountering any British troops to tell them, "You can't go into this area." If there was a ring around that town, one would have thought that ring consisted of posts around the main entry and exit points.'

Captain Eastough said, 'I can't answer that. I was given the task of showing the road, and that's what I did.'

Walker concluded, 'The failure to adequately plan for and warn of the dangers was in my view a contributory factor to their deaths. If the proper procedures had been followed, no one should have been allowed to use that route. Headquarters knew that it was a dangerous area, and they were advising people not to go near that area.'

❖ ❖ ❖

The 1st Battalion, The Black Watch, prepared for desert operations with exercises in the snows of Fallingbostel in northern Germany before their Warrior armoured vehicles were shipped to the Gulf from the port of Emden. Lieutenant Colonel Mike Riddell-Webster led the 'Jocks' into Iraq with the future of their historic regiment in jeopardy – from disbandment, not the enemy. The Black Watch was tasked to quell resistance in Az Zubayr and relieve US marines from several key positions as the siege of Basra continued. When Lieutenant Colonel Riddell-Webster arrived in Az Zubayr, he found the regular Iraqi Army gone. But as Staff Sergeant Cullingworth and Sapper Allsopp discovered, it remained a hostile environment.

24 March 2003

Az Zubayr

Lance Corporal Barry Stephen

L ance Corporal Barry Stephen was born in Perth and raised in the nearby town of Scone, where ancient Scottish kings were crowned on a stone throne now housed at Edinburgh Castle. He had joined The Black Watch in 1997 and served in Northern Ireland before joining the recruiting team. He became a familiar figure in schools, colleges and army cadet centres in Perth. He rejoined mortar platoon in preparation for Operation Telic, deploying with many of those he had persuaded to enlist. Lance Corporal Stephen and his wife Shirley planned to start a family.

On 24 March 2003, mortar platoon was ambushed on the outskirts of Az Zubayr. With his fellow soldiers pinned down, Lance Corporal Stephen braved a hail of bullets to break through the hatches of his armoured personnel carrier and man the machine gun. He stood no chance of survival when the militia fired rocket-propelled grenades and small arms at him.

Lance Corporal Stephen, the first Black Watch soldier to be lost in combat for 30 years, and the first Scottish fatality of the war, was awarded a posthumous Mention in Dispatches, the British Army's oldest gallantry award. It took the form of an oak leaf attached to his Gulf War medal. The flag of St Andrew was flown at half-mast over regimental headquarters in his memory.

Sergeant Mark Hudson said, 'He was a wonderful husband and son as well as a great friend. I know he was very proud to be a soldier and to wear the regimental red hackle. He loved the army, and both his family and I take some comfort from knowing that he died a hero, doing the job he loved. We will miss him dreadfully.'

A lone piper played laments to the mourners at Lance Corporal Stephen's funeral, while his widow Shirley said, 'Barry worked hard and achieved so much in his short life, and we his family are very proud of him. He will be sorely missed for ever.'

24 March 2003

Az Zubayr

Sergeant Steven Roberts

Sergeant Steven Roberts was a proud Cornishman who emigrated from Wadebridge, 'Kernow', to Shipley, West Yorkshire. As G-day approached – the beginning of ground operations – Sergeant Roberts expressed disquiet about logistics issues in diaries he recorded on tapes that he posted to his wife Samantha. With his battle group 40 per cent short of its Enhanced Combat Body Armour requirement, precedence was granted to dismounted infantry and troops using 'soft-skinned' vehicles such as Land Rovers. As a tank commander, Sergeant Roberts was considered safe. On 21 March 2003, he and 26 others relinquished their Enhanced Combat Body Armour, a decision he accepted, as 'the guys on the ground needed it more than us'. Sergeant Roberts' mood darkened overnight: 'I have not got my combats [desert pattern] yet. Things we've been told we are going to get . . . we're not. It's disheartening because we know we are going to go to war without the correct equipment. It fills me with remorse. I think remorse is the right word because I know that we have received our orders [to cross the border]. It will be interesting to see what armour I actually get. I will keep you posted.'

His morale slumped further on 23 March 2003: 'It's disgraceful. We've got absolutely nothing. I can't really sleep because I am too nervous that I may never wake up.'

Sergeant Roberts was tired after four days with little rest. He and his colleagues were also apprehensive about forthcoming operations and the likelihood of paramilitary-style attacks from fedayeen posing as civilians. His voice choked with emotion as he signed off to Samantha: 'I love you so much, and I will speak to you when I can, probably tomorrow. I love you lots. Sleep tight, babe. Bye.'

As infantry soldiers were being used to guard the oil and gas terminals – the 'crown jewels' – it fell to the 'Tankies' to man vehicle checkpoints around Az Zubayr. Sergeant Roberts' 8 Troop was tasked to mount a vehicle checkpoint late on 23 March 2003 until the following morning. Its purpose was to prevent the egress of armed civilians towards the Coalition Forces' Main Supply Route Tampa, which ran close to the city. Challenger II tanks were positioned either side of the main road, with Sergeant Roberts' tank manoeuvring towards vehicles. Traffic was light, with only two civilian cars searched before 0230. Wearing a helmet and a semi-protective jacket without ceramic plates, Sergeant Roberts volunteered for this duty – he felt obliged to, given his status as the troop's most experienced soldier. Sergeant Roberts carried a 9-millimetre Browning pistol as a sidearm and was covered by a dismounted soldier armed with a rifle. When Sergeant Roberts completed the search of a white saloon, he ordered the dismounted soldier to return to the tank and position it across the central reservation.

Dressed in black robes and with his face painted or chalked white to mark himself as a martyr, Zahir Zabti Zaher picked up a rock and threw it at Sergeant Roberts' head, dislodging his helmet. Shaken, Sergeant Roberts turned to see Zaher standing five metres in front of him. Though unarmed, he appeared threatening. Sergeant Roberts drew his pistol and held out his other hand to indicate that Zaher should back off. When he stood his ground, Sergeant Roberts attempted to fire a warning shot, but his Browning suffered a stoppage. In accordance with the standard 'immediate action drill', Sergeant Roberts backed away and dropped to one knee to clear the breach.

Sitting 15 metres away in a Challenger II, Sergeant Scott Manley ordered Trooper Gary Thornton to release a burst of warning shots with the tank's General Purpose Machine Gun. When Trooper Thornton's machine gun jammed, he switched to the coaxial-mounted L94 machine gun, a heavier weapon intended to engage targets at a distance of several hundred metres. Rounds from the L94 struck Sergeant Roberts and Zaher, who fell to the ground. As blood poured from wounds to Sergeant Roberts' chest and abdomen, a colleague rushed forward to give him medical aid, stripping open his combat body armour, ineffective when worn without plates, and undoing his flame-retardant tank coveralls. Despite a field dressing being applied to his worst wound, Sergeant Roberts slipped into unconsciousness.

His arm hanging off at the elbow, Zaher staggered to his feet and, clutching a rock, shuffled several paces towards Sergeant Roberts and his colleague. The soldier providing medical assistance shot the advancing Iraqi at point blank range with a pistol. With 'Rasputin-like' strength, Zaher stood up again before more shots were fired. There was no evidence or suggestion that Zaher or any other Iraqi opened fire. Rules of engagement only permitted British soldiers to engage non-combatants if they displayed 'lethal intent'.

Sergeant Roberts received cardiopulmonary resuscitation to no avail. The regimental medical officer arrived at 0350, and Sergeant Roberts and Zaher were declared dead ten minutes later.

After listening to her husband's voice recordings and learning that the body armour he sacrificed would have saved his life, Sergeant Roberts' widow sat in the public gallery at the House of Commons as Defence Secretary Geoff Hoon MP dismissed calls to take 'the only honourable way forward'. Samantha Roberts said her husband's passing left an 'unfillable void', while his mother, Marion Chapman, said when her son's body was repatriated, 'Just to have him home, to know he is back safe in this country and back in Cornwall, will be better. He used to fly a little Cornish flag on his tank. Steven was a Cornishman who became a soldier. Now he is a soldier who is coming home to be a Cornishman again.'

A week after their colleague's death, 8 Troop received their Enhanced Combat Body Armour. Other kit consignments destined for the 'Tankies' and other soldiers never arrived and were abandoned by delivery drivers in the desert. An investigation found barcodes on the boxes identifying the contents as body armour had rubbed off in transit. They were most likely confused with other items and sent to another battle group.

Attorney General Lord Goldsmith ordered an inquiry into the incident. Trooper Thornton told army investigators that he was unaware his L94 machine gun was so inaccurate at short range. Adaptations were made to the syllabus at the Armoured Fighting Vehicle Driving and Maintenance School to ensure that all future trainees were aware of the limitations of the L94.

When engaging targets at less than 200 metres, it was suggested that soldiers aimed off to the left. In early 2004, the Ministry of Defence decreed that all personnel should be issued with their own personal Enhanced Combat Body Armour before deployment to Iraq or Afghanistan.

A Board of Inquiry found that in the hours before the vehicle checkpoint, the Tankies were briefed on standard operating procedures for vehicle and personnel searches that included always having at least one soldier on foot with the man conducting the search, armed and ready to use his personal rifle at all times. The board uncovered failures at troop level to ensure these orders were followed. Lord Goldsmith considered criminal charges against six British soldiers in relation to the death of Zaher, but after a 16-month Metropolitan Police investigation they escaped criminal action. It was decided that there was no realistic prospect of conviction. The Crown Prosecution Service also interviewed five US soldiers and a number of Iraqi eye witnesses before concluding that the British soldiers had acted in self-defence. The Ministry of Defence admitted liability for Sergeant Roberts' death and agreed to pay his widow compensation – a rare admission. The principle of 'combat immunity' usually took precedence.

Six months before Sergeant Roberts' death, the office of the defence secretary had delayed an urgent request from army commanders for more sets of Enhanced Combat Body Armour, which in hindsight was a fatal error of judgement. According to the Ministry of Defence's own report, Hoon's delay led to an 'unachievable timeframe' for supplying and distributing vital equipment. The report said:

> In an attempt to provide Enhanced Combat Body Armour (ECBA) to personnel who might be required to deploy to Iraq on operations (if a political solution could not be achieved), an urgent operational requirement (UOR) was directed to the Secretary of State's office in September 2002. The Secretary of State's officer agreed to allow 12 out of the 16 UORs requested. The procurement of ECBA was not agreed at this time, as 'further advice required' was annotated against the [request].

Lieutenant Michael Fielder, Sergeant Roberts' platoon commander, assumed Sergeant Roberts was wearing an empty but padded combat jacket beneath his smock. Lieutenant Fielder also told a coroner's court that his pistol 'jammed more times than he could remember'. Coroner Andrew Walker asked him if he considered Trooper Thornton's use of the L94 appropriate: 'No, I did not, because it's quite an escalation to open fire with a machine gun when I have got one of my soldiers close to the person you are shooting at.'

Trooper Thornton and Sergeant Manley became emotional during questioning from Samantha Roberts' barrister, James Rowley, QC. Sergeant Manley said, 'Steve turned around and saw the guy quite close to him. He was obviously taken by surprise. I gave the order to open fire after seeing Sergeant Roberts attempt to fire his pistol, which jammed. If he had not drawn his pistol, maybe it would have been totally different, but he set the stage by drawing his own weapon and firing or attempting to fire. I was obviously very concerned for my friend. That's why I ordered Trooper Thornton to shoot. The Iraqi guy was hit, but at the same time I saw Steve fall to the ground. The only thing I was thinking about was trying to help my friend. That was it, nothing else.'

Sergeant Roberts' widow left the court during this exchange. Andrew Walker then asked Sergeant Manley if he felt using the L94 was his only choice. Sergeant Manley replied, 'I didn't really have much time. It was just a decision that was made at the time.'

Trooper Thornton added, 'The Iraqi got back up and I saw his arm, roughly at the elbow joint, hanging off. That's when I heard over the intercom that Sergeant Roberts was on the floor.'

When Brigadier David Martin, the officer responsible for channelling equipment to soldiers in Kuwait and Iraq, was asked to explain how Sergeant Roberts found himself in a war zone without adequate protective clothing, he said that he was not sure he could provide a full and comprehensive answer. Walker pressed him: 'But you were responsible for supplying what makes it over to Kuwait and to the troops? What was required was not making its way over there. What, from your point of view, went wrong?'

The Brigadier explained that it was decided in late 2002 that infanteers and vehicle-mounted personnel were to be equipped with Enhanced Combat Body Armour and that the aim was to stockpile 37,000 sets in time for March 2003. Walker asked if it was known at that time that there were insufficient stocks. The brigadier acknowledged it was a matter of public record that a number of operational requirements were absent: 'Whereas large stocks of equipment were kept during the Cold War and First World War, in today's "wars of choice" equipping for each and every likely option is unaffordable and unrealistic.'

The circumstances of Sergeant Roberts' death riled Walker: 'To send soldiers into a combat zone without the appropriate basic equipment is, in my view, unforgivable and inexcusable, and represents a breach of trust the soldiers have in those in government. I have heard justification and excuse, and I put these to one side as I remind myself that Sergeant Roberts lost his life because he did not have that basic piece of equipment. Sergeant Roberts' death was a result of delay and serious failures in the acquisition and support chain that resulted in a significant shortage within his fighting unit of Enhanced Combat Body Armour, none being available for him to wear.'

Samantha Roberts added, 'The loss of Steve cannot be measured. This has been the driving force behind our quest for answers, some of which we feel could have been provided earlier. The policy on Enhanced Combat Body Armour has changed, and this is Steve's legacy. But we must also ensure that these failures are not repeated with other basic kit.'

25 March 2003

Basra

Corporal Stephen Allbutt, Trooper David Clarke

Aged 17, Trooper David Clarke had left his job as a school caretaker to learn to drive a tank. Two years later, he was driving a sixty-eight-tonne machine across the Iraqi border, while back home his girlfriend and mother were pressing ahead with his wedding plans. He lived his life in a forward gear and set himself the target of promotion to sergeant before his 23rd birthday. To him, anything seemed possible – even to make his younger brother's wish come true that he would one day drive his tank up and down their street. Trooper Clarke's parents knew that he was not going to sweep corridors at Stafford College for long when he could join The Queen's Royal Lancers, whose motto was 'Death or Glory'. His last act before deploying to the Gulf was to bungee jump off Blackpool pier.

Trooper Clarke volunteered for the war because the alternative was to cover for striking firemen. Like many soldiers, he resented this task on the grounds that those taking industrial action and putting lives at risk were far better paid than him.

Trooper Clarke wrote home from Basra to tell his mother and father that it was 0230 and he was exhausted after driving his Challenger II all day and night. They were not to worry about him, however, as he knew that the Iraqi tanks and artillery were no match for the British.

Trooper Clarke's fellow trooper Andy Julien was 18, Lance Corporal Daniel Twiddy 22. His tank commander was Corporal Stephen Allbutt. At 35 years old, the stocky, battle-hardened corporal was a responsible, steadying influence and a Gulf War veteran returning to the same theatre 12 years on. Corporal Allbutt grafted as hard as his young crew members and did his share of nocturnal 'stag' duties. He was also self-motivated: having failed his school exams, he taught himself English and mathematics from textbooks.

Corporal Allbutt told his wife Debi that there were three loves in his life, in descending order: Stoke City Football Club, his family and the army. He was more romantic than that, and prior to his deployment secretly planted daffodil bulbs in the family garden to flower while he was away. He and Debbie were the proud parents of two boys: Joshua, fourteen, and Connor, eight.

In 1991, Corporal Allbutt had gone to war a youth and had returned a man. Between Gulf Wars, he completed three operational tours of Bosnia.

Trooper Andy Julien's parents had been against their son joining the army, but from the moment a recruitment officer visited Philips High School, Bury, he could not be dissuaded. Aged 17, he needed their consent to enlist. Initially, they refused, but when he told them that he would simply wait until his 18th birthday, they relented and approved his application. 'But what if there's a war?' his mother Avis told a recruiting sergeant. She said later that his response had been to laugh and tell her that the chances were 'nil'.

His love of sport, fitness and boundless energy made Trooper Julien an ideal recruit. A photograph captured a proud father and son on the day of Trooper Julien's passing out. His fellow crew member Lance Corporal Twiddy, from Staffordshire, was more laconic, with a philosophical outlook on life and the army. He was almost too tall for tank life and routinely slept on top of the vehicle, contorting his frame into a semi-comfortable position between the open hatches of the Challenger II and gazing up at the stars.

The Challenger II was the main battle tank of the British Army. It was also erroneously numerated, given that it was the third vehicle to carry the name. The first two were the A30 Challenger, a Second World War tank, and Challenger I, which Corporal Allbutt would have been familiar with from the 1980s and early '90s. Challenger II's primary armament fired 120-millimetre shells, and it was powered by a 1,200 horsepower CV-12 diesel engine. It was also protected by Chobham/Dorchester Level 2 armour, making it one of the most heavily armoured and best-protected tanks in the world.

On 23 March 2003, Corporal Allbutt's tank was used to seize bridges across the Shatt al-Basra canal on the city's western outskirts. His boundaries were then expanded to include responsibility for a dam one mile north of the last of the bridges, where they joined another Challenger commanded by Sergeant Kane Greenhill. The dam had only been discovered the previous day and was absent from maps and photographically generated ground traces used by the likes of B Company, 1st Battalion, The Black Watch, and its attached squadron of armour from the 2nd Battalion, Royal Tank Regiment.

At around 0030 on 24 March 2003, Lance Corporal Twiddy was seated inside the Challenger II when he heard a knock. He said later that Corporal Allbutt opened the lid and smiled. It was time for the senior rank to take over on sentry duty: 'Thanks for doing your stag.' They clambered over each other, and Corporal Allbutt added that Lance Corporal Twiddy should get some rest and that he would see him in the morning.

Lance Corporal Twiddy joined Trooper Julien on top of the tank while Corporal Allbutt climbed inside to join Trooper Clarke. On a balmy evening, the hatches were left open for ventilation. After a long day and evening, Lance Corporal Twiddy knew he would soon be asleep.

At 0050, Lance Corporal John Williamson of Egypt Squadron, 2nd Battalion, Royal Tank Regiment, identified 'hot spots' through his thermal-imaging sight. From his location on the eastern side of the Shatt al-Basra canal, he reckoned the position was an ammunition dump and saw human figures climbing in and out of a bunker. Lance Corporal Williamson heard Lieutenant David Pinkstone of the 1st Battalion, The Black Watch, check that no friendly forces were within three to five kilometres of his position. He then sought and was granted permission to engage. When Lance Corporal Williamson aligned his Challenger's primary armament and discharged one 120-millimetre high-explosive, squash-head round, the muzzle flash at the tip of the tank barrel illuminated the night sky.

At 0122, Corporal Allbutt saw a ball of fire speeding towards the tank and screamed, 'Incoming!' There was a huge splash of sand as the round landed short, but its force hurled Lance Corporal Twiddy and Trooper Julien from the tank onto the ground beneath a blanket of molten debris. Lance Corporal Twiddy suffered 80 per cent burns, while a piece of metal smashed his cheekbone, jawbone and teeth. Shrapnel lodged in Trooper Julien's skull and caused a brain haemorrhage. He was blinded and both his legs were crushed and broken. Corporal Allbutt's and Sergeant Greenhill's tanks were ablaze, while Sergeant Greenhill's sleeping bag and clothing caught fire as he was showered with, in his own words, 'molten Play-Doh'. The blast also threw a lance corporal from the top of Sergeant Greenhill's tank 15 feet and dumped him in the sand. The tank was left scarred and misshapen.

At this time, Sergeant Greenhill was heard to say over the radio, 'We are under enemy attack. RPG [rocket-propelled grenade] fire! At least three friendly casualties.' He ordered his crew to assist Lance Corporal Twiddy and Trooper Julien, who were rolling on the ground to put out the flames. Assuming more incoming enemy artillery was imminent, Sergeant Greenhill reversed his tank.

The first high-explosive, squash-head round was reported by observers as 'falling short'. Six minutes later, call-sign 110 reported an armoured vehicle (Greenhill's tank) moving in the same vicinity as the 'bunker' (Allbutt's tank). This armoured vehicle was then misidentified as an enemy T-55 tank and a second high-explosive, squash-head round fired. This round detonated on Corporal Allbutt's commander's hutch. Immediately on impact, high-velocity fragments entered the turret, setting it on fire and causing a huge explosion, which separated the turret, cupola and pintle mount from the main body. Corporal Allbutt and Trooper Clarke could not have survived the blast. As the ammunition on Corporal Allbutt's tank 'cooked off', call-sign 110 witnessed a small fire and assumed that the target was destroyed and the contact discontinued.

Lance Corporal Twiddy rose to his hands and knees. His face was 'mashed up' and his skin peeling off. 'Where's Clarkey?' Twiddy later remembered asking himself. 'Where's Steve?'

Sergeant Greenhill reversed his tank again and traversed its turret in the direction of the attack. Two Challengers appeared in his field of vision – 'the penny dropped'.

He sent a radio message: 'Ceasefire. You have just engaged my call-signs.'

On learning that he had engaged British call-signs, Lance Corporal Williamson asked to be relieved of his tank and returned to the B Company compound. As the proximity of the site to enemy positions precluded casualty evacuation by helicopter, Sergeant Greenhill escorted an ambulance towards what remained of the other Challenger II. A Royal Military Police investigation began as soon as surrounding enemy positions were cleared. Photographs of Corporal Allbutt's tank that were taken at this time were 'mislaid' before the Board of Inquiry sat.

On 25 March 2003, a family liaison officer broke the news to Avis and Trevor Julien that their son was critically injured and two soldiers were dead. Trooper Julien was flown back to hospital in Essex. Having feared the worst, they were simply relieved to know he was still alive and back in Britain. Avis and Trevor sat down to watch the TV news one evening, not long after the return of their injured son, when the telephone rang. An officer said they should be aware that the attack on their son's tank was a 'blue-on-blue' incident, something he omitted to tell them on his initial visit. The news bulletin included a report on a tragic British blue-on-blue incident, the same one that their son had been involved in.

To Avis, her son was an unrecognisable mass of blood and bandages. Surely the youth lying helpless in the bed at Broomfield Hospital was someone else? Trooper Julien was on a life-support machine, and, as a consultant explained, he would do well to survive the neurosurgery required to remove the shrapnel from his brain. The consultant advised her to pray for her son's life. Two days later, he was taken off a ventilator but remained unable to speak or see clearly. He also suffered hallucinations that he was still on his tank and on fire.

In the same intensive-care ward, Lance Corporal Twiddy lay wrapped in gauze with a large hole in his face. It was impossible for his loved ones to recognise him. He only regained consciousness a month after the incident. He opened his eyes to see his sister at his bedside. He was devastated to hear of the loss of his colleagues.

Such was the intensity of the explosion and his proximity to it that Trooper Clarke's remains were never found – an empty coffin was used at his funeral. A coroner's inquest only considered Corporal Allbutt's death.

'I want to say goodbye to them. At least one of them,' Lance Corporal Twiddy told his sister. He dragged himself to Corporal Allbutt's funeral at Holy Trinity Church, Stoke-on-Trent, where he met his commander's widow and their two sons. Corporal Allbutt's mother Mavis, a vicar at the church, said in her eulogy that she and her husband Colin knew from the moment they saw their baby son that he was 'a gift from God'. Lance Corporal Twiddy vowed that every year for the rest of his life he would lay wreaths at his comrades' graves and say hello to them.

Avis Julien was also among the mourners. She claimed that

a high-ranking officer came up to her and said, 'It's a terrible thing what the Yanks did to your son.'

She said, 'This man was supposed to be representing his regiment, and even he didn't seem to know who was responsible for the death of the man whose funeral he was attending.'

Friends recalled how the threat of friendly fire had been on Corporal Allbutt's mind on his return from the first Gulf War – during the conflict, nine British soldiers were killed in a blue-on-blue attack by a US aircraft on a British armoured patrol. War veteran Lee Goldstraw said, 'It was just so chilling that he was killed in this way when he was so passionate about these friendly fire situations. Stephen told me how he could not believe it could happen. He always said there should be more systems in place to stop this type of accidental killing at times of war. He was right, of course. More allied soldiers died through friendly fire in the last Gulf war than were killed in action.'

Corporal Allbutt's commanding officer, Lieutenant Colonel Charles Fattorini, recalled his 'reassuringly dry sense of humour': 'He was a real character and had a very promising career ahead of him, having been identified as a strong candidate for promotion to sergeant in 2004.'

The Board of Inquiry noted the failure to recognise panels on the sides of the Queen's Royal Lancers tanks identifying them as British, as well as profound communications failures. The families of the deceased claimed that the Ministry of Defence withheld information pertaining to the incident.

When he and Trooper Julien were medically discharged, Lance Corporal Twiddy expressed his grievances, which were entirely understandable given his experience: 'When I joined the British Army, I understood that it was their duty of care to support you through thick and thin. When you're at the passing-off parade, they say, "Not only is your son part of our family, you're all part of our family now." As soon as something like this happens, they toss you aside. Physically, I can heal up. What hurts the most is that I've been left. I'll always remember what they've done to me. It's something that should never have happened – friendly fire. They won't admit it. That's what makes me angry. They won't admit they've messed up.'

Under questioning as a coroner's witness, Lieutenant Colonel MacDuff, the senior officer involved in the incident, conceded that his decision not to pass news of the boundary changes to his men was 'a potentially serious failure'. There was no evidence to support Lieutenant Colonel MacDuff's claim that he had sent a radio message confirming the presence of two friendly tanks or that this had been acknowledged by his junior officers. Many recordings and radio logs pertaining to the incident were 'missing'. Lieutenant Colonel MacDuff was recalled after a series of witnesses disputed his evidence. Richard Hermer, the barrister representing the families, accused the lieutenant colonel of fabrication.

Coroner Andrew Walker admitted that he considered a verdict of unlawful killing before deciding it was impossible to apply the law necessary to reach such a verdict, as the deceased were engaged in combat operations. He returned a narrative verdict and described the events as a 'completely avoidable tragedy'. He said, 'There may be an innocent explanation for the loss of this radio log, but the centre of this tragedy represents a serious failing, and it will fall to others to question the fitness of this officer [Lieutenant Colonel MacDuff] to hold command.'

Corporal Allbutt's widow added, 'Maybe the mothers, fathers, husbands and wives of the soldiers in his regiment should question whether they want this man in charge. I hope that the people of the United Kingdom will stand by us and press for further action.'

28 March 2003

Ad Dayr

Lance Corporal of Horse Matty Hull

D Squadron of The Household Cavalry, The Blues and Royals, provided 16 Air Assault Brigade's armoured reconnaissance capability. On 27 March 2003, Major Richard Taylor learned a valuable lesson when, having pushed northwards of Basra, he spotted what appeared to be T-55 tanks. Although he guessed that they belonged to the Iraqi 6th Armoured Division, which at the time was in a state of disarray and dispersal, Major Taylor hesitated before calling in an air strike: the prevailing weather meant he could not identify the vehicles with absolute certainty. As US jets circled at 12,000 feet awaiting target instructions, Major Taylor feared that the tanks might belong to another unit from his brigade. A closer observation, conducted at great personal risk, revealed the targets to be 'dummy tanks' – drainage pipes stuck into the sand.

The morning of 28 March 2003 saw a number of skirmishes as Major Taylor's troop and a section from 23 Engineer Regiment (Air Assault) pushed north along Route Spear, the highway parallel to the Shatt al-Arab waterway. His men engaged 6th Armoured Division units before entering a village on the banks of the canal. Lance Corporal of Horse Steven Gerrard poked his head from the lead Scimitar to see locals clasping white flags. He waved but most were too scared to return his gesture. Lance Corporal Gerrard sympathised: they had been terrorised by the Iraqi Army and assumed the British Army had arrived intent upon doing the same. Trooper Chris Finney, an 18-year-old driver from Marple, Cheshire, brought the convoy to a halt. His friends Lance Corporal Al Tudball and Lance Corporal Matty Hull stopped in the second Scimitar. Lance Corporal Hull was a few days short of his 26th birthday and married to Susan, his childhood sweetheart.

Colonel Gus 'Skeeter' Kohntopp, an Idaho Air National Guard pilot flying an A-10 'Tankbuster', was also on the lookout for elements of the scattered 6th Armoured Division. The battlefield was 'porous', with numerous small groupings of enemy vehicles operating in 'shoot and scoot' mode. Colonel Kohntopp, a commercial airline pilot in civilian life, had already destroyed three Iraqi targets during his two-hour mission before a previously unsighted vehicle column attracted his eye. In order to avoid friendly fire from the skies, Major Taylor's two Scimitar and two Spartan armoured reconnaissance vehicles were draped in Union Jacks, sheets of orange fabric and day-glo orange panels.

Kohntopp's conversations with his wingman were recorded

and later made public. 'I've got a four-ship of vehicles evenly spaced out on a road going north,' Kohntopp radioed. 'Look down at your right,' he told his wingman. 'Two o'clock, at ten o'clock low, there is a left ten o'clock low. Look down there north along that canal, right there? Coming just south of the village . . . They've got something orange on them . . . I think they're rocket launchers?'

Having been told by his forward ground controller, 'Manila Hotel', that he was 'well clear' of friendly forces, Kohntopp continued, 'They've got orange rocket launchers on them. I think killing these damn rocket launchers, it would be great. We got visual. OK. I want to get the first one before he gets into town?'

'You roll in. It looks like they are exactly what we're talking about. Get him, get him,' Kohntopp's wingman replied.

'All right, we've got rocket launchers. Number two is rolling in from the south to the north and two is in . . .'

'Get it!' the wingman urged as Kohntopp rolled in for his attack run, turning his A-10 into a vertical dive to strafe the column below.

As if from nowhere, Lance Corporal Gerrard heard a quiet, rolling thunder. As his ears adapted to the sound, it sharpened and increased in volume until it became an eardrum-shattering staccato. The earth shook as a volley of 30-millimetre depleted-uranium rounds landed.

'Good hits!' chirped Kohntopp's wingman.

Trooper Finney heard the noise and felt the impact. His instinctive reaction was that he was under enemy attack, he guessed from rocket-propelled grenades fired from the village. In fact, a US 30-millimetre shell had scored a direct hit on top of his vehicle, exploding on the turret. Fearing he was going to be burned alive, Lance Corporal Gerrard pulled himself clear and saw the two fuel-laden Scimitars ablaze. Ammunition on each vehicle was 'cooking off', with loud bangs every few seconds. Trooper Finney got behind the controls of his vehicle, but in the pandemonium reversed into the Scimitar behind him, which was also alight. When he jumped down, Trooper Finney saw Lance Corporal Al Tudball wounded and trapped half out of his hatch. He ran over and, ignoring the flames, pulled him clear. As he administered first aid, Trooper Finney saw sparks coming from the ground then felt the sensation of being kicked extremely hard in the back of his leg. The pain became a burning sensation. He was wounded.

Corporal Ashley Bell realised that it was a blue-on-blue situation and reached for his vehicle radio: 'Stop, stop, stop. Check fire!' There was no response.

Sergeant Andrew Sindall released red smoke housed in canisters on the vehicles. Four soldiers were wounded, and Lance Corporal Hull remained trapped inside his vehicle. The call-signs were stranded 20 miles from supporting British units.

Kohntopp observed the chaos, with soldiers running through fire to save their colleagues. 'It looks like he's hauling ass,' he said.

British soldiers waved their arms and shouted at the US planes. When the US Tankbusters swooped again, Corporal Bell repeated his radio plea: 'Stop! Stop! Stop!'

'OK, I'm in again from the south,' said Kohntopp.

Lance Corporal Hull was strafed on the A-10 Tankbuster's second run. Trooper Finney fought the intense heat, smoke and the risk of incoming fire in a bid to pull Lance Corporal Hull clear. The flames beat him back from the burning turret. Ignoring his own injuries, Sergeant Sindall hauled other wounded to safety.

A US Marine Corps forward air controller sounded a belated note of caution: 'Lightning 34, be advised that in the 3122 and 3222 group box you have friendly armour in the area. Yellow, small armoured tanks. Just be advised'.

'Ah shit,' replied Kohntopp's wingman. 'F***! Got a smoke [the smoke fired by the Household Cavalry to warn of a blue-on-blue situation].'

'You got a . . .' said Lightning 34 tentatively. 'Looks like we might have a blue-on-blue situation. The A-10s are running against friendlies. Abort, repeat, abort.'

When US air controllers received the news that at least one 'friendly' was killed and others were wounded, Kohntopp was ordered back to base. 'We're f***ed. God damn it, f*** me dead,' he said.

'They did say there were no friendlies,' suggested his wingman.

'Yeah, I know,' Kohntopp replied. 'That thing with the orange panels is going to screw us. They looked like orange rockets on top.'

'Got to go home, dude . . . We're in jail, dude . . . I'm going to be sick.'

The ordeal was far from over, as Iraqi tanks now appeared and advanced at speed. Lance Corporal Mick Flynn and Corporal Dave Telling drew the enemy fire for half an hour, while Major Taylor supervised the evacuation of Lance Corporal Hull and the wounded. Corporal Telling expended 140 rounds on his 30-millimetre cannon.

The following day, the squadron held a brief ceremony in Lance Corporal Hull's memory before continuing to take the fight to Iraqi forces. Over subsequent days, the men endured several enemy contacts, with Lance Corporal Flynn distinguishing himself during a four-hour engagement with five T-55 tanks. He was awarded the Conspicuous Gallantry Cross and Corporal Telling a Mention in Dispatches.

The tragedy shocked Lance Corporal Hull's friends, close comrades and thousands of British soldiers encamped in Iraq. Royal Military Policeman Corporal Russ Aston wrote home to his wife Anna in Derbyshire:

> Well, the Americans have just blown up one of our tanks with an A-10 Tankbuster. We've just heard about it, so I suppose there is more dead there. They always f***ing do it, don't they? So it's all a bit shit, really.

The words of Trooper Finney's George Cross citation echoed across the Buckingham Palace ballroom as the medal was pinned to his tunic: 'For his clear-headed courage and devotion to his comrades, which was out of all proportion to his age and experience. Acting with complete disregard for his own safety, even when wounded, his bravery was of the highest order throughout.' A sore and limping Lance Corporal Al Tudball, whose life he saved, was among those present.

While the British Board of Inquiry criticised Manila Hotel's guidance to Kohntopp as 'scant', it had been Kohntopp's responsibility to inform 'Manila Hotel' of his identification of a potential target and to gain clearance to engage prior to his attack. He had failed to do so and was accused of a 'single-minded pursuit of UK vehicles'. The board found that the day-glo panels the crews fitted to their vehicles were identified by the US air crew as orange rockets and noted that it was unhelpful that the most powerful visual aid available to Kohntopp and his wingman was a pair of 12x magnification binoculars. VHF radios used by British Forces were inferior to those issued to US personnel, and their range was 'severely limited'.

The findings of the US investigation were classified, but no personnel were brought before court martial. The US Air Force was sympathetic towards Kohntopp, highlighting his 'cognitive and physical task overload and ineffective communication systems', which 'hindered timely and accurate decision making'. The United States Defense Department cleared him formally of any wrongdoing.

When the inquest convened four years later in Oxford without US witnesses, Harriet Harman MP, the constitutional affairs minister, said that the UK government was not in a position to compel them to attend. A 19-minute-long cockpit video and audio transmission was subsequently declassified after it was leaked to *The Sun* newspaper. Coroner Andrew Walker ruled Matty Hull's death unlawful: 'The attack on the convoy mounted to an assault. It was unlawful because there was no lawful reason for it, and in that respect it was criminal. The pilot who opened fire did so with disregard for the rules of engagement and acted outside the protection of the law of armed conflict.

'I am satisfied, having given careful consideration to all the evidence that I have heard in this inquest, that this is a case where I can properly consider whether an unlawful action and manslaughter applies here. Despite request after request, the court has been denied access to evidence that would provide the fullest explanation of the sequence of events that led to and caused the tragic loss of Lance Corporal Hull's life. I believe that the full facts have not yet come to light.'

The Pentagon responded, 'The [US] investigation determined that the incident took place in a complex combat environment. The pilots followed applicable procedures and processes for engaging targets, believing they were engaging enemy targets.'

Mrs Hull paid tribute to her late husband: 'I could go on for ever about his personal strengths, and I know all of us could. He was full of fun, just smiled all the time, and was always happy, even in the face of things that were difficult and trying. We need time to move on. It's been a long and painful time, and we need to move forward. I think all of our family feel it was the right verdict. It's what we've waited four years to hear. There is a great sense of relief that it's over. I hope the US pilots are at peace with themselves and that they can move on with their lives. I am sure they are full of remorse for what they did. I hope so, anyway. Perhaps it sends a message to other pilots about how they need to be trained and the enormity of what they're doing, because their actions can have grave consequences.'

30 March 2003

Al-Faw Peninsula

Marine Christopher Maddison

The covert unit 539 Assault Squadron, 3 Commando Brigade, was raised to launch night-time raids behind enemy lines. To the chagrin of many of its most experienced non-commissioned officers, its role in Iraq necessitated daylight patrols of waterways that were obvious targets for enemy forces. Sergeant Eddy Cochrane expressed his concerns about the lack of protection against rocket-propelled grenades, given that 539 Assault Squadron's fleet of mini-hovercrafts were without armour-plating.

After setting up camp at an abandoned Iraqi naval base, the main effort was to explore a large marsh delta and the Khawr az Zubayr river to ensure neither provided a route behind British lines. The first nine days of the war were spent patrolling empty rivers. Late on 29 March 2003, the order was received to identify the source of an encoded signal emanating from the marshes. Colour Sergeant Howman led a team of eight Marines from 539

Assault Squadron to infiltrate the area with Mk4 landing craft. No enemy were spotted, and the following morning headquarters approved their withdrawal.

At 0810 on 30 March 2003, the boat came under fire and sent an emergency radio message to base requesting immediate support: two crewmen were missing. As a quick-reaction force, which included Corporal John Hiscock and radio operator Marine Christopher Maddison, prepped their weapons, they were advised that were they to see Iraqis on the water they should identify persons as hostile before opening fire. They made fast for the area.

Corporal Hiscock was standing in front of the wheelhouse of his landing craft when its windows shattered and an incoming missile hurled him forwards. He pressed his hands against his face to find he was bleeding profusely. He was relieved to be alive but 'did not think he had a face left'. Marine Maddison, a 24 year old from Scarborough, was also wounded and in a serious condition. Corporal Hiscock steered towards the bank to deposit those struck by enemy fire before joining Colour Sergeant Howman's crew to locate the missing marines. It was assumed that they had swum into the reed beds to find cover following the blast. First to be found was Marine Kevin Jones, who was hauled aboard with shrapnel embedded in his leg. He was in agony. The second marine was found later, wounded and exhausted. There was no positive sighting of enemy forces, even by a British helicopter circling above.

As the two hovercraft approached Crossing Point Anna, gunfire echoed over the marines' heads. Amidst the pandemonium, three mud huts on a central spur of the river were identified as the source of the incoming fire. Shots were returned, and Sergeant Cochrane radioed a contact report to 539 Assault Squadron headquarters.

When Colour Sergeant Howman saw 'enemy forces' hiding in the wreck of a tug downriver, he and his men engaged 'with everything we had'. Their weaponry included machine guns and L94 rocket launchers. Sergeant Cochrane then spotted a Union Jack flying from the rusting ship and shouted, 'Friendlies on the wreck! Check fire.'

With the missing marines accounted for and the wounded

requiring immediate extraction, all personnel were ordered back to base.

Marine Joe Lidster held Marine Maddison's hand as he lay dying in front of him. A true marine, Maddison fought until the end, pumping Marine Lidster's hand, determined not to give up. He died at 34 Field Hospital, Shaibah Airbase. Major Nick Anthony, the commanding officer of 539 Assault Squadron, described his death as 'absolutely tragic'.

Captain Jason Durrup was the first officer to suggest that Marine Maddison might be the victim of friendly fire. In all likelihood, Royal Marine call-signs equipped with MILAN anti-tank rockets had mistaken his craft for an enemy vessel. Major Anthony called in the Special Investigation Branch of The Royal Military Police – the military equivalent of a civilian CID department – who exonerated the MILAN crews and suggested that Marine Maddison's craft had been out of range of their weapons systems. The finding of an inflatable craft loaded with Russian-made Sagger anti-tank missiles 35 kilometres downriver supported the conclusion that unseen Iraqi forces had been responsible. The Special Investigation Branch duly closed its investigation, convinced that Marine Maddison had been killed in action by enemy forces. However, a BBC television crew embedded with 539 Assault Squadron questioned the findings, as by its own measurements Marine Maddison's boat had been 1.6 kilometres, not 2.6 kilometres, from the MILAN crews. Executive producer Simon Ford said, 'The Royal Military Police report might have been written in haste, but in the interest of Chris, his family and his colleagues in the Marines, we believe our evidence justifies reopening the investigation.'

Following the broadcast of the BBC documentary *Fighting the War*, The Royal Military Police executed a prompt U-turn and agreed it was 'most likely' that a MILAN missile killed Marine Maddison, while an inquest later heard that those marines protecting Crossing Point Anna had been unaware of the movements and intentions of the night patrol from 539 Assault Squadron. Senior officers from other units within 3 Commando Brigade had failed to share information and a liaison officer should have been stationed on the ground. Marine

Maddison's craft had been declared hostile, as there had been no evidence to the contrary. It had been engaged from two firing positions: on Crossing Point Anna and on the Khawr Abd Allah estuary.

Lieutenant Colonel Anthony (promoted from major) told Oxford Coroners' Court, 'We were working eight to ten days, all on fighting operations. We were tired, and we were tense. There was no doubt about that. I think the communications set-up was clearly a failing at some point between various locations. But I also think people were doing their very best at the time in a very, very confusing situation.'

In Coroner Andrew Walker's words, Marine Maddison was 'let down by those in command and by the communication system in operation at the time. The first investigation, which concluded he was killed by enemy forces, was a farce.'

Marine Maddison's father Les Towell said, 'We are disappointed that some of the witnesses did not accept their responsibility and accountability, and in our opinion embellished the truth to try and justify their actions. A catalogue of errors resulted in tragic consequences, but this does not detract from the professionalism and integrity of the vast majority of forces personnel.'

Marine Maddison's mother Julie agreed: 'If a senior officer or officers had ensured that all procedures and orders necessary and usual had been in place before the initial task force was sent out, the resultant confusion would not have taken place. This omission resulted in catastrophe and the creation of a dangerous situation that ultimately led to the death of our beloved son. It was senior officers' responsibility and duty to ensure a foresight of risk. Leadership fell far below what could be reasonably expected in the circumstances. The lack of duty of care to possible risks and consequences that even I, as a lay person, could have foreseen, effectively created an obvious chain of events that could have led to further loss of life.'

❖ ❖ ❖

Marine Maddison was one of three British fatalities on 30 March 2003. Fellow commando Major Steve Ballard died of a heart attack while coordinating battle operations at 3 Commando

Brigade headquarters. Lance Corporal Shaun Brierley of the Royal Corps of Signals died after a traffic accident on Main Supply Route Tampa. On 31 March 2003, Sergeant Chris Muir died while attempting to defuse cluster bombs. The following day, another road traffic accident cost the lives of Lance Corporal Karl Shearer and Lieutenant Alexander Tweedie. Their deaths brought the number of British fatalities to twenty-nine, of which only three were attributed to enemy fire. This led former SAS commander General Sir Peter de la Billiere, the officer commanding UK forces during Operation Desert Storm, to question the degree of preparedness prior to the invasion, while 'complacency' was later highlighted as a contributory factor after the two Sea Kings crashed off HMS *Ark Royal*.

Given the lack of Iraqi resistance and the devastating effectiveness of the campaign, some degree of complacency was perhaps unavoidable. This was a war against a country bereft of air or sea power and whose tanks belonged in museums not on battlefields. As the bodies of Iraqis rash or jingoistic enough to resist the allied onslaught lay dead in the sand, there was little sign of a messy endgame. The internal struggle between Shias and Sunnis, and rival factions within each, was expected to peter out over the forthcoming weeks.

30 March 2003

Basra Province

Major Steve Ballard

L ucy Ballard harboured grave doubts about how being on operations would affect her husband's rare condition. Major Steve Ballard, from Plymouth, suffered from primary cardiomyopathy, a weakening of his heart muscles. Knowing this would effectively end his military career, Major Ballard failed to pass on the details of his heart condition, which had been revealed by electro-cardiogram, to his commanders. He received a standard precautionary medical before flying to

Kuwait, but consultant trauma and orthopaedic surgeon Nigel Rossiter only had access to his military medical records, which made no reference to his cardiomyopathy. He signed off Major Ballard as fit at his word – a standard procedure, as he suggested later. Hugh Watkins, professor of cardiovascular medicine at John Radcliffe Hospital, Oxford, told a coroner's court this was a 'serious failing' to provide basic medical care.

Major Ballard had deployed as a staff officer in 3 Commando Brigade headquarters, where his heart stopped beating after a long stint in the operations centre.

His family said, 'Stephen joined The Royal Marines in 1994 and was promoted to the rank of major in 2001. He was passionate about his life and proud to be a Royal Marine. One of four sons, he loved his family. Stephen and Lucy had been married for 18 months and were thrilled at the prospect of the arrival of their first child later this year. Stephen's family, colleagues and wide circle of friends are devastated by his death, which leaves a great void. He was a courageous man who wanted to serve with and for his men.'

Lucy Ballard subsequently gave birth to a daughter, Connie.

30 March 2003

Main Supply Route Tampa

Lance Corporal Shaun Brierley

When Lance Corporal Shaun Brierley contacted his local newspaper, the *Batley News*, calling himself 'George Cross' and asking for pen pals to write to him in the Gulf, his own grandmother was one of those hoodwinked into posting him a letter. He found this hilarious. Based in Herford, Germany, with 212 Signal Squadron, Lance Corporal Brierley was well known for his cheeky sense of humour. Having served in Kosovo and Bosnia during a ten-year army career, the twenty-eight year old had settled into life on the Continent, marrying a local girl, Birgit Reisenbeck, with whom he had a son, Patrick.

On 30 March 2003, Lance Corporal Brierley found himself on Main Supply Route Tampa when the Land Rover he was travelling in struck a piece of rubble and overturned. The driver had failed to see the masonry because an infra-red plate attached to the front grill as an anti-friendly fire device partially blocked the headlights. Lance Corporal Brierley was not wearing a seat belt and suffered fatal head and abdominal injuries.

A Gurkha piper, Lance Corporal Thambahadur Armaja Pun, led 400 mourners at the funeral and played 'Flowers of the Forest' as Royal Corps of Signals soldiers carried the coffin into Batley Parish Church. Lance Corporal Brierley was described by his local vicar, Reverend Andrew Johnson, as 'A rough diamond, someone big, brash and loud, someone who would always fight for the underdog.'

Hundreds lined the streets of Batley following the hour-long service after Lance Corporal Brierley's coffin was carried by soldiers from the Royal Corps of Signals. Mechanics, bank staff, road sweepers and other employees ceased work to pay their respects as the funeral passed along Upper Commercial Street and Blakeridge Lane to Batley Cemetery.

Reverend Johnson added, 'He never missed an opportunity to wind people up, particularly his parents Peter and Christine, his brothers Craig and Graham, and his sister Helen, as well as his partner Birgit, her children Andrea and Nicole, and their own son Patrick.'

Major Jim Wood said, 'Lance Corporal Shaun Andrew Brierley was a member of 212 Signal Squadron, which provides communications for HQ 1 UK Armoured Division. He was a radio systems operator of nine years' experience and was a highly regarded and well-known member of the squadron. He will be greatly missed by all who knew him.'

Lance Corporal Brierley's parents accepted an invitation from the Prince of Wales to attend a reception at Highgrove. They were presented with their son's war medals, including the Queen's Jubilee Medal and four operational tour medals. A verdict of accidental death was recorded.

31 March 2003

Basra Province

Staff Sergeant Chris Muir

Bomb disposal experts Staff Sergeant Chris Muir and Corporal Glen Roberts were en route to make safe an abandoned tank when Iraqi farmers asked for their assistance to clear hundreds of unexploded M42 'bomblets' from their tomato fields. Dropped by US forces, the bomblets were designed to explode when they struck buildings or vehicles but often failed to detonate on soft ground. Horrified to see so many of these lethal weapons lying about, entangled in the vegetation, Staff Sergeant Muir set to work, briefing his colleague on the safest method of making them safe. As Corporal Roberts recalled, 'I took one side, and Sergeant Muir went towards a large well, measuring 20 metres by 60 metres at the opening. Two hundred bomblets were placed there by the locals. At about midnight, I heard a large bang, and I knew it was not good.'

Staff Sergeant Muir, who was newly promoted to his rank, had been kneeling over the munitions when one exploded. When Major John Balding visited the scene, he saw M42s lying in the dust and hanging from tomato crops two feet high. A squadron of Spanish engineers was already scheduled to visit the area. As Major Balding told a coroner's court, 'I guess Staff Sergeant Muir felt he could help the peasant population to be safe and to clear the bombs so that they could harvest. He felt he was experienced enough to help these people and decided to do so.'

Staff Sergeant Muir had deployed to Iraq from the Army School of Ammunition at Kineton, Warwickshire. He made his home nearby with wife Gillian and their young son Ben. In accordance with his wishes, the Monty Python song 'Always Look on the Bright Side of Life' was played as Staff Sergeant Muir was carried from All Saints Church, Burton Dassett. Gillian said her late husband was blessed with a fantastic sense of humour and could always 'light up a room'. His funeral was followed by a private family cremation.

1 April 2003

Basra Province

Lance Corporal Karl Shearer, Lieutenant Alexander Tweedie

Four days after Lance Corporal Matty Hull's death, D Squadron of The Household Cavalry suffered the loss of Lance Corporal Karl Shearer and Lieutenant Alexander Tweedie. They were trapped inside their Scimitar armoured vehicle when it slipped off a crossing point in the marshes. The incident was recalled by its only survivor, Trooper Wayne White. 'Pull to the left,' Lieutenant Tweedie shouted, moments before the Scimitar slid down a bank and overturned onto its turret. Trooper White, Lance Corporal Shearer and Lieutenant Tweedie were locked inside the dark cabin as it filled with water. The vehicle began to sink. Initially, the water pressure prevented Trooper White opening the vehicle hatch. Finally, he pulled himself clear. There was no escape for his two colleagues, who slipped unconscious beneath the water. The second-in-command of D Squadron, Major Edward Haward, admitted that vehicles were becoming bogged down in ditches and slipping off crossings on a daily basis.

Lance Corporal Shearer, from Windsor, was survived by his wife Suzie and their daughter Lauren. They had been together for nine years. She said her husband was proud to be doing his job and that she did not think the accident could have been prevented. His commanding officer, Lieutenant Colonel Mark van der Lande, said, 'Karl was a popular and very able soldier, whom I had recently promoted. He demonstrated the very best of what it is to be a soldier of The Household Cavalry and will be greatly missed. Karl was a brave, courageous man who died doing his duty to his country under very difficult conditions. He and his comrades have been heavily involved in operations in Iraq and showed outstanding courage, determination and professionalism to defeat the enemy. My thoughts and those of the whole regiment are with his family.'

Coroner Selena Lynch recorded a verdict of accidental death

while on active service. She hoped it would be of some comfort to the soldiers' families that neither had suffered pain.

Old Etonian Lieutenant Tweedie had served with The Blues and Royals for two and a half years. He was brought home for treatment but died in an Edinburgh hospital without regaining consciousness on 22 April 2003. His family said he was a wonderful, loving son who brightened everyone's lives. He was proud to serve with The Household Cavalry and a promising career lay ahead of him. Lieutenant Colonel van der Lande described his death as a 'tragic loss to the regiment'.

6 April 2003

Basra

Lance Corporal Ian Malone, Piper Christopher Muzvuru

After two weeks of probing, British forces seized control of Basra on 6 April 2003, and Lieutenant General Robin Brims achieved his ambition of capturing the city without 'undue attrition'. Number 1 Company, 1st Battalion, Irish Guards, was at the tip of the spear.

On the morning of 6 April 2003, Piper Christopher Muzvuru serenaded his comrades with traditional tunes on his chanter, a small pipe. Among them was Lance Corporal Ian Malone, from Dublin, an Irishman proud to be a British soldier. The Irish Guards had been raised by Queen Victoria in 1900 to mark the bravery of Lance Corporal Malone's brethren who fought for Britain in the Boer War.

As armoured infantry mounted in Warriors, 1 Company, Irish Guards, headed for enemy positions around Basra University, Lieutenant Daniel O'Connell manoeuvred his platoon and engaged several enemy bunkers before dismounting and breaking into buildings. After supporting the next assaulting platoon, Lieutenant O'Connell remounted and cleared five more buildings, driving his men on and placing himself in great personal danger. He personally led each house clearance. While most Iraqi soldiers were long gone, the buildings contained pockets of fedayeen fighters, paramilitaries loyal to Saddam.

As the light faded, 1 Company formed a defensive perimeter around the college complex. It was then that men dressed in civilian clothing sprayed rounds towards guardsmen huddled near an armoured vehicle. Piper Muzvuru and Lance Corporal Malone were killed and two other soldiers wounded. Lance Corporal Malone was hit twice, through the neck and head. Lieutenant O'Connell, who later received the Military Cross, organised the extraction of the deceased and wounded.

While 40 family members and friends were present at RAF Brize Norton for his repatriation, Piper Muzvuru was denounced as a 'traitor' in Zimbabwe. The pro-Mugabe newspaper the *Daily Herald* published a cartoon of Piper Muzvuru headed 'Buffalo Soldier', a reference to the 10th Cavalry Regiment, the first all-black US regiment, raised to fight Native Americans. The Harare-based *Daily Mirror* called him a 'mercenary' fighting for a country that was 'virtually at war with Zimbabwe'. Former Zimbabwean cabinet minister Dr Ibbo Mandaza said, 'Throughout history, Africans have fought on behalf of Britain in return for cash, and I regret that this tradition continues today.' Piper Muzvuru's family, including his grieving mother, were subsequently questioned by Zimbabwean secret police. As many as 200 Zimbabweans were serving with the British Army at the time. In 2001, Piper Muzvuru had become the first black piper in the 103-year history of The Irish Guards.

The commemoration of Lance Corporal Malone's passing brought together communities on both sides of the Irish Sea, and the sight of his coffin carried by six guardsmen in British Army uniforms through the staunchly Catholic suburb of Ballyfermot, Dublin, was symbolic of reconciliation. Pall-bearers from 1st Battalion, The Irish Guards, were joined by soldiers from the Republic en route to the Church of the Assumption as the Irish capital saw its first British military funeral since 1922. Among the 1,000-strong congregation were the British chargé d'affaires, the British military attaché and representatives of the United States Embassy. Lance Corporal Malone had retained his Irish citizenship, and there were no Union Jacks or firing party.

Lance Corporal Malone, described as a man of faith, philosophy and integrity, had served in the Irish reserve force, the An Fórsa Cosanta Áitiúil, from the age of 15. He had joined The Irish Guards in 1997, aged 21, after considering the more 'romantic' option of joining the French Foreign Legion. Lance Corporal Malone beat his officers at chess with an ease that made some wonder if the right man was in charge. He had always been intellectual, if not academically inclined; one year at school he refused to sit his exams, suggesting to his family that they were a waste of time.

His mother May said that her son was proud of his regiment and enjoyed every moment of military life: 'It was a great honour to meet his colleagues who came to visit me in Dublin. For his sake, I try not to be bitter. I don't think the war should ever have happened. It was not necessary. There was no need for it. But I cannot go through life being bitter, because Ian wouldn't have wanted that, so for his sake I try not to be.'

6 April 2003

Basra

Fusilier Kelan Turrington

Fusilier Kelan Turrington of The Royal Regiment of Fusiliers was another tragic victim of friendly fire. The fatal shots were fired from a machine gun mounted to an armoured vehicle belonging to The Queen's Royal Lancers. The Royal Military Police's report into his death was passed to the Army Prosecuting Authority, and a Queen's Royal Lancers lance corporal was questioned under caution. No charges were pressed. Men from The Queen's Royal Lancers had been unaware of Fusilier Turrington's movements, and when he and three others advanced into their sector, they were assumed to be enemy. It was said that rounds from The Queen's Royal Lancers' position struck a grenade carried by Fusilier Turrington as he approached an enemy trench. The teenage infanteer, at the time the youngest

British serviceman to have died in Iraq, was awarded a Mention in Dispatches.

Like so many boys who grow up in a service environment, Fusilier Turrington had joined his father's regiment. His mother knew that he wanted to be a soldier from the age of four, and as a child he wore his father's beret and hackle. John Turrington, a serviceman for 23 years, was working at the Army Training Centre, Bassingbourn, Cambridgeshire, when his son died. They were 'best mates'. Kelan's battalion was stationed in Germany. When he last saw his parents, he had assured them that he wanted to go to war and that they were not to worry because 'the British are the best'. The West Ham supporter had left school aged 16 and was 18 years and 131 days old when he died. At his funeral, his beret and hackle were placed on top of a Union Jack draped over his coffin. They fitted better than his father's all those years before.

His mother said, 'We did not try to change his mind about joining the army, but we did not encourage him, either. All through his school life, he just wanted to be a soldier. He used to wait in the driveway at home for his father to come home from the base. We sent Kelan parcels, and I wrote to him all the time to say I loved him. He said that when letters arrived, the lads were like kids running to the ice-cream van. I just hope he received the parcels, too, so he knew how much we loved him.'

30 April 2003

Maysan Province

Lance Corporal James McCue

On 30 April 2003, Lance Corporal James McCue, a Royal Electrical and Mechanical Engineer who belonged to 16 Air Assault Brigade, died in Maysan when a shell fired, possibly accidentally, from an abandoned Iraqi tank landed inside a British base. Lance Corporal McCue, a single man from Paisley, Scotland, was found with a pen in his hand. 'Jamesy' had been writing a letter home when the warhead struck his tent. He bled to death from shrapnel wounds to his chest and liver. Coroner Nicholas Gardiner noted that he just happened to be sitting in the wrong place at the wrong time. Sergeant Martin Carrahar later suggested that there had been a 'distinct lack of urgency' in response to the shelling.

Lance Corporal McCue, a father of two and former Scottish international sprinter, had joined the army in April 1999 and served in Germany and Kosovo. His letters home touched on his sadness at the poor conditions in which so many Iraqi children lived.

His funeral took place at St Charles Roman Catholic Church, Paisley, followed by an internment at Hawkhead Cemetery. Six soldiers from Lance Corporal McCue's company were flown back from Iraq to carry his coffin, which was draped in the Union Jack. One wreath inside the hearse read 'Dad' in white carnations. An accompanying message read, 'Daddy, thank you for making the world a safer place for us to grow up in. Big hugs, Alexander and Hannah.'

Father Peter McGarry told mourners, 'He was a fit, lively, cheerful, fun-loving man who also had his serious side. In one of his last communications home to his family, he spoke with compassion of the difficult conditions in which many found themselves. Our prayers today turn to those closest to James. Our hearts go out to them.'

A twelve-man firing party fired three volleys of shots and a bugler sounded the last post. Finally, a lone piper played the traditional lament 'Flowers of the Forest'.

His mother Mary said, 'The family and all of James's friends were shocked and saddened to hear of his death. He was a wonderful son, and those that knew him will remember his maturity and lively sense of humour. He talked often about how much he loved serving with The Royal Electrical and Mechanical Engineers Air Assault Battalion and was extremely proud when he was promoted to lance corporal, which was only at the beginning of this year. Words cannot express the depth of our grief, but mixed with our profound sadness there is pride in the knowledge that he died a soldier while serving his country. He will be remembered for ever by all who knew him.'

Lieutenant Colonel Mark Armstrong said, 'Despite the relatively short time that he had been with the battalion, he had made a lasting impression on all of his colleagues. He had shown himself throughout to be highly competent, both as a soldier and as a tradesman, and he expected everyone to achieve the same high standards that he set for himself. He maintained the highest levels of physical fitness, and as a qualified physical fitness instructor many within the unit have benefited from time spent under his instruction. Lance Corporal McCue was a strong character who displayed a great sense of pride in everything he did, qualities that gained him respect and admiration from all members of the unit. He was a credit to his corps and will be sadly missed by all.'

6 May 2003

Camp Sparrowhawk, Maysan Province

Private Andrew Kelly

The airborne fraternity suffered another misfortune on 6 May 2003 when Private Andrew Kelly of A Company, 3 Para, shot himself while cleaning his personal weapon. Witnesses at Camp Sparrowhawk were adamant that he suffered a negligent discharge – when a round is released inadvertently from a soldier's weapon. They attempted to save him, but he died of his accidentally inflicted wounds.

Private Kelly, from Tavistock, Devon, was eighteen years and five days old when he deployed, two months after his older comrades. At the time of writing, he remains the youngest victim of the British war in Iraq.

Private Kelly was remembered as a humorous, courageous teenager who achieved his dream of becoming a paratrooper. He was buried with full military honours at the Church of St Mary and St Julian in the village of Maker, Cornwall, where a Union Jack flew at half-mast. Private Kelly's belt and maroon beret were presented to his mother by Colour Sergeant Mark Willetts. A gun party fired three volleys of shots, and a long bugler played reveille and sounded the last post. His coffin was carried from the church to his place of rest by members of his battalion, and the cortege was led by Private Kelly's father Robert, from Callington, Cornwall. Mr Kelly served in the Royal Navy for 24 years and was present in the South Atlantic throughout the Falklands War. He said that he understood the need to take up arms when it was justified but could see no justification for the war in Iraq.

Private Kelly's mother, Helen Yallop, said, 'Andrew's loss is deeply felt by all the family. We are devastated. He was a wonderful, fearless and confident son, always well-mannered, and who, even as a young boy, desired only to be a para. He turned 18 on 9 March this year, and within days was on his way to the Gulf. Even at school in Tavistock, he was single-minded about an army career, knowing it would fulfil his ambitions for travel and sport. He loved swimming, rollerblading and skiing, and had enjoyed many family trips abroad. In his last call to me just days ago, he said, "Don't worry about me, Mum. Paras always go to heaven." He will be missed sorely, too, by his two dogs, especially Roxy, a Staffordshire terrier, who senses a terrible tragedy has befallen us all. Andrew remains alive in our thoughts and memories. It will always be so.'

She said that her son carried with him a poem about paratroopers entitled 'The Maroon Machine'. It began:

> These men defy fear and jump from the skies,
> Striking fear into their enemies' eyes.
> They jumped into Arnhem and fought to the death,
> They recaptured the Falklands, unleashing their wrath.

Lieutenant Colonel Matthew Lowe, commanding officer of 3 Para, said, 'The loss of Private Andy Kelly is especially tragic. He was a young man full of energy and life, with a long career in The Parachute Regiment ahead of him. Andy had recently joined the 3rd Battalion, having come from the Infantry Training Centre, where he had completed basic training, and proved himself to be fit, mentally agile, professional and highly determined. It had always been Andy's ambition to be a Parachute Regiment soldier, and he was welcomed from the moment he arrived. He had just started to make new friends and settle down into post-war operations. Andy was quiet but confident and likeable.'

8 May 2003

Ali al-Saleem Airbase, Kuwait

Gunner Duncan Pritchard

Gunner Duncan Pritchard, who was based at RAF Honington, Suffolk, fell from the back of a Land Rover when the vehicle struck a ridge near Ali al-Saleem Airbase. He suffered severe head and back injuries and was 'medivaced' back to Britain. A post-mortem gave Gunner Pritchard's cause of death as a cranial-cerebral injury; a coroner recorded a verdict of accidental death. The court paid its respects with a minute's silence in his honour. Commander Andrew Knowles of The Royal Air Force paid tribute to Gunner Pritchard as a fine young man.

19 May 2003

Kuwait

Corporal David Shepherd

Corporal David Shepherd died of natural causes in Kuwait. A Ministry of Defence statement read, 'Our thoughts and prayers are with his family at this very difficult time.' His family requested that no further details be made available.

22 May 2003

Location Undisclosed

Leonard Harvey

At the time of writing, Leonard Harvey, aged 55, remains the oldest victim of the conflict. The divorced father of three from Wattisham, Suffolk, was an avid Ipswich Town supporter who volunteered for the Defence Fire Service for thirty-three years. Operation Telic was his third operational tour overseas. He was taken ill in the Gulf and returned home for treatment, where he died in hospital. David Marsland, assistant chief officer at the headquarters of the Defence Fire Service (Army), said, 'As a civilian firefighter in the Defence Fire Service (Army), Len volunteered to go to the Gulf, which speaks highly of his sense of duty and dedication. One of his greatest passions was his football, playing regularly in his youth as goalkeeper. He followed Ipswich Town's fortunes through thick and thin. As part of the fire-service team, he will be sadly missed by all his working and retired colleagues.'

❖ ❖ ❖

Prime Minister Tony Blair became the first coalition leader to visit 'post-war' Iraq and adopted his 'at ease with the soldiers' routine until one young paratrooper quipped, 'Where are you sending us next, sir? Korea or Iran?' Blair told the massed ranks their conduct was a 'model of how armed forces anywhere in the world should conduct themselves', which would serve as 'a lesson for armed forces the world over'. The downscaling of British forces began on the day of his visit, and responsibility for Maysan Province shifted from 16 Air Assault Brigade to its largest component part, a supersized battle group built around 1st Battalion, The Parachute Regiment, commanded by Lieutenant Colonel Tom Beckett.

24 June 2003

Majar al-Kabir

Corporal Russell Aston, Sergeant Simon Hamilton-Jewell,
Lance Corporal Benjamin Hyde, Lance Corporal Thomas
Keys, Corporal Paul Long, Corporal Simon Miller

On 24 June 2003, six Royal Military Policemen belonging to
the 1 Para battle group were executed at a police station in
Majar al-Kabir. Five years on, their deaths remain shrouded in
controversy, with so many questions unanswered, seemingly no
prospect of those who shot them being brought to justice and
the families seeking the intervention of the European Court of
Human Rights in a bid to force the government to conduct an
independent inquiry. The Red Caps' deaths are perhaps the most
evocative and symbolic of the Iraq campaign, as the six were
essentially non-combatants, lightly armed, plucky but passive;
they only visited the town to train the local officers and to hand
over funds for the repair of the station.

While it is impossible to determine their exact time of death,
Sergeant Simon Hamilton-Jewell and his colleagues Corporal
Russ Aston, Corporal Paul Long, Corporal Simon Miller, Lance
Corporal Ben Hyde and Lance Corporal Tom Keys died within a
couple of hours of a riot in the market area of the town caused by
the presence of British paratroopers, who, acting in self-defence,
shot dead a number of armed civilians. While the Paras, led by
Sergeant Gordon Robertson, took cover in a family home, taking
its members hostage, the mob headed towards the police station.
Sergeant Hamilton-Jewell, from Chessington, Surrey, urged the
Iraqi officers to stand beside him in defiance of the protesters.
They fled, shots were fired and the Red Caps' Land Rovers set
on fire.

While Sergeant Robertson's men radioed for assistance and
a quick-reaction force was dispatched from Camp Abu Naji,
misunderstandings and communications failures meant that the
rescue party was unaware of the Red Caps' presence and no effort
was made by British forces to reach the police station, where,

according to witness testimony, Sergeant Hamilton-Jewell's men had been forced to retreat to a storeroom and plead for their lives. They were not only executed but ritually slaughtered, with full magazines of 30 rounds expended into their bodies.

Sergeant Robertson fought heroically to lead his men out of the town to a checkpoint established by Major Chris Kemp. It was to there that an Iraqi doctor drove an ambulance shortly after midday to alert British forces to the presence of their colleagues at the police station. The doctor's first account said that the Red Caps were being held hostage. He returned a short while later with tragic news of their deaths.

Sergeant Hamilton-Jewell's mother Teresa and half-brother Tony said, 'A nod, a wink or a smile – 100 per cent human being, dedicated to life in full. He was a man keen to help anybody, a fearless man, biker, hiker and climber, but above all a man dedicated to the army, his regiment, his unit and his comrades. He gave 20 years of service defending others in so many locations and was a selfless, ultra-fit man to the last. A son and brother beyond belief, "H.J.", "Hammy" or "Simon" all meant the same – a top man, friend and soldier. A man's man and a soldier's soldier. He was a very human person who will be dearly missed for the rest of our lives. For a soldier never afraid to do his duty – we love and miss you. God bless. In our own grief at the loss of Simon, we are also remembering his colleagues who died with him, and offer our sympathy and condolences to their families and friends. We are both very grateful for the dedicated and caring support that so many ranks and agencies of the army have given to us and the rest of Simon's direct family, without which managing would have been so much harder.'

Lieutenant Colonel Eddie Foster-Knight said, 'Simon was an excellent soldier and military policeman – highly motivated, professional and dedicated in his approach. He handled himself with great credit during the whole operation and was a fine leader of his section. He was extremely well respected by all with whom he served.'

Corporal Aston, a former grenadier guardsman, was a fitness fanatic who ran marathons for charity and was one of only a small number of Royal Military Policemen to pass the Parachute

Regiment's P Company selection course. He doted over his daughter Paygan and told his wife Anna that this tour would be his last. In his letters home, he spoke of joining the prison service and returning to his native Derbyshire from Colchester, where the Red Caps were based. Corporal Aston, who was second in command to Sergeant Simon Hamilton-Jewell, was respected for his soldiering ability, humour and generosity. He was also mischievous and was described by one colleague as being 'as cunning as a shithouse rat'. Hundreds of his family, friends and comrades packed into St Mary's Church, Coton in the Elms, Derbyshire, for his funeral.

His widow Anna said, 'Russ was a very handsome man, loved by everyone who knew him. He was such a kind and special person, with a smashing sense of humour. He could get on with anyone he met. He was a doting father who had lots and lots of friends. When he walked into a room, he filled it with his height and presence.'

His father Mike said, 'I shall always miss him and shall never, never get over his death. But I stand proud, because few will ever equal what he achieved.'

Captain James Hibbert of The Royal Military Police said, 'To us, Russ was invincible. Surely no one like him could simply die? He seemed too quick, too strong, too full of life. He seemed impervious to danger. He was also a loyal friend, an outstanding soldier and an exceptionally proud father.'

Corporal Long attended Blackmoor Church of England Primary School and All Hallows Roman Catholic Comprehensive in Aldershot before moving to South Shields, where he attended Hebburn College. He joined the regular army in April 1999, having served two years with the Territorial Army, and was posted to 156 Provost Company in March 2000. A member of the Parachute Provost Platoon, he was a qualified radio operator.

His mother Pat said, 'The army was his life. He wanted only to help others less fortunate than himself. Paul leaves behind a loving wife, Gemma, and a baby son of 11 months, Benjamin David, and our devoted mother Patricia.'

Corporal Miller's parents John and Marilyn said, 'Simon was promoted to corporal just before he left for Iraq, and we were all really proud of him. He loved motorbikes and rode an army bike out in Iraq as well as having his own back in the UK. He was due to finish his tour in July and planned to marry when he returned home. He was our life. He was a lovely lad and very close to his family and fiancée. Words can't describe how much we all love him and miss him. At 12 years old, he attended Sunderland AFC School of Excellence. Later, he had trials for Cambridge United, and he went to the team's ground regularly for training before deciding to join the army and become a Red Cap. But he continued to play football for his unit, 156 Provost Company, and for The Royal Military Police team. Thank you for the 21 wonderful years you gave us, Si, the bravest man we ever knew. We will miss you and think of you every second of the day until we meet again.'

Lance Corporal Hyde's father John, a hospital porter, said, 'Ben was an extremely charismatic person who lightened the mood whenever he walked into a room. All he ever wanted was to be a military policeman, and he worked very hard to become one. He was very career-minded, with bags of potential, and he had been recommended for early promotion. The red beret was all he ever wanted. It was his life, so he gave his life doing the job he loved most. He was also a loving son who will be sorely missed.'

Lance Corporal Hyde's cousin Jenny Singh said, 'Ben and I grew up together. He wasn't just my cousin, he was really my big brother, and I worshipped him. He was fun, cheeky, incredibly charming and brave.'

Captain James Hibbert added, 'It was impossible not to like Ben. He was a guy bursting with character. Someone who did not just exist but who was bursting with life.'

Lance Corporal Keys' father Reg said, 'Five years ago, we gave the army a rather shy, introverted young sixteen-year-old boy. Sadly, what we see here before us today is not how we expected the army to return him to us – not the homecoming we had planned for Tom. On a more positive note, the army developed this boy into a brave young man brimming with self-confidence and a very rounded, resourceful individual. The day Tom was killed along with his five brave friends, he was just four days short of his 21st birthday. Cards that had arrived for Tom remain unopened – our wounds from the pain of his loss are still too raw to undertake such a task. To me and Sally, Tom was one of two perfect sons. Never once did he bring trouble to our doorstep. He was a quiet lad of whom we are immensely proud. I am sure Tom will in future be telling me to "take a chill pill" as we search for the truth behind the tragic events that unfolded that day.'

Captain James Hibbert said, 'Tom transferred to The Royal Military Police to fulfil a strong desire to take up the challenges of police work. We were delighted to receive him; in fact, from the moment he first expressed a desire to join us, every effort was made to get our hands on him as soon as possible. I recall the note made by his interviewing officer, who described Tom as "confident, articulate, fit and robust. He is precisely the kind of volunteer who will succeed in The Royal Military Police." Tom was an impressive guy and a consummate professional.'

18 July 2003

Az Zubayr

Captain James Linton

Captain James Linton, from Warminster, Wiltshire, died on 18 July 2003 following a training run at the British base at Az Zubayr. He served with 40 Field Regiment, Royal Artillery. A Ministry of Defence spokesman said, 'He was married with three children. Our thoughts are with them and Captain Linton's friends and colleagues.'

13 August 2003

Camp Abu Naji

Private Jason Smith

> 'The heat was unbelievable. It was like putting your oven
> on to the highest temperature and chucking your head
> in it. We were driving around in Saxons [armoured cars].
> They were like microwaves on wheels. There were guys
> chucking water over their drivers to keep them cool so
> they didn't pass out. There were pallets and pallets of
> water everywhere, but it was like drinking from a hot
> bath. There was no cold water.'
>
> Private John Horseman, 1st Battalion,
King's Own Scottish Borderers

As temperatures in Maysan touched 55 degrees Celsius, Private John Horseman collapsed and was flown back to Britain. Exposure to such extreme heat left him permanently disabled, and he was medically discharged. He was relatively fortunate, as his friend and colleague from the same battalion, Private Jason Smith, suffered a fatal cardiac arrest induced by heatstroke on 13 August 2003.

Private Smith's legacy might be the better protection of soldiers. Using his death as a test case, a High Court judge ruled five years later that human rights legislation could apply to military personnel on active service. Mr Justice Collins said that service personnel were entitled to legal protection 'wherever they may be', while 'to send a soldier out on patrol or, indeed, into battle with defective equipment could constitute a breach' of Article 2 of the European Convention on Human Rights, which enshrines the right to life. While he acknowledged that soldiers could not receive 'absolute protection', the judge added that they did not lose all protection simply because they were conducting operations in hostile territory. The Ministry of Defence had argued that it was impossible to give soldiers the benefit of the Human Rights Act in such circumstances.

After Andrew Walker concluded that Private Smith's death had resulted from a 'serious failure to recognise and take appropriate steps to address the difficulty he had in adjusting to the climate', the Ministry of Defence applied to the High Court to forbid coroners from using phrases such as 'serious failure' in their verdicts and summaries. This intervention was described by legal professor Gary Slapper of the Open University as 'an act of arrant insolence'. In the aftermath of any serviceman's death, Walker's duty was to conduct a full, fair and exacting investigation and to identify any failures in the organisation with a duty of care towards him. Justice Collins rejected the application.

Thirty-two-year-old reservist Private Smith left the home in Hawick he shared with his mother to attend the Reserves Training and Mobilisation Centre at Chilwell, Nottinghamshire, on 30 May 2003 to undertake training for Operation Telic. His weight was recorded as 112 kilograms and his height as 180 centimetres. These statistics gave Private Smith a body mass index of 34, which a Board of Inquiry later noted was 'in the upper end of the scale for obese'. In spite of his poor physical conditioning, and that it had been suggested he was inclined to 'give up easily' on tasks, neither a formal physical assessment nor an occupational-risk assessment were conducted prior to or during his deployment. There was no record of him passing any physical fitness test later than February 2002.

On 17 June 2003, Private Smith, of the 52nd Lowland Regiment (Volunteers), began his attachment to C Company of the 1st Battalion, The King's Own Scottish Borderers, as they acclimatised for ten days in Kuwait. During this period, it was noted that Private Smith spent more time than most on an air-conditioned bus made available for periods of rest when the heat became too intense. On 28 June 2003, C Company headed north, and Private Smith and his colleagues moved into the athletics stadium at al-Amarah, Maysan Province. It was the hottest period of the year in Iraq, yet there was no air conditioning at the facility. Even at night, the temperature rarely fell below 30 degrees Celsius. With 20 to 30 soldiers collapsing daily, it was feared the company would be left short of men to fulfil its duties and pre-arranged weeks of annual leave entitlement would have to be postponed.

On 9 August 2003, the C Company medic overheard a conversation in which it was suggested Private Smith was struggling with the heat and 'not performing well'. When Private Smith said he was not sleeping well at night and felt unwell, he was offered advice on hydration and nutrition, excused heavy duties and told to wear the minimum dress state. He was also ordered to report to the company medic every twenty-four hours and returned to normal duties after three days. It was a blessing for Private Smith when his multiple was tasked to guard a local power station: the building was air-conditioned, and he slept for six hours.

The next day, 13 August 2003, was more arduous. His multiple deployed on Operation Spey, the control of fuel distribution to petrol stations in al-Amarah. It was extremely hot on the station forecourts, and the locals were furious about fuel shortages. At 1500, Private Smith returned to the stadium and was seen filling his water bottle. Three hours later, he was found collapsed in a corridor in his accommodation with blood pouring from his nose. When questioned by colleagues, his speech was slurred. They poured water over him, fanned him and covered him in damp cloths. He was lifted onto a stretcher and carried to a battlefield ambulance, where an intravenous drip was attached to his arm.

'Don't drop me,' Private Smith was heard to say.

En route to Camp Abu Naji, he became more anxious and aggressive, 'as if he was having a fit', as the driver Corporal Jim Black described it after witnessing Private Smith rip the drip from his arm. His behaviour worsened to delirious on arrival at the military hospital, where his body temperature was measured at just below 42 degrees Celsius. Private Smith's medical condition worsened during treatment, and he suffered a cardiac arrest. In spite of numerous attempts to resuscitate him, he was pronounced dead at 2010.

Captain Stewart Murray of the Royal Army Medical Corps was dismayed his patient was not given oxygen en route to hospital: 'For a patient of any sort, the immediate response to those symptoms would be to give him high-flow, high-rate oxygen. This didn't happen. Jason had been ill for some days before the day he died, but the record-keeping seemed to be appalling. Jason's illness was not picked up. I feel very strongly that if his early onset illness was diagnosed and managed, he would still be alive today. I am utterly convinced of that. The level of medical competency was very low, shockingly low. This occurred to me very soon after I deployed. The problem was that once soldiers have done their medical training, you get little or no experience of injuries and illnesses until you are sent on operations, and then you are expected to react appropriately by yourself.'

Corporal Black insisted there that were no drugs in the ambulance besides aspirin and that only a few drops of oxygen remained in the cylinders. He said, 'By then it was too late anyway. We'd done about a mile when he had a seizure.'

A Board of Inquiry noted the high tempo of operations and lack of manpower to cover the tasks conducted by Private Smith and his colleagues; the latter point was made by every witness who gave evidence, from the officer commanding the company to the most junior private soldier. The board noted that duties at the petrol station had involved dealing with 'a disgruntled and frustrated public trying to get fuel for their vehicles. This duty was very stressful and very hot, spending time on the forecourts.' Private Smith had been subjected to drinking parades prior to and after each patrol, when the soldiers stood in a line and were made to drink from their water bottles while junior non-commissioned officers observed. Private Smith's accommodation, a concrete block at the stadium, was criticised as being 'of very poor quality, with no windows, doors or power, and no air conditioning or fans available'. There was also 'next to no natural wind'. The Board concluded, 'The lack of such facilities [at the stadium] caused suffering, and it should be noted that the officer commanding C Company had repeatedly requested air-conditioning systems and infrastructure support.'

As Private Smith had not been identified as suffering from a heat-related illness on the day of his death, no monitoring of his condition had taken place. The cause of his death was hyperthermia and was exacerbated by four factors, according to the board: 'He was very overweight, his probable lack of fitness, the extreme temperatures and lack of air-conditioned accommodation.'

Private Smith's inquest in late 2006 highlighted the inadequacy of the deceased's pre-deployment training, the failure to monitor the progress of soldiers during the all-too-brief acclimatisation period and the fact that the advice given to them on hydration was 'seriously wrong'. The coroner added that, given the controversial circumstances surrounding Private Smith's death, it was 'totally unacceptable and unforgivable' for the army to have lost his medical records.

14 August 2003

Basra

Captain David Jones

On Remembrance Sunday, November 2002, Captain David Jones had laid wreath at his village church in memory of fallen British service personnel. It was the same Lincolnshire church that saw his wedding to Isobel that summer. In February 2003, he deployed to the Gulf with The Queen's Lancashire Regiment as a civil–military liaison officer. He returned to Britain on leave in May ahead of starting a second tour the following month in Basra.

Even in the first weeks after liberation, half of the city's 1.5 million citizens considered the British Army as occupiers, according to a survey by the Iraq Centre for Research. By the autumn, this would swell to three-quarters of adult men and women.

As Captain Jones's commanding officer Lieutenant Colonel Jorge Mendonca bemoaned, the size of the British presence in southern Iraq was being reduced: from eighteen thousand in May 2003 to nine thousand five hundred just three months later. A proportion of these troops was stationed in Basra itself, where, as Lieutenant Colonel Mendonca put it, his battalion was the 'only show in town'. He knew the locals were angry that the 'water supply was iffy, there was insufficient fuel and the electricity supply had gone from bad to worse'.

Lieutenant Colonel Mendonca was one of the army's rising stars, and by his own reckoning 'no also-ran lieutenant colonel'. Having been promoted to his rank aged just 36, he could justify his arrogance better than most. He thought that there should have been more, not fewer, troops on the ground than had participated in the war-fighting phase. To his chagrin, this scenario contrasted starkly with the size of the British Army in Belfast during the height of the Troubles, when nine infantry battalions patrolled the streets. While neither Captain Jones nor Lieutenant Colonel Mendonca were predisposed to accept their mission as an inevitable failure, privately the latter cursed the British government's 'naivety' and the line of thought that the Shias would be so delighted to be rid of Saddam that they would bear the shambles with smiles.

When the locals staged their first major uprising in Basra on 9 July 2003, Lieutenant Colonel Mendonca's men were beaten with sticks, stoned and stabbed. Twenty-two soldiers required hospital treatment. The restraint displayed by their uninjured colleagues impressed the commanding officer. While gung-ho soldiers might have sought revenge and taken life, the rebellion was quelled peacefully.

During the same month, The Queen's Lancashire Regiment established a holding facility at their barracks to screen those suspected of violence against Coalition Forces. Major Antony Royce, the internment review officer, reported to Lieutenant Colonel Mendonca on legal issues pertaining to the treatment of captives being primed for interrogation. As Lieutenant Colonel Mendonca was told, the Ministry of Defence approved the hooding of suspects and the use of stress positions 'in certain situations'.

On 14 August 2003, Captain Jones was surrounded by a hostile crowd and stoned. He climbed into an ambulance to be driven to a field hospital for treatment. During the journey, a remote-controlled bomb planted at the foot of a lamp post was detonated, killing him and injuring two other soldiers. When army spokesman Major Charlie Mayo pledged to hunt down the perpetrators and bring them to Iraqi justice, he could not have imagined how many British servicemen would die in similar circumstances over the following years as improvised explosive devices became the insurgents' weapons of choice.

While Captain Jones was described by Lieutenant Colonel Mendonca as a 'courageous, warm-hearted officer who would be sorely missed', his widow Isobel added that she was 'extremely proud of Dai'. She said that he was 'a wonderful husband who served his country with great courage'. Captain Jones's funeral took place in the church where just over a year before they had married. On this solemn occasion, his comrades from The Queen's Lancashire Regiment carried his coffin into the packed All Saints Church, South Elkington, near Louth, Lincolnshire. The service was also relayed to 100 mourners outside. Major Adrian Peters' eulogy spoke of Captain Jones's love for his fellow servicemen. He was buried with full military honours.

Isobel's mother and father, Mr and Mrs Myers, added, 'Our daughter Isobel and Dai were married on 13 July 2002. It was the most perfect day. He was a beautiful person, both inside and out. His kindness, warmth and generosity of spirit touched everyone he met. They were immensely happy. Our family is finding his loss very hard to bear, but we take some consolation in the knowledge that he died doing the job he loved in the service of his country.'

❖ ❖ ❖

A month after Captain Jones's death, ten local men were arrested after a swoop on a Basra hotel and brought to The Queen's Lancashire Regiment base for screening. Lieutenant Colonel Mendonca witnessed their treatment briefly but trusted his junior commanders to handle the prisoners with dignity. Their treatment as he witnessed it was unrepresentative of that received over 36 hours by hotel receptionist Baha Mousa. In spite of his office and accommodation being only 29 metres from the hostage suite, Lieutenant Colonel Mendonca was adamant he did not hear Mousa scream or cry as he was beaten and kicked by Corporal Donald Payne and others. According to witnesses, the father of two pleaded for mercy, crying out, 'Blood, blood, I am going to die.' But there was no let up in the barbarism as he was beaten with bars, kicked and forced to drink his own urine. Payne even conducted 'choir practice': hitting the captives in sequence so that they cried out a tune. Mousa's post-mortem revealed 93 separate injuries.

Lieutenant Colonel Mendonca never saw Mousa's corpse but launched an investigation and visited his family – the victim's children were the same age as his own. Lieutenant Colonel Mendonca did not visit Mousa's family out of guilt, as he later made explicit. He felt it was his duty to confront them and to pledge that justice would prevail. He doubted at that point that he himself would end up in the dock.

Corporal Payne became the first British soldier for several decades to admit to a war crime – the inhumane treatment of detainees – for which he received a one-year prison sentence. He was discharged from the army. Weaknesses in the Crown's case at his court martial assisted Corporal Payne's escape from charges of manslaughter and perverting the course of justice. Mr Justice McKinnon said that he was 'compelled' to accept a motion of no case to answer and tore into the prosecution witnesses, describing Private Jonathan Lee as 'useless' and his evidence as 'incapable of belief, a catalogue of unexplained inconsistencies and downright lies'. Private Lee was also the main witness against Lance Corporal Wayne Crowcroft and Private Darren Fallon, whom the judge ordered to be cleared of inhumane treatment, and Sergeant Kelvin Stacey, who was found not guilty of assault occasioning actual bodily harm.

Colonel Mendonca – he had been promoted – should have been aware that the abuse was taking place, according to Julian Bevan, QC, who told the court at Bulford, Wiltshire, 'As commanding officer, Colonel Mendonca had a duty towards all detainees held by soldiers under his command. One of those duties was to do all that might be expected of a reasonably capable and careful colonel to ensure that detainees were not ill-treated. The sound of the prisoners' screams must have been heard, but nobody saw fit to question them, let alone report the goings-on. Why? The only answer is because it was considered normal practice. The result was that Corporal Payne and other soldiers were left to act as they wished without any adequate directions and without any supervision.' Julian Bevan also noted that the death of the popular Captain Jones 'contributed to the tension and increased hostility' towards the locals.

Major Royce's testimony that he sought and received guidance from his brigade headquarters on the handling of prisoners was key to Colonel Mendonca's acquittal. He also insisted that Colonel Mendonca had sought to satisfy himself that the conditioning process was acceptable under the laws of armed combat and the Geneva Convention. Major Royce's evidence proved that the British brigade – the umbrella organisation above Colonel Mendonca's battalion – sanctioned the conditioning process; the Crown sought to prove otherwise. Mr Justice McKinnon said, 'This case is remarkable for the fact that no witness has given any evidence to the effect that Colonel Medonca did not do anything that he should have done, or that he did anything he should not have done.'

Colonel Mendonca was angry to be tainted by the darkest chapter in the British experience in Iraq. He resigned his commission, claiming that while at battalion and unit level the British Army remained 'an extremely capable and laudable organisation', there were issues 'higher up' with which he was uncomfortable. He said that for that reason the British Army 'was not in good shape'. Colonel Mendonca, who was decorated for his service in Iraq, accused the attorney general of making him a scapegoat. Lord Goldsmith had reminded the Army Prosecuting Authority that those in command could be held equally responsible as their men in cases of abuse. As Colonel Mendonca paraphrased, the message on the evidence of the Mousa case was 'to make sure the commanding officer was on trial'.

Colonel Mendonca dismissed claims that as commanding officer at the base when the torture took place it was his responsibility to uncover such appalling misconduct. As far as he was concerned, he was entitled to expect junior commanders to get on with their jobs – they knew right from wrong, and no soldier who kicked or punched Baha Mousa needed him to tell them that their treatment constituted abuse. Any suggestion that they needed him to breathe down their necks was 'frankly ridiculous'.

Colonel Mendonca told the BBC, 'Had I heard anything like that, I would have been over there in an instant. I would have leaped upon it. I am tainted by the fact my case went to court martial and the impact it had upon my family, my career and me.

This issue is still very much with me, and in a sense I am fighting to clear my name. It is a fact that individuals will commit crimes, and the use of force against those in custody was illegal. If every commanding officer whose men did something wrong resigned, the British Army could not function. He has to delegate until he sees anything to the contrary to what he has ordered. Under no circumstances did I allow a culture of impunity. While I did not authorise the use of stress positions designed to cause pain, the use of sandbags seemed to me to be reasonable. I understood it was also legally acceptable.

'I don't know how it [Mousa's death] happened. I was often in my own base, but I did not hear anything, and nobody brought anything untoward to my attention. My soldiers had maintained their discipline while under great strain. Not one of my soldiers killed an Iraqi on the day the whole city rose up against them.'

Four months after Mousa's death, the Ministry of Defence disclosed that it had paid compensation to his family, although it denied any liability. In early 2004, the government rejected calls for an independent inquiry. In March 2007, the six-month court martial, which cost the British taxpayer £20 million, ended with acquittals all round. Mousa's family were aghast and released photographs of his body to remind the world of the brutality to which he had been subjected. In June 2007, they brought a civil action against the Ministry of Defence. Law lords ruled that UK human rights laws did apply to Mousa.

In the same month, it was announced that Colonel Jorge Mendonca was quitting the army. His wife said her husband's decision was influenced by fears that he could face a fresh investigation were he to remain in uniform. Louise Mendonca's interview with the *Daily Mail* was the latest move in Colonel Mendonca's media campaign. Mrs Mendonca, herself a Territorial Army officer, claimed, 'There are those within the army who are still determined to make him a scapegoat for the failings of others. My husband has decided he will not be hounded any more and would rather leave than face further injustice. If my husband's acquittal had been the end of the matter – as it should have been – then he would have continued with his career.' Mrs Mendonca described the army's treatment of her husband as a 'betrayal'.

In March 2008, the Ministry of Defence admitted breaching Mousa's human rights and those of eight other Iraqis. Two months later, the ministry announced a formal inquiry into Mousa's death. In July 2008, the Ministry of Defence agreed a £3 million compensation package with Mousa's family and nine other prisoners who endured the same treatment.

23 August 2003

Basra

Corporal Dewi Pritchard, Major Matthew Titchener, Warrant Officer Class 2 Colin Wall

The Royal Military Police were as vulnerable in Basra as they were in Maysan Province. Less than two months after the tragedy in Majar al-Kabir, the number of Royal Military Policemen killed in Iraq rose to nine. One of the British Army's smallest corps had sustained the highest number of fatalities.

On 23 August 2003, Major Matthew Titchener, Warrant Officer Colin Wall, Corporal Richard Lay and Corporal Dewi Pritchard set off in a rented civilian 4x4 vehicle to visit police stations in Basra. Warrant Officer Wall was a father of three. Prior to his deployment, he told neighbours in County Durham he was going to Iraq on a peacekeeping mission to help the locals rebuild their lives. Wall was described as 'open, cheerful' and 'someone who had time for anybody and was always happy to chat'. Corporal Lay had been due to leave Iraq but stayed on, as The Royal Military Police were short of men. Corporal Pritchard was nervous. Having pulled his gun several times in recent weeks, he was counting down the days to the end of his tour. On his most recent visit home, the reservist had confided in his wife Tracey that security was deteriorating. The father of two belonged to 116 Provost Company (Volunteers). His day job was at the Bosch electronics factory at Miskin, near Llantrisant, South Wales. Corporal Pritchard had married Tracey in 1996. They had a daughter, Kira, and a son, Ethan. Tracey said, 'He felt proud that he was going over there, and he felt he had a job to do. My husband was a very brave man, and he would not let anybody down.'

Four gunmen pulled up that day alongside the Red Caps' Nissan Pathfinder. They threw a grenade, which missed, before opening fire with a machine gun mounted on a two-legged frame on the rear of the pick-up. As glass shattered, a disorientated Corporal Lay screamed at Corporal Pritchard to 'put your foot down'. There was no response. More shots were fired, fatally wounding Major Titchener and Warrant Officer Wall. The vehicle smashed into a wall.

Mohammed Hussein, a baker, saw what happened: 'There were two men in the front and two in the back. The grenade they threw exploded in the street. Then they started firing many rounds, and after the British vehicle crashed, they fired into the air to celebrate, including the driver, who was holding a pistol.'

The only survivor, Corporal Lay, spent two days in a field hospital before being flown to England. He was treated for severe lacerations and received trauma counselling. He told an inquest, 'I would not swap a single day of my experience out there apart from that particular day. The first thing I remember was hearing gunfire and the windows coming in, but I could not tell where the gunshots were coming from. I shouted at Dewi but heard nothing back.'

Raqual Titchener had not been able to sleep the night before her husband died. The following morning, she read the headline on Teletext: 'Three British soldiers killed in ambush'. When she read that the three deceased belonged to The Royal Military Police, she knew that her husband would be among them. She hurried her son upstairs, and they dressed quickly, anticipating the dreaded knock from an army officer.

She said, 'I had always said I would never answer the front door, because if I didn't, they couldn't tell me. But I saw the man and opened the door before he had time to knock. I said straight out, "It's Matt. He's dead, isn't he?"'

Raqual was carrying Angel, born four months after her husband's death. She said later that only her pregnancy saved her from drink or drugs. She recovered to join the Army Widows'

Association and volunteered for the Forces Children's Trust, a charity set up to raise funds for the offspring of deceased service personnel. She described the 150 Provost Company commander as a 'perfect husband' and a 'brilliant dad' who was delighted at the prospect of becoming a father again. His mother Val described Angel's birth as 'like having a little bit of Matthew back in some ways'.

Sergeant Steve Brown of The Royal Military Police told the congregation at Corporal Pritchard's funeral, 'Dewi returned to Iraq after a period of leave with his family knowing that the situation was getting worse. A lesser man would have found an excuse not to return.'

Corporal Pritchard's commanding officer, Lieutenant Colonel House, said, 'Corporal Pritchard epitomised everything that we hold dear in The Royal Military Police and was a popular and loyal member of the Territorial Army. He joined The Royal Military Police in 1996, and from the outset of his service was an outstanding junior non-commissioned officer. He was awarded the Provost Marshal's Gold Whistle & Chain for Best Recruit on his course and had continued to show true professionalism and dedication throughout his time in The Royal Military Police. He will be greatly missed by his colleagues, all of whom held him in the highest regard. As soldiers, we never forget our comrades who are no longer by our side. We can only hope to uphold their example when it is necessary to do so.'

Warrant Officer Wall was a father of three and, like Pritchard, a Territorial Army volunteer. A train driver in civilian life, he lived with Patricia, his wife of eight years, their baby son, Alexander, and two children from his previous marriage, Lauren and Robert. Warrant Officer Wall enlisted in 1985 and subsequently joined The Royal Military Police. He was stationed at Catterick Garrison and had served in Kosovo and Northern Ireland.

His mother and father, Barry and Joan, said, 'Colin was a loving son, and we are very proud of him. He loved his family and enjoyed spending time walking in the Weardales.'

His cousin John Harrison said, 'He was a true professional who will be deeply missed. He loved the army, and he lived for it. It is difficult to talk about it because the whole thing is so sad. I will always remember his sense of humour. He was such a funny lad.'

Captain Sean O'Brien said, 'Colin was the epitome of a company sergeant major and made a real difference to the operational effectiveness of the company. His untimely death is a blow to all in The Royal Military Police family and to all those who worked closely with him here at Catterick. He had many friends in the company and will be sorely missed by all who knew him.'

27 August 2003

Ali al-Sharqi

Fusilier Russell Beeston

Unemployed Fusilier Russell Beeston, from Govan, Glasgow, belonged to the 52nd Lowland Regiment and was attached to the 1st Battalion, The King's Own Scottish Borderers. As Fusilier Beeston had received a mandatory summons, he was depicted by the media as a conscript soldier who did not want to serve. This may or may not have been true, but either way he passed all the tests at the Reserves Training and Mobilisation Centre. In an email to fellow former students at the Glasgow College of Nautical Studies on 4 July 2003, Fusilier Beeston wrote:

> Well, as of a couple of weeks ago I was still living in Glasgow. However, I have been called up for service, and I am currently serving with the army out in Iraq. If you want to get in touch with me, you can do this by emailing. Bye for now.

On the evening of 27 August 2003, Fusilier Beeston was returning to base through the town of Ali al-Gharbi. The route back took him through Ali al-Sharqi. When the Land Rover convoy encountered large crowds, Beeston and the other soldiers were ordered to dismount and form a cordon. The mob closed in and warning shots were fired. The Iraqis returned fire with interest, striking Beeston in the chest. He died of his wounds at the scene. Another soldier was shot in the hand. The King's Own Scottish Borderers arrested ten protesters before withdrawing to Camp Abu Naji.

Fusilier Beeston's funeral at Killermont Parish Church, Bearsden, just north of Glasgow, was attended by 200 family members and friends. The lesson was read by Lieutenant Colonel Jim Wilson, the commanding officer of the 52nd Lowland Regiment. After a 30-minute service, pall-bearers carried Fusilier Beeston's coffin, draped in a Union Jack, from the church on the first leg of its journey to Maryhill Crematorium. Police halted the traffic, and local people stopped where they stood to pay their respects.

Lieutenant Colonel Jim Wilson said, 'Personally, I am very saddened. I knew Russell reasonably well, and it is a day of deep sadness across the regiment. Our sympathies of course go out to his family. The Beestons have shown themselves to be towers of strength. They are an immensely strong family, and they are pulling together very, very strongly. While we have lost a colleague, they have lost one of their own. He was a well-liked and popular man who was utterly dedicated and had a good Territorial Army career ahead of him.'

A family statement read, 'Russell was a soldier doing his duty in Iraq. He will be sadly missed.'

23 September 2003

Shaibah Logistics Base

Sergeant John Nightingale

Sergeant John Nightingale, an electronics expert from Guiseley, West Yorkshire, was a driver with The Royal Logistics Corps. He went through the same process at the Chilwell Mobilisation Centre with his friend and 217 Transport Squadron colleague Lance Corporal Ian Blaymire, a 23-year-old plumber from Leeds.

As he had failed his weapons handling test, Lance Corporal Blaymire's deployment should have been deferred in accordance with army regulations.

On 23 September 2003, Sergeant Nightingale and Lance Corporal Blaymire were messing around in their accommodation at Shaibah Logistics Base when Lance Corporal Blaymire pointed his rifle at Sergeant Nightingale, who grabbed the muzzle and yanked it towards him. Lance Corporal Blaymire said, 'I pulled away and stood back on my left foot. As I stood back, the weapon rose and a round came out of the chamber, shooting John in the chest. He fell back onto a table. The rifle did not have a magazine attached, so I thought it was empty. I shouted, "No!" I could not believe it. As soon as I heard the weapon go bang, I realised a round had come out.'

Lieutenant Colonel John Bevan, Sergeant Nightingale's commanding officer, said, 'He was a good man, a strong character and an excellent senior non-commissioned officer who had an impact on the working and social lives of many in the unit during our tour. He will be sorely missed.'

Sergeant Nightingale's fiancée Lucy, a non-commissioned officer in The Royal Air Force, and Sergeant Nightingale's family said that he was proud to serve Queen and country. He had a passion for cars and motorbikes and was a member of Otley Rugby Football Club.

Lance Corporal Blaymire was questioned by The Royal Military Police and charged with manslaughter. His court martial exposed the poor preparation prior to deployment of many non-infantry reservists and their lack of weapons handling skills. Lance Corporal Blaymire was reputedly among an estimated 2,300 Territorials who failed gun tests yet were posted to Iraq. Weapons instructor Captain Andrew McIntyre acknowledged it became an 'accepted policy' along his chain of command that soldiers who failed or received only an average mark in weapons handling should be approved for deployment, even though this represented a contravention of the Army Operational Shooting Policy. Sergeant Major John Drain told the court that his concerns about some reservists were so great that he had written letters to their units warning about the dangers they posed in theatre. Concerns over the standard of reservists deployed were compounded by the fact that the Territorial Army at the time provided one in four of the eleven thousand soldiers in Iraq. While the best were a match for their full-time colleagues, standards across the army differed markedly. A final, fatal error prior to Sergeant Nightingale's death was the failure to act upon a recommendation to provide remedial weapons training to all Territorial Army personnel based at Shaibah.

When Lance Corporal Blaymire was cleared, Assistant Judge Advocate Paul Camp accused the army of lying in an attempt to prevent the exposure of the 'very poor training and very poor leadership' to which he and many reservists were subjected. He said, 'Blaymire was undoubtedly very badly let down by the army, and blame for this incident does not rest on his shoulders alone.'

Lance Corporal Blaymire's court martial was also notable for revealing that American military planners had told their British counterparts in October 2002 when the war was going to start, almost to the exact day. The confidential communication gave key dates, known as 'P Day', 'A Day' and 'G Day'. P Day was 15 February 2003, the day US president George Bush would announce his decision to go to war, A Day was to be the start of air strikes and G Day the start of the coalition's ground offensive. When the army sought permission to begin build-up training in December 2002, the request was blocked. Lieutenant Colonel Christopher Warren told the court martial that the Defence Crisis Management Organisation – a committee that included the prime minister – ruled that mobilisation could not be seen to begin. Lieutenant Colonel Warren said, 'In December [2002], there was a world interest. If the UK had mobilised whilst all this was going on, that would have shown an intent before the political process had been allowed to run its course.'

As a result, Territorial Army build-up training began two months late and regular army training a month late.

31 October 2003

Northern Iraq

Corporal Ian Plank

On 31 October 2003, Corporal Ian Plank became the first Special Forces fatality of the war. A Royal Marine who had joined the Special Boat Service based in Poole, Dorset, he was involved in operations that were intended to capture Saddam Hussein. The announcement of his death was delayed for operational reasons. Director of The Royal Marines, Colonel Jerry Heal, described him as 'extremely popular and greatly admired'. He added, 'He was particularly well known for his resilience and robustness under pressure, when his leadership, example and sense of humour were especially valued.' Corporal Plank was working with US Special Operations Forces in northern Iraq when his section came under heavy fire.

6 November 2003

Basra

Private Ryan Thomas

A week later, Private Ryan Thomas, from Resolven, near Neath, Gwent, died after the Land Rover in which he was travelling was hit by a car at high speed on an unlit road on the outskirts of Basra. As Private Thomas's driver Private Stuart Pemberton slowed on approaching a junction, a local vehicle with no headlights came speeding towards him, shrouded in darkness. Second Lieutenant Sean Williams said, 'I saw the vehicle as I looked through a side window. He was going at some speed and didn't seem to brake or swerve to avoid us.' The saloon struck the right-hand side of the Land Rover at approximately 80 miles per hour, tipping it over. Second Lieutenant Williams added, 'I felt the collision with a lot of force. Things happened very quickly, and it was very confusing.'

Private Thomas, of the 1st Battalion, The Royal Regiment of Wales, was providing top-cover. He was thrown 30 feet on impact and landed on the roadside, suffering multiple chest and abdomen injuries. Those responsible for the crash were never identified; investigators concluded that it was an accident.

Coroner Nicholas Gardiner said, 'Had an incident of this sort occurred in this country, I have no doubt that had the culprit been tracked down there would have been a charge of manslaughter or causing death by dangerous driving. However, one has to bear in mind that the standard of driving in Iraq is quite different and vehicles there don't tend to have lights.'

Private Thomas, a keen rugby player, was the fifth Welsh serviceman to perish, following the deaths of Lance Bombadier Llewelyn Evans, Lance Corporal Thomas Keys, Captain David Jones and Corporal Dewi Pritchard. In 2007, Welsh nationalists Plaid Cymru calculated that of the countries providing service personnel to fight in Iraq, Wales's death rate per head of the population was second only to the United States. Private Thomas was the 53rd and last British fatality of the war in 2003, of whom only 18 were killed by the enemy.

2004

1 January 2004

Baghdad

Sergeant Norman Patterson, Major James Stenner

Among The Special Air Service soldiers celebrating the New Year of 2004 was the regiment's operations officer in Baghdad, Major James Stenner. The married 30 year old was a rising star who had followed in his father Alan's footsteps when he joined The Special Air Service from The Welsh Guards. The previous year he had won a Military Cross while serving as a troop commander with D Squadron, 22 SAS, in Iraq. Toasting Hogmanay with him was Sergeant Norman Patterson, a 28 year old who had joined the regiment in 2003 from The Cheshires. Beer and wine flowed at the party thrown by US Special Forces soldiers, with whom The Special Air Service men were working as part of Task Force 77.

While Major Stenner and Sergeant Patterson were seen drinking, neither was considered drunk. From the party, they drove with another Special Air Service soldier, identified at a coroner's inquest as 'Soldier A', to a residential complex, where more alcohol was offered. Major Stenner was keen to leave. Neither he nor Sergeant Patterson wore a seat belt as their unmarked 4x4 vehicle approached a concrete chicane that had been installed to protect troops from suicide bombers at the entrance to the Green Zone. Visibility was poor, as the street lights were extinguished for security reasons, and the air was thick with fog.

It was 0140 on New Year's Day when US soldier Justin Gondeiro heard a loud bang and observed a white four-door vehicle embedded in the security barrier. When he called for back-up, US medic Jamie McCurry leaned into the wreckage but found no pulse on either Special Air Service man. They were rushed to a hospital one kilometre away, where they were certified dead. Major Stenner died from head and chest injuries, Sergeant Patterson from a spinal injury. Sergeant Patterson, the driver, was two-and-a-half times over the UK drink-drive limit. Oxfordshire deputy coroner Selena Lynch recorded verdicts of accidental death: 'There are many causes for this accident, and there is no doubt that Mr Patterson had been drinking. The level was high, and it impaired his ability to drive. I do get the impression that he could tolerate a good amount of alcohol, but he was not capable of driving, and he would have been impaired by the alcohol he consumed.'

Sergeant Patterson, from Draycott in the Clay, Staffordshire, was single. He went to school in Widnes, Cheshire, and was a fanatical Everton supporter. He was survived by his father, also Norman, brother Sean and sister Julie. His former commanding officer, Lieutenant Colonel John Donnelly of The Cheshires, described him as a natural leader and the embodiment of a regimental soldier, greatly respected and popular among his men. He had served in Bosnia and Northern Ireland before volunteering for the Special Forces.

❖ ❖ ❖

When Prime Minister Tony Blair and US Ambassador Paul Bremer visited Basra on 4 January 2004, they were briefed on plans to step up 'security sector reform'. The Iraqi Civil Defence Corps, later renamed the Iraqi National Guard, had been identified as key to the future stability of British-controlled provinces and a foil for the militias loyal to Moqtada al-Sadr and the Iranian-backed Supreme Council for the Islamic Revolution in Iraq. Crucially, Iraqi Civil Defence Corps recruits were to be paid – 70 per cent unemployment in Maysan would drive the project. Thousands volunteered, with those who had previously held rank in the Iraqi Army entrusted with command. While the US only embedded Special Forces with indigenous recruits, the British chose The Argyll and Sutherland Highlanders for the same task. The mission, as outlined to the battalion's commanding officer Lieutenant Colonel Jonathan Gray, was to raise, train and deliver a 5,000-strong operational brigade of the Iraqi Civil Defence Corps for internal security duties within six months. By his own admission, Lieutenant Colonel Gray and his company commanders knew little about the prevailing cultural, tribal, religious and social issues in the provinces in which they were to operate.

7 January 2004

Basra

Lance Corporal Andrew Craw

The Argylls returned early from Christmas leave and left Howe Barracks on 5 January 2004. They arrived in Basra at midnight on 6 January 2004, and deployed to Braemar Ranges at 0700 on 7 January 2004 for a live-firing and weapons-familiarisation package. This took place in appalling weather under the supervision of Captain William Scrase-Dickins. The officer was surprised to be told that a three-day training exercise was now to be compressed into one day.

As the torrential downpour continued, Captain Scrase-Dickins considered cancelling the live firing; aware of time pressures, he pressed on. With raindrops bouncing 18 inches off the ground, Lance Corporal Andrew Craw was handed a Minimi light machine gun, a weapon with which he was unfamiliar but eager to fire. When Lance Corporal Craw suffered a stoppage, he shouted to Sergeant Callum Wilkinson, who instructed him to cock the weapon to see if a live round was trapped in the chamber. Lance Corporal Craw propped the weapon upright and leaning over the barrel he trod down with his boot on top of the cocking lever. As his friend Lance Corporal Gary Bell looked on, the weapon released a round that shot through Lance Corporal Craw's jaw and into his brain. There was no ambulance or medic present, and as no signal was showing on Captain Scrase-Dickins' satellite phone, more than an hour passed before Lance Corporal Craw received medical treatment. Finally, he was airlifted to hospital by helicopter, but it was too late.

Ministry of Defence safety expert Paul Adams told Lance Corporal Craw's parents, 'They'd been going for 48 hours, and they had probably got into bed at 0330 hours. Their breakfast was at 0700. To a man, they slept on the coach going to the range. They had got up at a time when their body clocks were telling them it was four in the morning.'

Senior Argylls officers admitted that with the benefit of hindsight the exercise should not have gone ahead. Battalion second-in-command Major James Scott told an inquest, 'It was unusual but not unheard of for soldiers to carry on with such little sleep. It was not ideal, and there are issues that come out of having that little sleep, but we operate like that on exercise. I would not be content for soldiers to drive a car in that state, but when the range is well-run and properly supervised and soldiers follow strict procedures when using weapons, then yes.'

Lance Corporal Bell's level of excitement had kept him awake: 'I was quite tired, but it was my first time in Iraq, so the buzz kept me going. You don't need much sleep sometimes. It's just the way it is.'

Coroner Andrew Walker said, 'It has been suggested that his death was the result of an unthinking moment on his part or a lapse of concentration [with regard to Lance Corporal Craw's unauthorised method to clear the stoppage]. I do not agree. There were, according to the evidence, serious failures in the planning for the Braemar Range, and on the day that Lance Corporal Craw was injured a cavalier approach to the standing orders put in place to provide for the safety of those using the range was adopted. The training he was given was just too short in time to allow him to complete the appropriate weapons-handling test and be allowed to fire the weapon on the range. The range did not comply with the standing orders because no communication link had been established, and there was an absence of appropriate medical facilities to respond to a casualty.'

Captain Scrase-Dickins conceded that it had been a dereliction of his duty to ignore the strict regulations. The coroner concurred: 'Had you done your job properly, no soldiers would have fired on that range that day, and Lance Corporal Craw would not have died.'

The final ignominy for Lance Corporal Craw's parents was to discover that had their son died after 6 April 2004, they would have received £73,992 in compensation – four times what they received because he died three months earlier.

His parents James and Ray said, 'The family and all of Andy's friends were shocked and saddened to hear of his death during active service in Iraq. He was a wonderful son and brother, and all those who knew him will remember his maturity and lively sense of humour. He talked often about how much he loved serving with the 1st Battlion, The Argyll and Sutherland Highlanders, and was extremely proud when he was promoted to lance corporal during the summer of 2003. Mixed with our profound sadness is a pride in the knowledge that he died while serving his country. He will be remembered by all who knew him for ever.'

Lieutenant Colonel Gray said, 'This is a tragic incident in the first few days of the battalion's six-month operational tour in Iraq. Andy was a bright and promising soldier who will be sorely missed by all in the regiment. At present, our thoughts are with his family.'

21 January 2004

Al-Amarah

Rifleman Vincent Windsor

Rifleman Vincent Windsor, from Cowley, Oxfordshire, died from head injuries on 21 January 2004 while on patrol in al-Amarah. As Rifleman Richard Whitlock of the 2nd Battalion, The Royal Green Jackets, told an inquest, Rifleman Windsor died as their convoy passed beneath a metal girder at the end of a 63-metre-long pontoon bridge on the River Tigris. He heard a thud and turned to see Rifleman Windsor lying on the floor of the vehicle in a pool of blood.

The soldier's mother Linda Darby listened in tears as Oxfordshire coroner Dr Richard Whittington noted that there had been a time when top-cover soldiers were given a warning as they went under these girders, but there was no evidence of anyone being told to duck that day. Her son was engaged to a woman he had met while based at Paderborn, Germany. Dr Whittington recorded a verdict of death by misadventure.

Lieutenant Colonel Harry Emck described Rifleman Windsor

as an 'enormously popular and likeable soldier with a great sense of humour who would be sadly missed by his colleagues and comrades. Rifleman Windsor joined A Company of The Royal Green Jackets in 1999 and served in Bosnia and Iraq.'

31 January 2004

Basra

Sapper Robert Thomson

Before he deployed to Iraq for his second tour, Sapper Robert Thomson told friends that he hoped to 'make a difference' to the lives of ordinary Iraqis, a common sentiment among junior British soldiers from humble backgrounds who were taken aback by the poverty and deprivation that surrounded them. The Ministry of Defence never publicised the circumstances surrounding his death at Basra Palace on 31 January 2004. It was suggested that Sapper Thomson was run over while collecting soil samples in a trench. He belonged to the armoured troop of 37 Engineer Squadron, and his skills as a plumber were in great demand in Basra. His commander Major Alex Hilton said, 'Known to us all as "Rab", he was a popular soldier with a ready wit and a natural enthusiasm. He made friends easily. His sudden death shocked us. He was a close friend and a brother-in-arms.'

Sapper Thomson had joined the army from Whitburn Academy in 1998 and supported Motherwell Football Club. The year after his death, Sapper Thomson's medals were stolen from his mother's house while she was at home. She said, 'He was a wonderful son who lived life to the full. He is sorely missed by us, but we are also extremely proud of him for being a soldier. He was much looked up to by his younger brother Stewie.'

12 February 2004

Shaibah Logistics Base

Corporal Richard Ivell

Corporal Richard Ivell, a married father of three from Doncaster, South Yorkshire, died in a road traffic accident at Shaibah Logistics Base on 12 February 2004. No Iraqi vehicles were involved. His funeral service was conducted by his father Robert, the vicar of Wadworth and Loversall, and attended by his wife Jane and children Jonathan, Chelsea and Charlotte. Reverend Ivell was sanguine about the role of British forces in Iraq: 'I think it's a difficult situation. There is always a risk with the kind of role responsible countries have in peacekeeping. I feel for the families who are in the same situation as us. The army was very supportive of us, for which we were very grateful. My parishioners were very supportive, too, and in a way it has brought us closer together.'

❖ ❖ ❖

As spring became summer in 2004, the British Army redoubled its efforts to find those suspected of executing Sergeant Simon Hamilton-Jewell's men. Among them was Naseer Zachra Abdu Rufeiq, described by one British officer as 'local hate figure number one'.

Maysan was hotting up, literally and metaphorically, as The Light Infantry handed over responsibility for the province to the 1st Battalion, The Princess of Wales's Royal Regiment, led by Lieutenant Colonel Matt Maer. Its tour of duty would be remembered for Private Johnson Beharry's Victoria Cross, the siege of the Civil Military Cooperation House in al-Amarah and the 'Battle of Danny Boy'. They would return to barracks with a record haul of gallantry medals, but without Private Chris Rayment and Private Lee O'Callaghan.

Two buzz phrases heard time and again as the battalion enforced its authority were 'Smile, shoot, smile' and the 'Three Block War'. Each encapsulated the versatility required of soldiers fighting a war among the people. While the first phrase is self-explanatory, the second reminded commanders that their soldiers might be delivering humanitarian aid in one block, an armed patrol might be progressing in a second block, and a no-holds-barred engagement between insurgents and occupying forces could be under way in a third. It was harder for soldiers to smile after being shot at. Smiles were also less persuasive after Coalition Forces had used brutally effective means to restore order hours before.

Friday, 14 May 2004 saw the biggest battle of the post-war period and one that became the subject of claims in 2007 and 2008 that Iraqi civilians were abused and executed in British custody. The nature of the battle, with tanks deployed in support of British troops, led some officers to concede that the battle for hearts and minds had been lost in Maysan and that too much force was being used when dialogue would have been more appropriate. Personal accounts of the Battle of Danny Boy attest to the incredible violence of the day. It was highly fortunate that no British lives were lost.

The battle began with an ambush by 25 to 30 insurgents on a vehicle patrol led by Major Adam Griffiths of The Argylls and his company sergeant major, John McNab. After surviving gunfire, their Land Rovers were attacked by gunmen armed with rocket-propelled grenades.

Major Griffiths used his mobile phone to call the operations room at Camp Abu Naji. His contact report was relayed but misinterpreted at Camp Condor, a satellite facility used to train members of the Iraqi Civil Defence Corps. The Argylls rescue force was greeted on the highway with a volley of rocket-propelled grenades. As they dismounted, they observed gunmen sprinting into positions dug into the crusty brown landscape. By then, Major Griffiths had reached Camp Abu Naji. The base came under mortar fire as rescue forces were scrambled.

Sergeant 'Pete' Perfect of the 1st Battalion, The Princess of Wales's Royal Regiment, recalled, 'Like a squadron of Second World War fighter pilots, the platoon ran for its Warriors, and once mounted sat and listened on the radio net before moving to the front gate. I was told to go and help the patrol in contact. I remember thinking that it would just be the usual: roll up, collect any casualties and dismounts, kill the enemy, and go home. I was wrong. What happened was a lot different and nearly ended in disaster.'

Sergeant Major Dave Falconer of the same battalion described how he and his men were 'bayoneting and slashing and using everything – kicking, head-butting, punching, the lot. Effectively, we were in a close-quarter battle lane. As I was coming up the trench, I saw two things that looked like sacks of spuds up the track. They were like dark ovals on the ground. I crouched down and looked through my SUSAT [magnified rifle sight], thinking, "What's that?" It was two enemy lying on the deck. I opened up and killed both of them. The enemy had an RPG and an AK-47. The end of an AK is cut diagonally, so it is not like our rifles. I could see the end of the weapon poking out of a bush, and it was moving as the firer took aim. I turned and emptied a magazine into the bush. The worst bit was there was one bloke who was looking at me. He was lying in the bush, and a round went straight into his forehead. His mouth fell open, and he gasped. Then, just as suddenly, blood started coming out of the hole, and it wasn't pumping or oozing – it sprayed. I felt quite sick.'

Sergeant Perfect was soon in as much trouble: 'I pushed on 800 metres towards the checkpoint. Almost immediately after the initial contact, the gunner Private Williams returned fire with his chain gun, but it jammed irreparably. He then used the main armament to fire high explosives at the pockets of enemy along the trenches. Unfortunately, this weapon also jammed after firing only 12 rounds. I was spotting with my rifle, and, hearing the inspiring word "stoppage" from the gunner, I told the two dismounts to open the mortar hatches and return fire as we moved the final 400 metres towards Danny Boy.'

One of Sergeant Perfect's dismounts was Private Hoolin, who recalled, 'I heard my platoon sergeant ask me to open the hatches and suppress the enemy with my Minimi. When I opened them, I saw the enemy and fired. They saw me, too, and fired back. As the vehicle was moving backwards, I saw a blinding flash in the corner of my eye and heard a deafening bang. Private "Danny" Danquah said, "He's dead, he's dead." There were flames all around, and I started shouting, "Fire, the back is on fire." We grabbed the fire extinguishers and sprayed dry powder. We were coughing and spluttering. The whole crew were choking on it. I could see Danny's eyes popping out of his head. Sergeant Perfect shouted to see if we were OK. He climbed out of his turret and ran around to open the back door. He kept banging hard for us to let him in, but we couldn't hear him. He was under enemy fire at the time, so he was not best pleased to be locked out. When he got in, he had a few choice words for me and told me to hand him a Minimi. We drove through the ambush, and suffice to say we took a few on the way. South of the checkpoint [Danny Boy], there was one lonely RPG man exposing himself. He fired and got the favour returned.'

Sergeant Stuart Henderson led The Argylls' assault on a derelict building and the main enemy trench, actions for which he received a Mention in Dispatches.

During this attack, The Argylls took a prisoner of war – a boy they guessed was aged between 13 and 15 years old. While his life was spared, his treatment was less than fair, as Private James Lawrence recalled: 'I could see what was happening because I was wounded in the hand and not taking part in the battle at that stage. The kid was about 14 and dressed in rags. He was crying, had defecated himself and must have thought he was going to die. The stress of the situation got to a few of the guys, because he was hit with rifles and kicked and had stones thrown at him. Then he was dunked in a water-filled trench, with his head kept under water for about 20 seconds at a time. This was going on in the middle of a firefight. It was not like he was in a cell or something. The rounds were still going down around us. People should understand what the stress was like at that time before they judge.'

As the air above them filled with exploding mortars, The Argylls finished off the enemy themselves and began the gruesome task of loading the bodies of the deceased onto their Land Rovers. The dead gave off the most inhumane, repulsive aroma that none of the soldiers would forget. The state of the bodies gave rise to suggestions that the Iraqis had been shot at close range and their corpses brutalised while in British custody. In fact, it was the potency of the General Purpose Machine Gun that had mutilated the bodies.

Lance Corporal Muir of The Princess of Wales's Royal Regiment attempted to save a gunman's life, as his colleague Captain Marcus Butlin described: 'He was tending to one of the four prisoners. The man was lying on his front when they got into position, and a large gash was clearly visible on his right shoulder. The wound was about eight inches long, and his clothes were soaked in blood. When he was further examined, an entry wound was found on his front where a bullet had hit him in the chest and torn a chunk out of him. He had what is known as a sucking chest wound: each time the casualty breathes, air bypasses the throat and is sucked directly into or forced out of the wound. This caused bubbles of blood to emerge from the man's chest. Lance Corporal Muir placed a chest seal over the wound, but it only just covered it. The man's lung was collapsing, and Lance Corporal Muir struggled to keep him alive, giving him oxygen.

'He continued his efforts to save the man for the next 45 minutes while exposing himself to enemy fire. It was hopeless, and the man drowned in his own blood, but it demonstrated the professionalism and compassion of British soldiers. The prisoners were shifted into place face down behind the sergeant major's wagon, where they were afforded some protection from the incoming fire. The men were moved quite forcefully. There were few men on the ground, and the prisoners had to be controlled with the minimum number of guards. A private stood watch over them with orders to shove their heads back down into the ground if they tried to communicate.'

While The Argylls drove the deceased to Camp Abu Naji in the cargo holds of their Land Rovers, The Princess of Wales's Royal Regiment used the back of a Warrior armoured vehicle. To remove them was not as straightforward as it seemed, as Sergeant Chris Broome explained: 'With the electrical door broken, there was no way we could open it from the outside. The only way we could open it was from the inside. This meant someone had to climb in through the driver's tunnel and get underneath the bodies and release the catch in order for us to open the door. The cargo hold of the Warrior was full of blood, and the eight bodies on top of the release catch were really starting to smell. My driver climbed inside to perform this task. It made him very ill. In his defence, he did an excellent job. He was given an order, and he just cracked on and did it.'

The corpses were handled respectfully. Captain James Rands, who photographed the bodies and searched their pockets for anything of intelligence value, said, 'Though I had seen dead bodies before, I had never handled one, and it was extremely disconcerting to move a body's arm in order to get at a pocket and then have the thing close back to exactly where it had been. But the blank, staring eyes won't stay with me nearly as long as the weirdly unpleasant smell.

'Many of the bodies had shat or pissed themselves as they died. A good number had sneezed absolutely vast quantities of snot over their face. The quantities were huge, more than I could ever imagine coming out of one person. There was also lots of blood and brain tissue. Padre Myatt said he was shocked. He too had seen dead bodies before but never so many in the one place. When the second set of bodies came in, it was already growing quite dark, and the flash on my camera struggled to deal with the light conditions, so it took ages to get each photo.

'As we went down the line, we could see that there was a mix. Some of them were fighters kitted out in Madhi Army uniforms of black pyjamas and olive green chest rigs, making them look like Viet Minh. Others had probably just joined the fight from whatever their daily routine was and had not changed. The youngest was probably only about 14 or 15. Their pockets were empty. I suspected they had sanitised their kit before battle, as usually when we made arrests the people had something on them. Naseer Zachra was not amongst the dead.'

Lieutenant Colonel Maer explained the repatriation policy: 'The logic behind the decision was that a particular individual whom we had come close to capturing [understood to be Naseer Zachra Abdu Rufeiq] was wanted in connection with the murder of the six Royal Military Policemen in Majar al-Kabir in June 2003. It was felt that there having been a large battle near the village, he was very likely to have been involved. If he had been killed, we could identify him, and it would clarify the matter.'

❖ ❖ ❖

Relations between The Royal Military Police detachment at Camp Abu Naji and the incumbent infantry battalion were no better over the summer of 2004 than the previous year – when The Royal Military Police had found themselves 'falling through the cracks' of the battle-group structure in Maysan Province, with fatal consequences. In response, The Princess of Wales's Royal Regiment did not mince their words. They found it irksome that The Royal Military Police reported to divisional headquarters in Basra and not the battle group hierarchy in Maysan.

Lieutenant Colonel Gray saw his grand and noble plans for the Iraqi Civil Defence Corps kicked into the dust. It was the circle that could never be squared: fail to train the Iraqis to maintain security and the British did not have an exit strategy; teach them too well and the rogue elements among them put into practice what they were taught against British forces. The Iraqi Civil Defence Corps was infested with insurgents eager to learn British Army tactics, and to be paid for it, something which might have dissuaded Lieutenant Colonel Maer from embracing their potential. When instructors got wise to their ulterior motives, the recruits were only taught to 'go left flanking' when under fire. Such adaptation to their teachings was a matter of self-preservation for the British training teams.

28 June 2004

Basra

Fusilier Gordon Gentle

Nineteen-year-old Fusilier Gordon Gentle became the first British soldier to be lost in hostile action for ten months when a roadside explosive device in Basra tore through his Land Rover on 28 June 2004. His mother and sister bemoaned his lack of protection – a task issue order for The Royal Highland Fusiliers to collect detection equipment had been issued two weeks previously but had not been acted upon. Fusilier Gentle, from Pollok, Glasgow, died instantly. Electronic jamming devices were installed in Land Rovers just days later.

'This device was sitting in an army storeroom, and it was because of laziness and carelessness that it was not fitted to their vehicles sooner. I am not prepared to let this go. I don't want any more MoD [Ministry of Defence] cover-ups,' said Rose Gentle, Fusilier Gentle's mother. She rose to prominence as an anti-war campaign spokeswoman but lost a High Court bid to challenge the government's refusal to stage an inquiry into the decision to go to war. Her daughter Maxine wrote to Tony Blair: 'My big brother died at the age of 19 and for what? A war over oil and money. That's what I think this war is all about. There was no such thing as weapons of mass destruction.'

19 July 2004

Basra

Flight Lieutenant Kristian Gover

Flight Lieutenant Kristian Gover had joined 33 Squadron, Royal Air Force, in Basra after its commander Squadron Leader Martin Cowie raised the maximum temperature at which his fleet of six Puma helicopters were permitted to fly from 43 to 50 degrees Celsius, a decision born of tactical necessity, but which also increased the strain on the engines. On another sweltering morning, Flight Lieutenant Gover acted as co-pilot on his maiden Iraq mission. Having successfully inserted troops into the desert, he and Flight Lieutenant Daniel Brook approached Basra Air Station after 1030 on 19 July 2004. The pilots were then disorientated by a sudden increase in wind speed from ten knots to twenty-two knots.

As they turned downwind, their Puma ran out of power and plummeted. Flight Lieutenant Gover increased power in a bid to pull out of the drop, but a hydraulic fault reduced the level of power reaching the blades when the controls were changed, and the rotor speed decelerated. Flying Officer Wes Healey watched from the air traffic control tower as the helicopter fell out of the sky: 'It was as if someone had a helicopter and just dropped it.'

The Puma hit the ground, veered back up by ten metres and then landed on its side and burst into flames. Flight Lieutenant Brook and Flight Sergeant Pedrick escaped, but Flight Lieutenant Gover was trapped inside and died of smoke inhalation.

Group Captain Nigel Wharmby, The Royal Air Force commander at Basra International Airport, said, 'This is a tragic accident in which a very professional and well-respected pilot has lost his life. All the servicemen and women in Iraq operate with the very highest level of professionalism, none more so than our helicopter crews who perform magnificently in arduous circumstances. Kris's death has hit everyone at Basra very hard, even those who only knew him briefly. Our thoughts and sympathy go out to his family and friends at this extremely difficult time.'

At the inquest, Flight Lieutenant Brook said, 'I think I misinterpreted the wind. I am not sure if we had the wrong Met information, but I believed it was a light northerly wind. We started moving down and very, very suddenly. Shortly after that, it went through the roof, and the ground rush was enormous. It was clear we were going to hit the ground.'

Coroner Andrew Walker could not understand how two highly competent pilots with 1,000 flying hours between them had ended up in such a situation. He suggested it reflected badly on their training. A Royal Air Force investigation found that the crash was caused by an inappropriate downwind approach to land. Squadron Leader Cowie said the pilots and the helicopters had been accustomed to flying fully loaded and in the heat.

4 August 2004

Al-Amarah

Private Christopher Rayment

According to one of his colleagues, Private Chris Rayment had lost count of the mortar, rocket-propelled grenade and small-arms attacks he had survived prior to 4 August 2004. He was killed by a falling security barrier at the Civil

Military Cooperation House in al-Amarah. The 22-year-old Londoner from Y Company, 1st Battalion, Princess of Wales's Royal Regiment, had been steadfast under almost constant bombardment and was described by Lieutenant Colonel Maer as 'a soldier of irrepressible vigour, boisterous humour and infectious optimism. He was also tremendously committed, zealous and showed considerable courage, self-discipline and the highest standards of professionalism over an exceptionally testing and hazardous period.'

❖ ❖ ❖

By the admission of senior Princess of Wales's Royal Regiment officers, the defence of the Civil Military Cooperation House had continued beyond the date when it ceased to be a tactical imperative. A presence was maintained there as a demonstration of military force and strength of will. This coincided with Moqtada al-Sadr's declaration of war against Iraq's 'invaders'. He sought to draw a parallel between the British 'occupation' of Basra and the southern provinces with the presence of US forces in the shrine city of Najaf.

Heavy fighting broke out in Basra following the expiry of a deadline to release four of his supporters arrested by British soldiers. In spite of this, Major David Bradley, the officer commanding of B Company, 1 Princess of Wales's Royal Regiment, felt there was little desire on the part of the Iraqis to see the religious elements take over, particularly by violence and lawlessness. He trusted to the maxim that no terrorist campaign could continue at high tempo indefinitely without a groundswell of support, and over the summer of 2004, no single grouping emerged sufficiently powerful to exert control over the city. As Major Bradley saw it, the majority of citizens wanted to 'make a bit of money and provide for their families in a safe environment, free from the intimidation of any extremist group'. Meanwhile, the Iranian influence remained distrusted, and al-Sadr's brand of Islam was too militant for the moderate majority, many of whom enjoyed 'Western' pleasures, such as the cinema, and turned a blind eye to the use of alcohol.

9 August 2004

Basra

Private Lee O'Callaghan

Private Lee O'Callaghan was killed in Basra on 9 August 2004, a day that saw the winning of two Conspicuous Gallantry Crosses, the award second only to the Victoria Cross.

That lunchtime, Major David Bradley was summoned to the operations room to be told that nine soldiers from The Royal Horse Artillery led by Sergeant Terry Bryan and Sergeant Matt Oliver had been reported trapped in a house surrounded by 200 gunmen. The company commander was instructed to join the rescue party en route to the old Ba'ath Party headquarters, a former British location handed back to the Iraqi police. The office of Moqtada al-Sadr's political party was next door. The Royal Horse Artillery personnel had been forced to go to ground after their armoured Land Rovers were destroyed by a succession of rocket-propelled grenades that blew up the wheels.

Sergeant Bryan and Sergeant Oliver's men were junior soldiers only a year out of basic training. They ran from the blazing vehicles and dived into ditches, where they fought off the mob before Sergeant Bryan followed Sergeant Gordon Robertson's example in Majar al-Kabir the previous summer and found a family house to use as shelter. With gunmen sprinting after them and rounds kicking up dust at their feet, The Royal Horse Artillery had burst inside the urban semi-detached house and ushered the terrified local family into the cellar. As Major Bradley drove towards the scene, he could see the plumes of black smoke given off by their abandoned Land Rovers. The noise was deafening as his own Warrior column came under rocket-propelled grenade attack.

The Royal Horse Artillery were in a life-or-death siege: nine men against a mob of heavily armed insurgents. Sergeant Bryan saw gunmen on rooftops lobbing grenades at him and his men as rounds fired from AK-47s missed his head by inches. His mind turned to the worst-case scenario: 'As I distributed my last 200 or so rounds of 5.56 millimetre, I could see Olly [Sergeant Oliver] shrugging his shoulders. He'd given the base a grid reference for the house, but we both had the feeling they wouldn't be able to find us. Once we ran out of ammunition, or if the enemy attacked in even greater numbers ... well, that did not bear thinking about. We didn't need to say much. We all knew about the six Red Caps who'd been surrounded and killed in Majar al-Kabir the year before. I could see us getting overrun and then either shot, or, worse, maybe dragged through the streets by our feet behind vehicles, paraded, tortured, beheaded on TV, that sort of thing. Olly and I decided that if we were about to be overrun, we would take our own lives. We'd shoot the young lads and then each other. We were absolutely certain about that.'

Meanwhile, Major Bradley's vehicle was fired at from all directions. When he poked his head through the turret, he was struck by a rocket. He did not realise that the warhead and fragments of his rifle had been blasted through his body armour and into his chest. When he lifted his right hand, he saw it was severed in half. Another rocket struck the Warrior as one of his junior soldiers closed the metal lid. 'The bullets sounded even closer with ricochets coming off the vehicle,' he said, 'and the constant crackle of high-velocity rounds seemed to intensify as the Madhi militia tried to shoot me off. As I slid back into the turret, I saw the left side of my body armour was on fire. I patted it out. The thought of being badly burned terrified me.' Other soldiers in the same wagon were also severely wounded.

When a grenade landed inside the house occupied by Sergeant Bryan, the troop medic grabbed and squeezed it to prevent it exploding. He made his way to the window and hurled it towards the insurgents. With the soldiers close to tears of desperation, a car was driven fast into the front door and the wreckage set alight. The house slowly filled with smoke. The only positive was that the clouds rising from the vehicle would aid rescuers' efforts to locate the house.

As Major Bradley and his wounded colleagues were driven back to base, the remainder of the quick-reaction force used the chain guns mounted inside the Warriors to best effect. At this time, Private O'Callaghan was shot. Lieutenant Ian Pennells recalled, 'As we were manoeuvring out of position, I heard a shout from the back [of the vehicle]. Looking over my shoulder, I saw Private O'Callaghan fall back into the Warrior. My heart leaped into my mouth. I shouted at my driver to reverse at full speed onto Red Route. The medic shouted from the back, "Boss, he's bad. Get us out of here." Your mortality is thrust upon you all of a sudden when you see one of your men get hit.'

With the lives of scores of British troops in the balance, Corporal Terry Thomson and Sergeant Andre Pepper led dismounted troops towards The Royal Horse Artillery bolthole. Armed with Minimi light machine guns, Corporal Thomson and his colleagues accounted for 26 gunmen. As he later recalled, he and his men 'took a real malleting in there' and 'there was a lot [of lead] flying around'.

Sergeant Bryan's men burst from the house and onto the street. Scanning rooftops and behind cars for lone gunmen, they fired and manoeuvred towards the nearest Warriors. The soldiers jumped inside and lay on top of each other – there was insufficient room in the cargo holds on their journey back to camp.

Tears of relief were followed by tears of sadness when the news spread of Private O'Callaghan's death. He had always wanted to join the army and had only just finished his basic training. The soldier had been due to fly home in just a few days. The oldest of four children, Private O'Callaghan had lived with his parents Eugene and Shirley in Walworth, south London. His father had been so proud when his son was sent to Iraq. He had been on active service for four months. 'I can't believe this has happened,' said Eugene. 'This is a nightmare. My poor wife is inconsolable. He was a good, good lad.'

Gun battles continued for the following few days, with al-Sadr's militiamen roaming the streets. Sergeant Bryan and Corporal Thomson were awarded Conspicuous Gallantry Crosses and Sergeant Pepper a Mention in Dispatches.

Major Bradley was one of one hundred and twelve Princess of Wales's Royal Regiment casualties over the summer of 2004, of which forty-eight were wounded in combat. In addition to Private Johnson Beharry's Victoria Cross, The Princess of Wales's

Royal Regiment won two Conspicuous Gallantry Crosses and eight Military Crosses. Lieutenant Colonel Matt Maer and Major James Coote were awarded Distinguished Service Crosses. There were 16 Mentions in Dispatches.

After learning that her husband had been wounded, Lara Bradley spent the night clutching her husband's anniversary card, written before 9 August, which told her that he was praying harder than ever before in his life that he would be home soon. During open-chest surgery, Major Bradley suffered a massive haemorrhage and 'flatlined' twice. He woke up four days later at Selly Oak Hospital, Birmingham. As he recovered, Major Bradley cried a lot over Private O'Callaghan's loss. 'It was quite an emotional time,' he said, 'and I guess it took me about six months to get over that.'

12 August 2004

Basra

Private Marc Ferns

Private Marc Ferns died on 12 August 2004 when a roadside bomb blew up his Warrior armoured vehicle in Basra. The father of one from Glenrothes, Fife, joined The Black Watch aged seventeen and was remembered for his courage and professionalism. The explosion severely injured his friend Sergeant Kevin Stacey from Perth, who was 'casevaced' to Kuwait. Sergeant Stacey was the third generation of his family to serve with the battalion. His family joined him at a US hospital, where he received life-saving treatment.

Reverend Alan Sharp led tributes to the fallen soldier, who was on his second tour of Iraq: 'We are hurt and saddened by the loss of Marc. We can hardly begin to understand why this should be. All kinds of questions are raised within us, and our hearts are raw with emotion. Marc was very dear to all of us. He was a loving son, a dear grandson, a much loved brother and a devoted father to Amy-Louise, just 15 months old.'

Lieutenant Colonel James Cowan, Private Ferns's commanding officer, said, 'His tragic death saddened and shocked the battalion. Private Ferns had loyally served The Black Watch for three years and had a bright future ahead of him. He was an experienced, committed, professional and very popular soldier who will be sorely missed by all who knew him. Our sympathies and thoughts are with his family at this time.'

❖ ❖ ❖

Private Ferns's death was one of hundreds across Iraq within just a couple of days. Interim Defence Minister Hazem al-Shalan stated that 400 militiamen were either killed, captured or wounded fighting US forces in Kut, while more than 165 Iraqis died as fighting spilled over from the shrine city of Najaf. In Sadr City, named after Moqtada al-Sadr's father, 25 people died in clashes with US armoured columns.

17 August 2004

Basra

Lance Corporal Paul Thomas

L ieutenant William Follett's men were recovering a damaged Land Rover in Basra on the evening of 17 August 2004 when the officer heard a loud blast on a whistle, the signal for a pre-arranged ambush. Within seconds, soldiers of the 2nd Battalion, The Light Infantry, came under a hail of 5.56-millimetre rounds and rocket-propelled grenades. To the subaltern's chagrin, a white saloon screeched to a halt and the driver and passengers joined the fight. A third man sprinted to open the boot and urgently distributed AK-47s to passers-by. Lance Corporal Paul Thomas, from Welshpool, Powys, was shot in the neck by al-Sadr loyalists and certified dead on arrival at Shaibah Logistics Base. He was on his second tour of Iraq.

Lance Corporal Thomas's funeral was held with full military honours at St Mary's Church, Welshpool, and attended by

110 members of his regiment. His comrades carried his coffin shoulder-high into the church. Lance Corporal Thomas's body was interned at Castle Caereinion, where a three-volley gun salute was fired and the last post sounded. Lance Corporal Thomas had served in Basra from June 2004 and had been recommended for promotion to the rank of corporal.

Lieutenant Follett said, '"Taff" was a proud Welshman who had a passion for all sports. He was a keen rugby supporter as well as following his local football club, Shrewsbury Town. He was an immensely popular member of the platoon, widely regarded as its backbone, through his diligence, professionalism and unfaltering enthusiasm to the job and the soldiers under his command. His death has shocked the platoon, especially those soldiers who were with him when he died. He will be sorely missed, and our thoughts and prayers go out to his family and loved ones at this time.'

Lieutenant Colonel Ted Shields, Lance Corporal Thomas's commanding officer, paid tribute: 'He was one of the first to volunteer to go back [to Iraq], because he loved soldiering. There is no doubt he was a very experienced soldier and junior non-commissioned officer. He was unfailingly professional. There is some solace for his family in that they can look back on his eight years with The Light Infantry with considerable pride.'

Praising the bravery of the deceased soldier, Coroner Geraint Williams described the scene where he died as 'harrowing'.

10 September 2004

Camp Abu Naji

Fusilier Stephen Jones

Fusilier Stephen Jones, from Denbigh, North Wales, complained to his wife, 'They won't let me rest. I'm just knackered.' He and his colleagues from The Royal Welsh Fusiliers were working overtime at Camp Abu Naji in temperatures that had already cost lives. On 9 September 2004, Fusilier Jones had worked a 12-hour night shift the previous evening when he returned to duty at 1800 to join an operation to arrest a local bomb-maker. Fours hours later, as Fusilier Jones began his return journey to base, he winced and rubbed his eyes. His inquest heard that they were red from a mixture of sweat and insect repellent dripping into them. With one hand off the wheel, his Land Rover veered off course and flipped onto its roof. He was found bleeding heavily and leaning out of the window. A rescue helicopter was summoned, but Fusilier Jones was declared dead at the roadside from head injuries.

Fusilier Jones had married his wife Zoe just a few weeks before he had deployed to Iraq in April 2004. His funeral with full military honours was held at his parish church. An annual rugby match is now played in Fusilier Jones's honour between The Royal Welsh Fusiliers and North Wales Barbarians. He had joined the army aged 17 hoping to become a physical-training instructor.

His father Ian said, 'Stephen joined the army because he loved the sport – he didn't have a bad bone in his body. He wouldn't have wanted to go to war – to help, maybe, but not war. You never think it is going to happen to you. He joined The Royal Welsh Fusiliers straight from school. It is difficult to cope. We had received a letter from him telling us everything was pretty calm out there and he was looking forward to coming home.'

Coroner Nicholas Gardiner's greatest area of concern was the number of hours drivers and all soldiers were expected to work. He noted that soldiers were 'not notorious clock watchers' and that they were tempted to continue working when they were exhausted and required rest for their own safety. Gardiner said that fatigue 'might well have played a major part in Fusilier Jones leaving the road'.

28 September 2004

Basra

Gunner David Lawrence, Corporal Marc Taylor

When a rocket-propelled grenade struck Corporal Marc Taylor and Gunner David Lawrence's Land Rover, their colleagues saw a bright yellow flash moments before the vehicle burst into flames. Corporal Taylor, from Ellesmere Port, Cheshire, and Gunner Lawrence, from Walsall, West Midlands, died from blast injuries. The attack happened near Basra on 28 September 2004.

Corporal Taylor, of The Royal Electrical and Mechanical Engineers, was just days short of his 28th birthday and had been looking forward to returning to Britain. His wife Olivia was expecting their second child. She said her husband, nicknamed 'Spud', had enjoyed helping Iraqi people rebuild their lives and had been very positive about his time there. On the day he died, he had been escorting visitors to a new housing project. His grandfather Ted Roach, a former Royal Engineers warrant officer, said, 'We are all extremely proud of Marc and are just shattered by his death. From a young age, he always wanted to be a soldier, and I encouraged him because I know what a good life it can be. The last time I spoke to him, he promised me he would steer clear of trouble. But you cannot plan for the ambush like the one in which he died.'

Gunner Lawrence of the 1st Battalion, Royal Horse Artillery, was described as a 'proven Trojan' by relatives and friends. His funeral was held at Christ Church, Blakenhall Heath. The church was packed with 300 friends, comrades and family.

Reverend John Barnes told mourners, 'We come to express our grief, our sorrow and maybe our anger that David's life was tragically cut short at the age of 25. David must have known, as indeed all of our armed service personnel serving in Iraq must know, that each new day brings the possibility of death. I have it on good authority that David performed several heroic acts whilst on active service in Iraq.'

His troop sergeant, Harry Harrison, added, 'We were a family, a band of brothers, and we all feel for you, David's family.'

❖ ❖ ❖

In October 2004, Tony Blair was accused of using British troops to boost Bush's presidential election campaign when he approved the deployment of The Black Watch battle group to Camp Dogwood in the 'Sunni Triangle' near Baghdad – an area where nine US Marines had met their deaths and one hundred and ninety-seven been wounded in the previous three months. The 'relief in place' was to enable the US Marines to join the major assault of Fallujah. This coincided not only with President Bush's race against Senator John Kerry, but also with discussions at the Ministry of Defence on future infantry structures that looked set to make the 254-year-old Black Watch regiment extinct. Operation Bracken, as the temporary redeployment was codenamed, was unpopular back home. A survey conducted at the time suggested that, for the first time, less than one-third of British voters thought the decision to depose Saddam Hussein had been right.

The mission began on 27 October 2004 with the battle group's armoured personnel carriers and Scimitar light tanks packed onto low-loader transporters. Security concerns ruled out a road move for the 850 men of The Black Watch, Queen's Dragoon Guards and Royal Marines, who were flown north. They touched down and immediately began filling sandbags. The locals did not disappoint, and rockets were fired at their base within hours.

An email written by a serving Black Watch officer expressed commonly felt fears: 'I hope the government knows what it has got itself [into]. I am not sure it fully understands the risks.'

However cautionary his note, its leakage to the *Daily Telegraph* was condemned, as it came at a time when security and morale were paramount. It was suggested that further damage was done by junior soldiers who used television interviews to complain about the task at hand and the revelation that within hours of Operation Bracken's first fatality the deceased soldier's colleagues had telephoned newspapers in a bid to sell information.

As one defence chief commented, 'The Black Watch is coming across as an unprofessional unit. It has some very good officers and soldiers, but at the moment they are doing themselves an injustice.'

General Mike Walker saw it differently, suggesting that the media made it easier for insurgents to attack British troops: 'I think the contribution towards the initial attacks was certainly enhanced by, if you like, a media picture that was being laid across a number of channels.'

29 October 2004

North Babil Province

Private Kevin McHale

Private Kevin McHale was killed on 29 October 2004 when the Warrior armoured vehicle he was driving overturned as a road bridge in North Babil Province collapsed under its weight. He was on his second tour of duty, having been one of the first British soldiers to cross the Kuwait–Iraq border in 2003. As his family made clear, Private McHale had accepted the mission readily. He had assured them in a phone call just days before the start of Operation Bracken that he was not scared.

Private McHale was buried at St Patrick's Roman Catholic Church, Lochgelly, Fife, with full military honours in recognition of his five years' service with The Black Watch. His oak coffin lay before the altar draped in a Saltire, the regimental flag of The Black Watch, and was topped by Private McHale's red hackle, regimental belt and campaign medals throughout the hour-long requiem Mass. The regimental hymn 'Lochaber No More' was played as he was lowered into the ground, and a bugler sounded the last post. His aunt Karen Cunningham said, 'We are all devastated. He was not reluctant. He was not scared. He took life as it came. He knew what he had to go and was looking forward to coming home. Being in the army was all he ever wanted to do.'

Lieutenant Colonel James Cowan said, 'Private McHale was a great character. He had served for five years with The Black

Watch and been in Kosovo and in Iraq the first time around. He had always been a friend of many. We will miss him deeply. Our thoughts are very much with his family at home tonight in Lochgelly in Fife, and in particular with his father Michael, who was a great friend of many in the battalion.'

❖ ❖ ❖

Late 2004 saw the first confirmed suicides of British soldiers in Iraq and the death of the first servicewoman. After Royal Military Police Staff Sergeant Denise Rose took her own life, the debate over the presence and role of female soldiers was muted. However, some old-fashioned views were aired when Flight Lieutenant Sarah-Jayne Mulvihill's Lynx helicopter was downed in March 2006. Given the invaluable contribution of hundreds of female personnel, the suggestion that there was no place for them on the frontline seemed strange. Female officers and servicewomen also won a clutch of gallantry awards, including a Distinguished Flying Cross in recognition of the courage and skill displayed by Flight Lieutenant Michelle Goodman, who landed her helicopter under heavy small-arms and mortar fire at night to save the life of a seriously wounded colleague with just 15 minutes to live. Aged just 19, Private Michelle Norris of The Royal Army Medical Corps also became the first woman to be awarded the Military Cross after giving her injured commander life-saving treatment while under fire in Maysan Province.

31 October 2004

Basra

Staff Sergeant Denise Rose

Staff Sergeant Denise Rose had dreamed about being a soldier as a child and had enlisted at the earliest opportunity after completing her studies in Liverpool. Fifteen years later, she was training the Iraqi police in Basra. As a member of The Royal Military Police's Special Investigation Branch, she was investigating allegations of abuses of Iraqi civilians by British troops.

Recently divorced for the second time, Staff Sergeant Rose knew that she had let herself down when she was seen drunk in uniform. This had led to a stiff rebuke from her commander, Captain Philip Neville. The following day, she was found dead at an army base in Basra, shot in the mouth. A 9-millimetre pistol with one round discharged was resting in her lap.

Captain Neville later told an inquest that she 'liked a drink' and 'was very much part of a male-dominated environment. Often within the SIB [Special Investigation Branch], she found herself to be the only female. She often wanted to be one of the boys. I knew she had recently gone through a messy divorce, but she did not seem in a low mood. The tour was very busy, and she had relished the challenge. She wanted to get her career on track and was keen to be promoted.'

Her mother Florence Barcas said, 'The family is struggling to come to terms with this tragic loss. We are a very close family, and Denise was adored by all of us. She will be terribly missed and will always remain in our hearts and thoughts.'

4 November 2004

Al-Anbar Province

Sergeant Stuart Gray, Private Paul Lowe, Private Scott McArdle

While The Black Watch had grown wearily accustomed to the booby traps, bombs and rocket-propelled grenades that characterised daily life in Basra, the threat of lone suicide bombers most concerned senior officers during their deployment to the Sunni Triangle. As the battalion discovered on 4 November 2004, they were virtually impossible to guard against.

At around 0100, a red Opel Omega accelerated towards a checkpoint installed by The Black Watch hours earlier as part of a cordon operation. Its hasty approach captured the attention of

Sergeant Stuart Gray, Private Paul Lowe, Private Scott McArdle and their interpreter. That day should have seen the interpreter's wedding in Basra, but he had volunteered to accompany the soldiers on their redeployment.

Without warning, a colossal explosion rocked the earth, lifting Private Andrew McMenemy off his feet and throwing him across the road. He looked up to see a fireball rising 100 feet in the air. It was also seen by a disorientated Major Robin Lindsay: 'Everything went blank, and all I could see was a [fire] ball. As it got closer, I felt a burning sensation on my face. I then heard a large blast.'

One of eight wounded men, Private McMenemy struggled to get up as his knees buckled beneath him. His left arm was mangled. Mortars rained down as he received first aid.

When Private Scott Pollard ran back to his Warrior to get his rifle, he saw a body lying face down on the road. He reached down and pressed his forefinger against Private Lowe's neck but could not find a pulse. The interpreter and three sons of Fife lay dead. The deceased and wounded were extracted by helicopter.

Commanding officer Lieutenant Colonel James Cowan said, 'Sergeant Gray, Private Lowe and Private McArdle were all killed instantly, as was the patrol's interpreter, whose name cannot be revealed for security reasons. For a close-knit family such as The Black Watch, this is indeed a painful blow, and all three of these soldiers were our friends. But as we mourn their deaths, so we remember their lives and give thanks for their contribution to the life of our regiment. While we feel this blow most keenly, we will not be deterred from seeing our task through to a successful conclusion.'

Sergeant Gray, from Dunfermline, left a wife, Wendy, and two children: Kirstin, twelve, and Darren, ten. Lieutenant Colonel Cowan described him as a 'sergeant of great experience'. Kirstin paid her own tribute when she laid ten roses in her father's honour at St Giles Garrison Church, Warminster, and a note in her handwriting: 'Dad, love you and miss you. Love Kirstin.'

His mother Mary said, 'He was an experienced and professional soldier, a loving husband, father, son and brother, and a proud member of The Black Watch. My thoughts are with

127

my daughter-in-law Wendy, her family and my two gorgeous grandchildren.'

Private Lowe, from Kelty, Fife, had wanted to join The Black Watch from the age of seven. An able, talented drummer while still at school, he continued his interest throughout his year-long training at the Army Apprentice College in Yorkshire and subsequent training at Catterick to join the regimental band. He deployed to the Gulf for a second time in July 2004 with his fellow pipers and drummers in their war-fighting role and had been due to return to Britain on leave just days after the blast. He was one of three family members to serve in Iraq, and in spite of his disagreement with the war he persuaded his younger brother Craig to enlist. The 18 year old returned to Britain from Iraq after his brother's death. They had been photographed in their desert combats with their cousin Barry.

Craig said, 'He [Private Lowe] didn't think he should be there because the regiment has already done its time over there, the first time. So, he didn't think they should have gone back. Paul thought George Bush was an arsehole for starting a war over nothing, trying to get oil and money.'

Reverend Scott Burton told mourners, 'We will not forget amidst our grief to give thanks to God for the magnificent man that Paul Lowe had become, and with the same honour that he gave to his regiment we honour this son of Scotland, this child of God, with our vow never to forget him. Those who watched him grow through the years will tell you that having joined up as a boy, Private Paul Aitken Lowe leaves now with full military honours as a man.'

Private McArdle had followed a family tradition when he joined The Black Watch. He had recently been promoted to the battalion's reconnaissance platoon and was about to become a father. He had proposed to his girlfriend Sarah McLaren while on operations. A message posted on the regiment's website read, 'The saddest thing is he had left the battalion but was recalled for this terrible and pointless mission.'

Reverend Alex Forsyth told those at his funeral, 'Scott was a brother in arms in a historic regiment that is proud of its traditions, its training, its soldiers and its record of service. Scott was serving his country and the regiment he loved alongside soldiers who enjoyed the sheer gladness of being in such company.'

8 November 2004

Camp Dogwood

Private Pita Tukutukuwaqa

Four days later, a roadside bomb detonated beneath Private Pita Tukutukuwaqa as he drove his Warrior armoured vehicle north of Camp Dogwood. He died of head, chest and pelvic injuries. Two wounded soldiers were taken by helicopter to a US airbase. The well-built Fijian had joined The Black Watch in March 2001 and had also served in Kosovo. He was an outstanding sportsman and sniper. The Prince of Wales visited his family in their Pacific Islands home to express his condolences.

26 December 2004

Shaibah Logistics Base

Sergeant Paul Connolly

On Christmas Day 2004, Sergeant Paul Connolly, of The Royal Mechanical and Electrical Engineers, confided to a close friend that he had been abused as a child. A divorced father of three, Sergeant Connolly, from Crawley, West Sussex, wanted to leave the army and start a new life in Canada with his fiancée Louise Wills. He was in considerable financial debt. On Boxing Day, he took a weapon from the armoury at Shaibah Logistics Base, marched into an empty aircraft hangar and shot himself. He was three months into his tour.

After basic training in 1989, Sergeant Connolly had specialised as a metalsmith and master welder. He was described as highly capable and popular. Lieutenant Colonel Nick Cavanagh,

Sergeant Connolly's commanding officer, said, 'Paul's death is a real tragedy and a terrible shock for his many comrades, both in the regiment and the wider family of The Royal Electrical and Mechanical Engineers. He was widely respected and admired. He will be sorely missed. Our thoughts and prayers are with his family at this most difficult time.'

❖ ❖ ❖

Sergeant Connolly's death, the last of 2004, brought the total number of fatalities among UK service personnel to 75. Only ten British soldiers were lost to hostile enemy action that year – as compared to seven hundred and nineteen US soldiers. The frequency of attacks against British forces was to intensify during 2005, 2006 and 2007.

2005

Sunday, 30 January 2005 was a day of celebration. Millions of Iraqis defied the insurgents to vote for their first elected assembly. This was a 'Kodak moment', to steal a phrase from President Bush, like the capture of Saddam Hussein almost a year earlier. Those who had suffered under his dictatorship and in the anarchy that followed its dismantlement voted in the naive hope that an end would come to the violence that was tearing their country apart. The disenfranchised Sunnis shunned the elections, and not until 2007 would Iraq begin to disentangle itself from a web of conflicts.

The advent of the elected assembly was chosen by former Labour foreign secretary Robin Cook, who had resigned on the eve of war, former Conservative foreign secretary Douglas Hurd and Liberal Democrat foreign affairs spokesman Menzies Campbell to call for British and United States troops to leave Iraq at the end of 2005 when the United Nations mandate expired. Cook called for a fresh direction for British policy:

> The starting point for any search for an alternative strategy is to be frank that the present one has failed. This is an opportune time to set out a change of direction. It must be so radical that it is seen by Iraqis as a new strategy and not as a continuation of the failed approach of the past two years. There can be no credible programme to reduce support for the resistance unless we convince the Iraqi people that we have an exit strategy within a realistic timeframe. Both the US and UK should inform the new assembly elected this weekend that we expect to leave by the end of that [UN] mandate. A target date is necessary to demonstrate to Iraqis that we do not intend to stay indefinitely.

That the elections passed peacefully in the British-controlled provinces was no great surprise, because although an intra-Shia civil war beckoned, the two largest parties in the south – the Supreme Council for the Islamic Revolution in Iraq and the Islamic Dawa Party – had joined forces. The 'Islamic Basra' combined ticket secured 33 per cent of the city's vote, while al-Fadhila, representing moderate followers of Moqtada al-Sadr, won 20 per cent there and topped the polls in Maysan.

30 January 2005

Balad

Chief Technician Richard Brown, Flight Sergeant Mark Gibson, Acting Lance Corporal Steven Jones, Squadron Leader Patrick Marshall, Master Engineer Gary Nicholson, Sergeant Robert O'Connor, Flight Lieutenant Paul Pardoel, Flight Lieutenant Andrew Smith, Flight Lieutenant David Stead, Corporal David Williams

> 'I would find it hard to constitute again such a thoroughly professional and experienced team as this one – they were the best.'
>
> Group Captain Paul Oborn, Royal Air Force

Flight Lieutenant David Stead and his crew had deployed to Iraq in the middle of 2004 as the Sunni–Shia conflict gained pace. Not a month passed without an atrocity: 37 Shiites killed at a mosque near al-Hillah in June; 70 Shiites killed queuing for jobs in Baghdad in July; 45 Shiite pilgrims killed at Kufa in August.

Flight Lieutenant Stead belonged to 47 Squadron, otherwise known as the 'Special Forces Flight', stationed at RAF Lyneham in Wiltshire. The married father of two had been decorated for his courageous flying in Afghanistan three years previously, winning the Air Force Cross after a mission to rescue wounded Afghan children near Kandahar. In horrendous weather, Flight Lieutenant Stead had flown on 'internal flying aids only', which as his citation confirmed was 'extremely dangerous and required exceptional skill'.

Flight Lieutenant Andrew Smith, Flight Lieutenant Stead's co-pilot and ten years his junior, had only joined 47 Squadron in November 2004, and this was his first operational detachment. Flight Lieutenant Stead's regular crew included: two ground engineers, Chief Technician Richard Brown and Sergeant Robert O'Connor; navigator Flight Lieutenant Paul Pardoel; air engineer

Master Engineer Gary Nicholson; air loadmaster Flight Sergeant Mark Gibson; and army signaller Acting Lance Corporal Steven Jones.

Flight Lieutenant Stead's Hercules C-130 Mk 1 had been built by Lockheed in 1967 and upgraded for Special Forces operations with the installation of Directional Infrared Countermeasures and a Missile Approach Warning System. Given its age and 24,200 flying hours, it was described in Royal Air Force parlance as 'mature'. Neither Flight Lieutenant Stead nor any other pilot had reported problems with the airframe in Iraq.

On 29 January 2005, Flight Lieutenant Stead flew for seven and a half hours, hopping back and forth between Baghdad International Airport and the US air base at Balad, forty-five miles north of the capital, where his final flight of the day touched down at 2200 local time. The following morning, his crew was joined by detachment safety equipment fitter Corporal David Williams, and at 1230 hours Flight XV179 flew to Baghdad, where a number of Special Forces personnel jumped aboard. Flight Lieutenant Stead landed at Basra at 1359, where the rear ramp was lowered and 125 kilograms of general freight, 126 kilograms of flares and 12 kilograms of 7.62-millimetre ammunition loaded aboard. The aircraft was refuelled with 17,500 kilograms of av-gas, taking its total weight to 59,236 kilograms. The heavy load gave the aircraft a contingency endurance were it to be re-tasked later that day. The fuel was carried in the aircraft's wing internal tanks. Special Forces passengers sat in the cargo hold as Flight XV179 took off at 1511, touching down in Baghdad an hour later. They disembarked to be replaced by visiting air advisor Squadron Leader Patrick Marshall, a 39-year-old former Tornado pilot usually stationed at Strike Command Headquarters, High Wycombe.

Unknown to Flight Lieutenant Stead or anyone aboard, at 1315 two US Black Hawk UH-60 helicopters had been engaged in flight by surface-to-air fire from ambush sites near al-Taji, 20 miles north-west of Baghdad – locations on XV179's intended flight path to Balad. This had been the first such attack in that locality for two months.

The flow of such mission-critical information was restricted, or, as Chief of the Air Staff Sir Jock Stirrup described it, 'compartmentalised', to prevent parties being 'overwhelmed' by intelligence, little of which was of immediate relevance. Of greater concern was the fact that British planners and intelligence staff had only limited access to the US's preferred computerised communication systems, such as Military Internet Relay Chat and Secret Internet Protocol Network. Instead, the British waited for general security updates by email, hours after the intelligence had gone live across the US network. When an outline of the attack reached The Royal Air Force's Air Component Headquarters at al-Udeid, Qatar, at 1515, precisely two hours after the incident, nobody there was aware of Flight Lieutenant Stead's intended flight plan, and hence its relevance was dismissed. Neither was there any method of passing real-time threat information from Air Component Headquarters directly to Flight Lieutenant Stead in the cockpit of his aircraft.

One hour before local twilight, cloud cover was minimal, visibility unrestricted and the temperature a clement 18 degrees Celsius. Flight XV179 departed Baghdad International Airport at 1624. Expected time of arrival at Balad was 1645.

When finalising route, altitude and flight speed, Flight Lieutenant Stead would have weighed operation-specific requirements against his squadron's standard operating procedures and tactical aid memos on hostile flying over flat, featureless terrain. Low-level flying increased the vulnerability of his aircraft to small arms but countered the threat, or so it was thought, posed by Man-Portable Surface to Air Weapon Systems.

Flight Lieutenant Stead's Hercules had a long history of operating in hostile environments. The duplication of its flying controls allowed Flight Lieutenant Smith to take over seamlessly. Either pilot could retain control in the event of engine and hydraulic power failure. The fact that small-arms attacks had only caused slight structural damage and minor fuel leaks in previous years had dissuaded The Royal Air Force from fitting a safety mechanism known as Explosive Suppressant Foam. This was designed to prevent fires or explosions when fuel tanks were pierced. The foam expanded, confining vapour ignition to the area closest to the spark and preventing an explosion. At £600,000 per airframe, Explosive Suppressant Foam failed The Royal Air Force's cost-versus-benefit test. This omission was highly controversial, given that 47 Squadron pilots had specifically requested its installation. It was also standard fitting on Australian and US Hercules.

On his return from Special Forces operations in Afghanistan in 2002, Squadron Leader Chris Seal's 'lessons identified' memo had requested Explosive Suppressant Foam be fitted to all Royal Air Force Hercules planes. Unknown to Squadron Leader Seal, and in all likelihood Flight Lieutenant Stead and his crew, the Defence Evaluation and Research Agency had concluded in 1994 that the UK was 'lagging behind the US' on Explosive Suppressant Foam. The agency's advice was not acted upon.

While loadmaster Flight Sergeant Gibson was in the cupola of the Hercules and the signaller Lance Corporal Jones sat at his communications station in the freight bay, it was standard practice for ground engineers Chief Technician Brown and Sergeant O'Connor to keep watch through the parachute doors. After take-off, Flight Lieutenant Stead opted to fly at low altitude, between 200 and 500 feet. His aircraft was observed by insurgents stationed at two ambush sites near al-Taji. They were in close proximity and on Flight Lieutenant Stead's right-hand side as his aircraft approached. The Iraqis, surprised perhaps that just hours after their attack on two Coalition Forces helicopters, a transport plane should follow the same flight path, primed their rocket launchers. The occasion was recorded for propaganda and posterity, a video camera capturing the moment when a finger pressed a button on an ignition device, sending two rockets skyward with corkscrew-shaped outlines of smoke trailing in the sky. These were unguided rockets, most likely adapted Russian S5s, steel-bodied missiles with high-explosive warheads fired from 57-millimetre tubes. There were elongated exhaust nozzles at the rear of each of the rockets, attached to which were eight forward-folding fins, which sprang up as they left the launch tubes. The S5s were capable of travelling 300 metres in just 1.1 seconds and burned brightly during flight. Eye witnesses later reported seeing 'fire balls' travelling towards the Hercules.

Either small arms or rockets, or both (the evidence remains classified), passed through the Hercules' right-hand aileron dry-bay and into the number four fuel tank ullage. Post-incident investigations were divided on whether a standard rocket-propelled grenade struck the aircraft at the same time.

Flight Lieutenant Stead's aircraft was in grave danger, as Lance Corporal Jones told Balad air controllers, 'No duff. No duff. We are on fire. We are on fire.' Moments later, with its number four fuel tank and right wing ablaze, communications aboard Flight XV179 were lost.

Flight Lieutenant Stead might or might not have been aware of an incident over the Falkland Islands when Flight XV206 managed a successful landing after its burning wing snapped off. On that occasion, the crew had survived because the outer wing had severed before the fire caught hold in the main body of the aircraft. A 23-foot section of Flight Lieutenant Stead's right wing was torn off, but a stump remained ablaze, and the fire spread rapidly. The aircraft was unstable verging on uncontrollable, putting the pilot in an invidious position: if he remained airborne, the fire would spread; if he decelerated in order to crash land, he would have lost any remaining control when his speed decelerated below 215 knots, sending his aircraft into a spin.

Flight XV179 came to ground 1.3 miles from where its right wing had landed, flooding the site with burning fuel, oil and hazardous pollutants that contaminated an adjacent irrigation waterway. None of the crew could have survived. At 1655, Flight Lieutenant Stead's Hercules was confirmed missing and US Apache helicopters scrambled from Balad in a bid to locate survivors across the sparsely vegetated area, decorated with small clumps of trees and now the blazing remains of a Royal Air Force transport aircraft. Insurgents won the race to the scene and found the dead body of Australian navigator Flight Lieutenant Pardoel. Born in Melbourne, he had enlisted at the Australian Defence Force Academy in Canberra in 1988, graduating three years later with a bachelor of science degree. In spite of his love of flying and rugby, his first passion was his family. He had met his wife Kellie at a Royal Australian Air Force summer ball in 1995. Their first child Jordie was born two years later, her brother Jackson in 1999, and later a sister, India. The militiamen stripped the deceased naked and filmed the spectacle. When the US ground forces arrived, personal effects and classified materials were spread over a wide area, and it took 150 heavily armed US Marines to secure the main crash site.

The following day, Al Jazeera broadcast a videotape provided by the Sunni terrorist group National Islamic Resistance in Iraq, which purported to show the shooting down of the aircraft. The footage was genuine.

The powder-blue flag of The Royal Air Force was lowered to half-mast at RAF Lyneham after the service's biggest single loss of personnel since the Second World War. Residents of the village and the base shared a sense of disbelief. Councillor Jenny Jardine spoke for her constituents: 'Our hearts bleed for the families. They were our first thought. The whole village will share the grief. The base and the village are very much one community.'

Flight Lieutenant Pardoel was the first of the ten victims to be named and the first Australian killed in Iraq. He lived opposite the base gates. Corporal Williams's widow Kathryn described the equipment fitter as 'caring and compassionate'. The 37 year old from Chippenham was the first to be laid to rest. The funerals of Master Engineer Nicholson and Flight Sergeant Gibson were held over the following days. Flight Sergeant Gibson had served in Sierra Leone and Afghanistan. The married father of one had joined The Royal Air Force aged 18, following his father's footsteps into the service.

The president of the Board of Inquiry ordered all manageable pieces of wreckage to be placed in an adjacent canal and the tail section to be blown up to prevent its use as a symbolic backdrop to another video. The smaller, teardrop-shaped crash area 1.3 miles to the south-east also had secrets to reveal, but much of the wing had been hauled off to the local villages before the site was sealed. Ten to fifteen locals observed picking through the remains fled when American troops arrived. It would have taken a major offensive and probably cost more lives to recover the missing pieces; instead, a radio appeal was issued. In spite of the reward on offer, no components were returned.

Missing parts, a lack of creditable witnesses and the absence of an Accident Data Recorder aboard the Hercules hampered crash investigators as they began to examine possible causes.

Prospective scenarios included a bomb placed aboard or that the C-130 had been mistaken for an incoming missile on approach to Balad and been shot down by US forces.

The Board of Inquiry criticised the failure to disseminate mission-critical intelligence, which had led to Royal Air Force elements flying in ignorance of essential information:

> Maintaining an up-to-date picture of the threat situation is a continuous and complex process. The intelligence staff were enthusiastic about their work and were obviously striving to provide the best service they could within their areas of responsibility. However, looking specifically at the ground-to-air threat, a number of factors reduced the effectiveness of the collection and dissemination process. In essence, each stage in the process appeared to work but the links between stages were less robust. The procedure for reporting SAFIRE [Surface-to-Air-Fire] activity was laid down in the Special Instructions, but units of different services and commands appeared to interpret these instructions in a manner that best served their needs . . . Once reported, details of a SAFIRE event would progress up the reporting chain in the form of a Mission Report, which would be interpreted and analysed before being included in the 12-hourly Mission Summary and forwarded to units. As this was a human process, there were delays at every stage.

The board hinted at the expectation of the crew to be told what they needed to know, when they needed to know it:

> As the crew had good communication equipment onboard and a dedicated signaller, it is reasonable to suppose that they were confident that any time-sensitive threat information would be passed directly to them. However, the crew of XV179 remained unaware of the earlier attack and, once airborne, flew close to the SAFIRE sites and crashed shortly afterwards. Ultimately, it is not possible to prove that the earlier SAFIRE and the loss of XV179 were linked; however, the fact that the aircraft took off on

a routine sortie without an accurate threat picture proves that the intelligence collation and dissemination system needs urgent review. [It] was a contributory factor in this incident.

The board found that those onboard died 'extremely rapidly, if not instantaneously' as a result of severe multiple injuries. However, their injuries differed and were 'assessed to be the result of the aircraft's tumbling break-up'.

The board suggested that the right wing had blown apart due to an 'internal over-pressure'. This conclusion was supported by the lack of bending or yielding in the metal structure and the fact that the separated wing section had not detached in one piece:

> The over-pressure that separated the wing must have occurred in the number four fuel tank, which extended from the wing tip to the right-hand outboard engine. The cause of this explosive event is most likely to have been caused by an ignition of the fuel/air mix in the space above the fuel, known as the ullage. Aviation fuel as a liquid will not explode; however, the ullage contains a fuel/air mixture that can explode if ignited under the correct conditions ... The fuel would have been relatively warm, due to the ambient air temperature, and aircraft manoeuvring could have agitated the tank contents ... There is evidence of sustained airborne fire on the section of wing at the separation point, which is also likely to have occurred after separation. The fire caused significant damage to the trailing edge of the wing.

The board concluded that XV179 was only in flight for 12 to 15 seconds following the explosion and found the decision not to fit Explosive Suppressant Foam was 'a contributory factor'. It recommended that 'the fitting of a fuel-tank suppression system for the C-130 should be considered'.

The Al Jazeera video 'certainly recorded elements of the incident if not all of it', according to the Board of Inquiry. Flight Lieutenant Pardoel's widow Kellie Merritt was horrified to find film footage of her husband's corpse being sold on eBay.

The families of the deceased campaigned for the fitting of Explosive Suppressant Foam, a process which hampered mission effectiveness, as each of The Royal Air Force's 44 operational Hercules had to be flown home for refitting. When Squadron Leader Seal was shown the Defence Evaluation and Research Agency document pertaining to Explosive Suppressant Foam, he said, 'I am gobsmacked, astonished. I had only found out about Explosive Suppressant Foam when a US pilot told me his aircraft had it. I had got into trouble after writing my lessons learned report, which voiced my concerns about Explosive Suppressant Foam, infrared countermeasures and night-flying tactics. I was reprimanded for not following proper staff procedures and censured thereafter. When you flag things up, all I can say is it does not do your career any good.'

The families were further dismayed when the Ministry of Defence insisted on a gagging order to prevent them from discussing classified evidence. They were told that they could only read documents if they agreed not to discuss them in public – the material was highly sensitive and the Ministry of Defence's position was understandable. An administrative error led Wiltshire coroner David Masters to bar Sarah Chapman, sister of Sergeant Robert O'Connor, from reading the texts because she had failed to register in advance to see them.

On 25 April 2008, the inquest into the deaths was adjourned 'part heard' until September 2008 when it was anticipated that it would take three weeks for the remaining evidence to be heard.

Sergeant O'Connor, from near Tamworth, Staffordshire, had joined The Royal Air Force in October 1985. On completion of his apprenticeship, he was posted to RAF Lyneham, where he spent the vast majority of his service career, excepting a short tour at nearby RAF Brize Norton. He was held in esteem by his work colleagues and superiors for his knowledge, dedication and professionalism. During his tours, he was an active sportsman and a keen participant in all aspects of station life. A Ministry of Defence spokesman said, 'He will be sadly missed by his loved ones, colleagues and friends, particularly the small section of engineers who worked closely with him. All our thoughts are with his family and loved ones at this time.'

Flight Sergeant Gibson, from Cardiff, had started his career on Hercules aircraft with 24 Squadron in July 1989. An early above-average flying category saw him posted to an instructor's tour with 57 Squadron in May 1993, then to 47 Squadron in January 1996. He accrued more than 7,300 flying hours, the vast majority of which were on Hercules, and saw action in many theatres, for which he was awarded operational service medals for tours of Sierra Leone, Afghanistan and Iraq. He married Sheila in October 1992, and their daughter Poppy was born five years later.

His friend Terry Dyer said, 'Mark followed his father into The Royal Air Force and made him very proud. They were a smashing family.'

A Ministry of Defence statement read:

> Throughout his career, Mark managed to combine his intelligent, hard-working approach to professional matters with an ebullient enthusiasm that made him a pleasure to work with. As an instructor, his depth of knowledge and ability to relate to all made him a natural. After becoming qualified in the tactical C-130 roles, he was rapidly assessed as being the best all-round operator in his section. Later, not one to rest on his laurels, he produced an ad-hoc new loading scheme that directly led to the success of a major operation during the Afghanistan conflict. 'Gibbo' was known and loved by all who worked with him, and he was known to be a bandit on the golf course, regularly playing ten below his handicap. He was requested by name by those he worked with and was renowned for his entertainments, such as the music he played to parachutists as they jumped out. In short, he was one of life's entertainers, a true character, a real giver – never a taker. Mark was a great husband and father and will be sorely missed.

According to his colleagues, Chief Technician Brown, from Tetbury, Wiltshire, had been totally dedicated and committed to everything he did. He was also always willing and eager to help others. More than 250 people attended a memorial service in his honour at the St Mary the Virgin Church in Tetbury. The service included a poem read by his fiancée Sharon Jones and tributes from his mother Lyn Kelly and colleague Graham Scott.

Reverend John Wright said, 'We in Tetbury are proud of him and what he was prepared to do. It is so easy to take it for granted. Today reminds us of the price that must sometimes be paid by loyal, brave and honest men and women. He was as he was: the same with everyone. He had the gift of taking each moment as it came, living fully, and he had the virtue of telling everyone straight.'

Master Engineer Nicholson, from Hull, East Yorkshire, had seen action in many theatres over 23 years of service and was known and loved by all who worked with him. A Ministry of Defence spokesman said, 'It was commented once or twice that you could hear him before you could see him. Seeing him was not a problem, either, as he was a giant of a man, with a giant heart and an ebullient nature. Indeed, Gary was the embodiment of a master air engineer and, in the finest tradition of the service, always put the interests of his subordinates before himself. Gary leaves behind two sons, whom he loved and nurtured with a tenderness rarely seen. He will be sorely missed.'

Flight Lieutenant Pardoel's mother Margaret said, 'He was lovable, and he was good at sport: cricket, tennis. He had an excellent personality, excellent. Paul had planned to finish up his contract with The Royal Air Force, and he and his wife Kellie and their three children planned to settle back in Canberra. He wanted to see the children more, and the job was getting far too risky. He was aiming to get out as soon as he could.'

A Ministry of Defence statement read:

> Paul 'Pards' 'Paulie' Pardoel was born in Melbourne, Australia, on 15 June 1969 and spent his youth growing up in the Australian city of Ballarat. He joined the Australian Defence Force Academy in Canberra in 1988 and graduated three years later with a bachelor of science degree. He completed navigator training with the Royal Australian Air Force the following year and was posted to 36 Squadron, flying Hercules aircraft in Richmond, outside Sydney. He served with distinction, flying

operational aircraft around the world for seven years. In 1999, he moved to Sale in Victoria, where he instructed at the School of Air Navigation, training future navigators for the Australian and New Zealand defence forces. In this role, Pards was an exceptional instructor, renowned for his ability to impart knowledge whilst maintaining a relaxed environment for his students.

Paul's love of and dedication to his family were obvious to all who were fortunate enough to know them. He had the relaxed, easy grace of someone who knew what was important in life and what wasn't worth worrying about. There is no doubt that Kellie and their children were the centre of his world. Between them, Paul and Kellie created a wonderful family. Pards' philosophy for life was reflected in his approach to fatherhood, where he was very much a 'hands-on' and active dad. His endless patience and gentle encouragement were a direct result of the pure joy he got from Jordie, Jackson and India. He was a gentleman and a proud Australian. The impact of his sad and terrible loss has devastated a close and loving family. His loss has affected all who knew him.

Flight Lieutenant Smith's brother said, 'He was a really funny guy, very loud and fearless. He loved abseiling and bungee jumping – he was a real daredevil. He was just so proud to have been in The Royal Air Force. It was what he had always wanted to do. It is all such a shock.'

Flight Lieutenant Stead, from Burley-in-Wharfedale, West Yorkshire, was born on 15 October 1969 and in his youth was a keen fell runner. After a short spell with a quantity surveying practice, he was commissioned as a Royal Air Force officer on 2 August 1990 and was posted to RAF Linton-on-Ouse, where he commenced flying training. He was awarded his pilot's wings in 1993 and joined the Hercules fleet in 1995. He completed his co-pilot's tour on 47 Squadron and rejoined the squadron as a captain on 18 December 1999. He amassed some 4,100 hours in the air, 3,800 flying Hercules, and was recognised as being one of the most capable captains within the fleet. Flight Lieutenant Stead was involved in operations around the globe, including in

Afghanistan and Iraq. Crews always showed a depth of trust and confidence in his captaincy that motivated them to give their all. He was married to Michelle and the couple had two daughters, Holly and Amelia.

Squadron Leader Marshall, from Ballymena, County Antrim, had joined The Royal Air Force in June 1990, serving 11 operational tours on the Tornado GR. He was awarded a General Service Medal for air operations in Iraq, an Operational Service Medal for Operation Telic and the NATO Medal for operations in the former Yugoslavia. His last job was as a staff officer at Strike Command Headquarters, High Wycombe, where he was part of a team responsible for coordinating Royal Air Force support operations. Although he thoroughly enjoyed his staff tours, he was eagerly looking forward to returning to his greatest passion, flying. He was a highly regarded and talented operational pilot. His family described him as 'full of spirit, but with a very kind and thoughtful side to his nature. He had a very positive outlook on life.' He attended Campbell College before Queen's University, Belfast.

Reverend Stephen Radley said, 'In the choice Patrick made to join The Royal Air Force, he chose to serve others, and through this choice we see a reflection of the character of God in Patrick's life.'

Squadron Leader Marshall was buried at The Royal Air Force chapel of St Michael and All Angels, Cranwell, Lincolnshire.

The family of Acting Lance Corporal Jones, from Fareham, Hampshire, said he was 'adventurous and fun loving. He will for ever be in the hearts of those who knew him.'

Corporal Williams, from Eyemouth, Scotland, had been a survival-equipment fitter serving with the engineering wing at RAF Lyneham, the base for all Royal Air Force Hercules. Married with three young children, Corporal Williams was a devoted husband and proud father. His colleagues remembered him as a happy-go-lucky character, with a mischievous personality and dry sense of humour. He had been a Royal Air Force serviceman for 17 years and had amassed a wealth of knowledge. Corporal Williams was honoured with a full military funeral at St Andrew's Church, followed by a low-level Hercules fly-past. His coffin was draped in the Union Jack, and former Royal Air Force colleagues acted as pall-bearers.

His widow Kathryn said, 'Dave was a wonderful and devoted husband and daddy. We had nine special years together and had three beautiful boys. The memories we share will be with us for ever in our hearts and in our minds, though our lives will never be the same. Dave was born in Dumfries and was the only child of David and Evelyn Williams, who live in Eyemouth. He was always proud to show us his home, and we have many happy memories of holidays with his family there. His love of Eyemouth was shown by his dedication to the lifeboats and their crew. He was a caring and compassionate man, with a great sense of humour, and was loved and respected by everyone who knew him. Though his smile has gone for ever and his hand we cannot touch, we shall never lose sweet memories of the one we loved so much.'

28 March 2005

Basra

Private Mark Dobson

On Easter Monday 2005, Private Mark Dobson, one of thirty-four reservists from The Tyne-Tees Regiment in Basra, took his rifle strap, wrapped it around his neck and strangled himself. Super-fit Dobson, a paramedic in civilian life, had given thought to his actions, planning his methodology and writing suicide notes to his parents and his colleagues. His mother said that her unmarried and childless son, while known for his sensitivity and kindness, was also 'serious-minded'. His last letter spoke of 'this evil world'. Jean Dobson insisted that before her son had deployed to Iraq, he had been impatient to get out there; he had thought it was the 'ultimate thing'. He had trained five or six evenings each week, running and working in the gym. When she had spoken to him a few days before his death, he had mentioned that he was looking forward to seeing his friends and family in Britain in a fortnight's time.

She said that she would have heard it in his voice if he had been particularly distressed.

'The army say they are as baffled as us,' she said. 'Everyone seemed to be stunned, because he was just getting on with his job and seemed happy. He was such a loveable and good person and had so much kindness in his heart. He would not hurt anyone, and I cannot believe he would do this to hurt us. He would get very emotional about problems such as world affairs and poverty. It was just the general situation in Iraq – there was something that was bothering him. I just wish he had said, and I just pray to God that we get some answers.'

Private Dobson's platoon commander spoke of him as a 'father figure' to younger soldiers. His final letter to them ended, 'Sorry to let you down, lads.'

His inquest returned a verdict of suicide. Coroner Nicholas Gardiner noted, 'Something was clearly troubling Mark Dobson, but, as his mother says, we shall probably never know exactly what it was.'

Lieutenant Colonel Ian McFarlane, Private Dobson's commanding officer, said, 'Private Dobson was an enthusiastic and popular member of B (Green Howards) Company of The Tyne-Tees Regiment based in Middlesbrough. He transferred into the infantry three years ago from another local unit in search of further challenge and to satisfy his thirst for adventure and passion for soldiering. Private Dobson always had a valuable contribution to make. He was a tremendously effective team member and could always be relied upon to give a full 100 per cent in anything he was tasked to do. He had recently qualified as a physical-training instructor, gaining a course award considerably better than others who were many years younger than him. He was a regular attendee at weekend and annual training camps, and had served since 1996 throughout the UK and in Cyprus. Private Dobson's death has come as a great shock to the many people who knew him, and he will be sadly missed.'

2 May 2005

Al-Amarah

Guardsman Anthony Wakefield

On 2 May 2005, Guardsman Anthony Wakefield became the first of ten soldiers to be killed that year by improvised explosive devices or roadside bombs. Guardsman Wakefield, a father of three from Newcastle, was on patrol in al-Amarah when insurgents struck. Guardsman Wakefield was on top-cover, sticking his neck out above the Land Rover when the bomb went off. In spite of his body armour, he suffered fatal neck and chest wounds. The same device left one of his colleagues wounded. It was suggested that had he been issued with the recently acquired Kestrel jackets, with added arm and neck protection, he might have survived.

A member of The Coldstream Guards, Guardsman Wakefield had deployed to Maysan in March with 12 Mechanised Brigade. His estranged wife Ann Toward described him as a 'very brave man' who was 'outgoing' and 'funny'.

Lieutenant Colonel Andrew Williams said, 'Guardsman Wakefield was a supremely fit and popular soldier who died doing his duty and amongst his friends. A proud Coldstream Guardsman, he was attached to The Staffords battle group and had made many friends during his time with us. To all those who were lucky enough to know him, it was clear that he loved his duty and had a very bright future ahead of him. He was already a qualified physical-training instructor and had been selected to attend a course for promotion at the end of the six-month tour. Guardsman Wakefield will be sorely missed by a great many people, and our thoughts and prayers are with his family and friends.'

❖ ❖ ❖

Ann Toward turned her anger towards Tony Blair, saying that were it not for his actions, her children would still have a father. As the hours counted down before the general election, the prime minister's approval rating of more than 90 per cent recorded after his 'People's Princess' speech seemed a very long time ago. On 5 May 2005, Reg Keys, father of Red Cap Lance Corporal Thomas Keys, won 10 per cent of the vote standing as an independent candidate in Blair's Sedgefield constituency. After winning a muted victory locally and nationally, the prime minister said that he had 'listened and [he had] learned'. Not only grieving family members blamed Blair personally for the deaths of British soldiers; it was also widely felt by many members of the general public that he was individually responsible for the British presence in Iraq.

29 May 2005

Al-Kahla

Lance Corporal Alan Brackenbury

Lance Corporal Alan Brackenbury was killed by a roadside bomb in al-Kahla, near al-Amarah, as troops travelled to a meeting with Iraqi security officials. Four other soldiers were injured.

Lance Corporal Brackenbury, from East Riding, Yorkshire, had been promoted earlier that year, having joined The King's Royal Hussars in 2000. His father said that his son had loved the army and had only ever wanted to serve on operations.

Lance Corporal Brackenbury's willingness to learn Arabic and his friendliness towards the locals had impressed his seniors, and he was expected to continue his rapid progress through the ranks. 'He made friends in many quarters,' said Captain Anthony Sharman, 'firstly because he was a committed professional, but secondly and most importantly because he was a good person. He had developed a sense of right and wrong and the moral courage to follow the just cause.'

Soldiers joined his family and friends for Corporal Brackenbury's funeral at Holy Trinity Church, East Cowick, with six of his comrades carrying his coffin inside for the service.

His family was joined by his fiancée Kirsty, who was planning their wedding. His father Stephen said, 'It is some comfort to us, as we grieve for Alan, that he died doing what he loved so much.'

Lieutenant Colonel Toby Bridge said, 'This is a desperate loss. He was a man of the future. Corporal Brackenbury lived life to the full. He had a passion for racing, football and fishing. Above all, we will remember his tremendous sense of humour and fun, and his willingness to try something new. His death will be felt by all those who have been privileged to serve alongside him.'

❖ ❖ ❖

Violence and hostility towards external authority were centuries-old traditions in Maysan, where Brackenbury's battle group commander Lieutenant Colonel Andrew Williams admitted in June 2005, 'British Forces are constantly looking at when we are going to draw down. We are not going to be here for ever. You have got to get to a stage where you are handing it back to the people. Would the Iraqi security forces be able to handle and keep a lid on the violence? Yes, I think they would. Maybe not today but in three or four months' time. By the end of the year [2005], I think we will be ready to pull out of Maysan.'

But when the British Army did hand over the province to the Iraqi Army the following year, the Madhi Army swept its soldiers aside. The city was retaken in May 2008 without a shot being fired by any of the thousands of Iraqi troops or US Special Forces after Moqtada al-Sadr ordered his men not to resist government forces. The chief of police in al-Amarah had fled a week before the operation, fearing arrest for his association with the Madhi Army. British Forces were not involved.

29 June 2005

Basra

Signaller Paul Didsbury

S ignaller Paul Didsbury, from Fylde, Lancashire, was fatally injured in an accident in Basra on 29 June 2005. Signaller Didsbury, of 21 Signal Regiment, was leaving his base to catch a helicopter when he suffered a negligent discharge. Lance Corporal Rory Gallagher heard a shot followed by his friend's screams. He said, 'At first I thought he had just made a negligent discharge of the weapon, and I told him not to worry about it, because it happened to everybody. But as I went round to his side of the vehicle, he fell out onto the floor, and I realised he must be injured.'

There was no suggestion that Signaller Didsbury committed suicide. His rifle discharged when he believed that the safety catch was engaged and that there was no round in the chamber. According to his colleagues, he cocked it by mistake in his haste to reach the helipad. An inquest heard that Signaller Didsbury had failed his most recent annual marksmanship test.

Like his father Stuart, the deceased soldier had played rugby for Fleetwood. He had always aspired to join the forces and had enlisted straight from school in 2003. At 18 years of age, he was one of the youngest British soldiers to die in Iraq.

Major Bob Lovett, Signaller Didsbury's officer in command, said he was a 'bundle of energy and enthusiasm' who made the most of his time. 'He always had a smile on his face,' he added, 'and volunteered for absolutely everything. He had arrived in the squadron in 2004 and had quickly become known because of his character. We will miss him.'

◈ ◈ ◈

The war in Iraq was supposed to make Britain safer. But on the morning of 7 July 2005, 52 people, a cross section of twenty-first-century Londoners, were killed and 700 injured when suicide bombers blew themselves up on the London Underground.

The day demonstrated Britain's vulnerability and gave implicit credence to those who saw the war as the single biggest mistake by a British government for 60 years.

16 July 2005

Al-Amarah

Private Phillip Hewett, Second Lieutenant Richard Shearer, Private Leon Spicer

Private Phillip Hewett was a 21-year-old soldier serving with the 1st Battalion, The Staffordshire Regiment. He wrote home:

> Hey, mother, I am fine, just really tired and worn out. We went on patrol the other day for eight hours and we sat down after about four hours for a breather and some old guy shot his AK-47 at us because he thought we were terrorists (old damn fool), it was such a rush. I dived into a brick trench and nearly broke my neck. It was so funny. In the end it was all handshakes and apologies. No one was hurt. Everywhere you go here there are dead dogs and donkeys on the roads. How disgusting, eh? Anyway, I love you and I will write again soon.

He did so on 22 June 2005:

> Hey, mother, I am so looking forward to coming home. I really need a big hug. I have got some stories for you and I've got some good pictures on a disc for you, nothing bad, though. I can't wait to see the family again. I've had so many close calls in the past three weeks it's getting sporty now. Anyway, I am on guard now so I will have to go. Give my love to the family. I love you, take care and I will see you in six days.

Private Hewett flew to Britain on leave, returning to Camp Abu Naji in early July. His colleague Private Leon Spicer was also from Tamworth; troop commander Second Lieutenant Richard Shearer was from Nuneaton. The Staffords were a solid county unit, its soldiers sharing relatives, friendships and a common heritage. Private Spicer maintained a positive attitude, having recovered from a broken leg to rejoin his regiment. He had wanted to be with his mates in Maysan, where he told his parents he thought the people 'lovely'.

Second Lieutenant Shearer had served with the French Foreign Legion and was described as 'no stranger to either danger or excitement'. On 16 July 2005, he commanded a patrol of three armoured Snatch Land Rovers on a visit to the Risaala neighbourhood of al-Amarah. Second Lieutenant Shearer and Private Spicer were standing guard at the rear of the vehicle, with Private Hewett behind the wheel, when a roadside bomb was detonated by infrared control. Second Lieutenant Shearer and Private Spicer died instantly, Private Hewett a short while later at the scene. Two severely wounded soldiers were taken to the field hospital at Shaibah Logistics Base.

After learning the blast which killed her son entered the window of his vehicle through nothing more protective than steel mesh, Sue Smith, Private Hewett's mother, described the Snatch Land Rovers as 'death traps'. Designed for use in Northern Ireland, they were nowhere near capable of withstanding such explosions but were used in preference to more robust vehicles, as they were less intimidating to the locals.

This attack was one of many blamed on Abu Mustafa al-Sheibani, who reportedly led a 280-strong militia and imported his military hardware from Iran. With little supporting evidence, it was also suggested that his men might have been involved in the deaths of the Red Caps in Majar al-Kabir two years earlier.

Lieutenant Colonel Williams said, 'There have been about 50 incidents involving terrorist action since the regiment took over responsibility for the area in April. Soldiers leave camp every day to help train the Iraqi security forces or to help coordinate the reconstruction of the province and have a reasonable expectation of being fired upon or, worse, being the target of some form of bomb. This year the terrorist has remained underground and is adopting a more conventional guerrilla-style insurgency, using sophisticated roadside bombs. These could be concealed anywhere amongst debris and litter.'

Private Hewett's funeral took place at St Editha's Church, Tamworth. The Reverend Alan Barrett said, 'Phil lived his life to the full. He always enjoyed everything he did, and it's wonderful that he had so many good friends who loved him so deeply. Phil died on active service. People should be free to live to enjoy the fruit of their own labour – we call it freedom and democracy – and Phil and his colleagues were engaged on behalf of the nation in trying to secure peace, freedom and democracy for a nation.'

The Ministry of Defence said, 'Private Hewett was Second Lieutenant Shearer's driver – a respected position of enormous responsibility only given to the best of senior soldiers. He was skilled as a driver of both Land Rovers and Warrior armoured vehicles and had been with the platoon since arriving in the 1st Battalion three years ago. A cheerful and intelligent young man with a natural air of confidence, Phillip had worked with the platoon throughout the build-up to the deployment to Iraq and was a well-established member of a very close team. His lively nature ensured he was always popular, and despite just returning to Iraq from leave in England he was full of good humour and stories. Private Hewett had marked himself as having a sound future in the army and had been selected to attend a promotional course in the winter. Exceptionally fit, he was also shortlisted to become a physical-training instructor.'

According to Lieutenant Colonel Williams, Second Lieutenant Shearer had established himself as a 'true soldier and a leader of men', whose passion for soldiering was 'infectious'. He added, 'Rich was highly respected by everyone. His men loved him and regarded him as much more than their platoon commander. One of the very best of his peers and an inspiration, he had only just been selected to run the next cadre for soldiers wishing to become junior non-commissioned officers. In the officers' mess, Rich was a popular friend to all, fun to be around and had a mischievous sense of humour.'

Bridie Spicer received her son's next-of-kin letter:

Dear Mum and Dad,

Right, if you're reading this, I've gone somewhere that all of you have not. Don't cry because if you do I'll have a word with God and tell him not to let you all in. Right then, I knew what could happen to me but it was my job and I wanted to do it. Remember that I love you all (and you and Dad more). Only joking.

Gerard is the best brother any brother could ask for and as Nina is my only sister, I love her to bits. So stop crying as I am as I write this.

I've had the best life out of anyone in the whole world. Right then, Mum, what can I say about you? If I wanted to say everything, I would need about ten million notebooks but I can put it into five words: 'The Best Mum in the World'. P.S. I need to count because I do believe that is six words. Now, Dad, you are 'The Best Dad in the World' and I hope you know it. I love you so much. We had everything in common but I think I took Scouting too far . . . I joined the army! Between you and me, we were the only ones that could survive in the woods. I loved everything that you did and wanted to do it from camping to being a leader.

See you all soon. I will be there waiting for you all.

Bridie Spicer said of her son, 'He was proud to be a Stafford and proud to serve his country. He was also full of life and lived life to the full. We hope our son died for a reason: for peace for those who really want it. He wanted to be in Iraq.'

❖ ❖ ❖

On 31 August 2005, 965 Shias died in the single biggest incident of the civil war to date after Sunni insurgents fired rockets into a huge crowd gathered near the shrine of the seventh Imam, Musa Kadhim, on the occasion of the anniversary of his death. Frightened worshippers ran towards the Aimma Bridge in Baghdad. There was a stampede after rumours spread that there was a suicide bomber on the bridge. Pilgrims were trampled to death and some drowned after jumping into the River Tigris.

5 September 2005

Az Zubayr

Fusilier Stephen Manning, Fusilier Donal Meade

According to his family, the young boy had gazed up in awe at Royal Air Force planes and wanted to be a pilot. Donal Meade's dream lived on after a volcanic eruption destroyed his Caribbean home and made his family refugees. Donal's name recalled the Irish sailors who had docked at Montserrat in the seventeenth century. When he left the West Indies for south London, he missed beach cricket and swapped his bat for a *Star Wars* lightsaber. After failing to achieve the academic results to win a pilot's scholarship, he joined the army. When he passed basic training, his mother Jacinta was so proud that she made him parade in his Royal Regiment of Fusiliers uniform at their Plumstead home. His sister Keisha was shocked when he volunteered to swap barracks life in Belfast for Basra.

Aged 20, Fusilier Meade settled into a routine of providing security escorts for United Nations and reconstruction convoys. 'Stop worrying, sis,' he would say when Keisha mentioned the dangers. As far as he was concerned, the threat was an intrinsic aspect of his job not to be bemoaned. It also irked him that less was made of the deaths of Iraqis than the passing of British soldiers.

Many of his fellow fusiliers had been recruited from south London, such as 22-year-old Stephen Manning. They spent their downtime at Saddam's Palace watching DVDs, eating crisps and looking forward to their periods of leave back in Britain. Fusilier Meade was due to return to Britain to give his sister away at her wedding. Keisha had asked him to wear his smartest army dress. While his commanding officer said that he enjoyed the excitement and camaraderie of life on operations, Jacinta wanted to see him home safely and ordered him to be careful.

On the morning of 5 September 2005, Fusilier Meade and Fusilier Manning were on top-cover, gazing across the crusty landscape surrounding Shaibah Logistics Base, when their Land

Rover was struck by an improvised explosive device. Both were killed.

Fusilier Manning's family described him as a loving son and grandson who would be deeply missed. He had been proud to be a soldier and had died doing the job he loved.

Major Matthew Thorp, the officer commanding C Company, said of Fusilier Meade, 'Those who knew him best and closest were most aware of his fantastic sense of humour, his ability to laugh or crack a joke in any situation. He and Fusilier Manning understood the dangers but were proud to be soldiers and recognised they were doing a difficult, occasionally thankless, but always worthwhile job. They were two fine young men.'

Keisha said, 'Mum was worried, but she knew that was what he wanted to do. He wanted to be a front-line man. As far as he was concerned, he was peacekeeping. That was what he was trained to do in Belfast. He was one in a million, and he just made me laugh. I can't go back to crying, because if my brother was alive, he would be angry with me. He would say, "Oh, sis, shut up."'

One of the last things Fusilier Meade had said to his mother was, 'I am a soldier and soldiers die.'

11 September 2005

Basra

Major Matthew Bacon

Six days later, another improvised explosive device, another British fatality. Major Matthew Bacon had been due to travel by Merlin helicopter from Saddam's Palace until a hydraulic fault forced him to travel by Snatch Land Rover. A roadside bomb tore through the vehicle's Kevlar and reinforced-fibreglass skin. Copper projectiles sliced through the legs of two other soldiers and wedged in Major Bacon's chest. A post-incident investigation suggested that the technology behind the infrared 'trip wire' device had come from outside Iraq, the most likely sources being the Iranian Revolutionary Guard or Hezbollah in Lebanon.

Major Bacon was dating a Royal Military Policewoman and had arrived in Iraq just days after his 34th birthday. He and Corporal Natasha McLennan had recently attended each other's best friends' weddings; their families hoped that theirs would follow. Major Bacon, nicknamed 'Biffa', had wanted to fit as much as possible into his life. Colleagues remembered his catchphrase: 'Come on, old boy, there's no time to waste.' Born in Aberdeen, he had joined the cadets aged 13 and the regular army aged 17. Having served in the first Gulf War, he was plucked from the ranks of the Army Air Corps to begin officer training. He changed cap badges and joined the Intelligence Corps. His obituary in *The Times* noted his passing of the All Arms Commando Course and his attachment to the Special Boat Service. He had served in the Balkans and had done three tours of Afghanistan. At the time of his death, he was stationed at the Coalition Forces Multinational Division, South-east, in Basra, where his work focused on intelligence analysis.

Lieutenant Colonel Andrew Barrow, Major Bacon's commanding officer, said, 'Major Matt Bacon did not waste a moment of his life. He loved soldiering, had a passion for physical exercise and in his spare time was studying for a law degree. He was hugely popular and a real contributor. His death is deeply felt by all those who were privileged to serve alongside him.'

Bacon's father Roger, a retired Metropolitan Police officer of 30 years, suggested that his son had been afforded little protection: 'The roadside bombs were a known threat. If they had used properly armoured vehicles, British soldiers would be alive today, and Matthew might be among them. It makes me very angry and sad.'

United States and United Nations personnel enjoyed the added protection of the RG-31: a Land Rover-type vehicle that the Ministry of Defence had ruled out due to its width and the poor performance of its prototype during trials in the Balkans.

15 October 2005

Basra

Captain Ken Masters

After Captain Ken Masters was found hanged in his accommodation at Waterloo Lines, Basra, his wife Allison suggested, 'If someone had done something, or there had been something in place, Ken would be here.' He was the second Royal Military Police officer to take his own life in Iraq. 'Depression is an illness, but they really need to look at the stress and having somebody out there to look after them,' she said. 'He loved his job, but he was under extreme pressure. The troops are overstretched and attitudes need to change.'

The father of two daughters, Captain Masters was the officer commanding 61 Section, Special Investigation Branch. He died on 15 October 2005, five days before he had been due to return to Britain.

One investigation in his in-tray had been into the deaths of seven Iraqis during an operation to rescue two SAS soldiers captured by local police. The pair had been monitoring the movements of corrupt police officers when they were waved down at a checkpoint. After a gunfight, the soldiers were accused of killing one police officer and wounding another. They were taken to the al-Jamiat police station, where Moqtada al-Sadr loyalists tortured the prisoners with electric drills. With the soldiers tied up and the Madhi Army guarding the station, the captors met pleas by the Iraqi Interior Ministry to release the British pair with demands to free Madhi Army leaders Sheikh Ahmad Majid al-Fartusi and Sajjat al-Basri. When the SAS men were smuggled to a nearby house, it was feared they would be killed. Their Special Forces colleagues used Warrior armoured vehicles to smash through walls and drive over parked cars to force their release. The incident soured relations with local leaders. Basra governor Mohammed al-Waili described the rescue operation as 'barbaric, savage and irresponsible'.

The level of corruption and the fact that militiamen were

COLOUR SERGEANT
JOHN CECIL
21 MARCH 2003

LANCE BOMBARDIER
LLYWELYN EVANS
21 MARCH 2003

CAPTAIN
PHILIP GUY
21 MARCH 2003

MARINE
SHOLTO HEDENSKOG
21 MARCH 2003

SERGEANT
LES HEHIR
21 MARCH 2003

OPERATOR MECHANIC
IAN SEYMOUR
21 MARCH 2003

WARRANT OFFICER CLASS 2
MARK STRATFORD
21 MARCH 2003

MAJOR
JASON WARD
21 MARCH 2003

LIEUTENANT
PHILIP GREEN
22 MARCH 2003

LIEUTENANT
ANTONY KING
22 MARCH 2003

LIEUTENANT
MARC LAWRENCE
22 MARCH 2003

LIEUTENANT
PHILIP WEST
22 MARCH 2003

LIEUTENANT
JAMES WILLIAMS
22 MARCH 2003

LIEUTENANT
ANDREW WILSON
22 MARCH 2003

FLIGHT LIEUTENANT
KEVIN MAIN
23 MARCH 2003

FLIGHT LIEUTENANT
DAVID WILLIAMS
23 MARCH 2003

SAPPER
LUKE ALLSOPP
23 MARCH 2003

STAFF SERGEANT
SIMON CULLINGWORTH
23 MARCH 2003

LANCE CORPORAL
BARRY STEPHEN
24 MARCH 2003

SERGEANT
STEVEN ROBERTS
24 MARCH 2003

CORPORAL
STEPHEN ALLBUTT
25 MARCH 2003

TROOPER
DAVID CLARKE
25 MARCH 2003

LANCE CORPORAL OF HORSE
MATTY HULL
28 MARCH 2003

MARINE
CHRISTOPHER MADDISON
30 MARCH 2003

MAJOR
STEVE BALLARD
30 MARCH 2003

LANCE CORPORAL
SHAUN BRIERLEY
30 MARCH 2003

STAFF SERGEANT
CHRIS MUIR
31 MARCH 2003

LANCE CORPORAL
KARL SHEARER
1 APRIL 2003

LANCE CORPORAL
IAN MALONE
6 APRIL 2003

PIPER
CHRISTOPHER MUZVURU
6 APRIL 2003

FUSILIER
KELAN TURRINGTON
6 APRIL 2003

LIEUTENANT
ALEXANDER TWEEDIE
22 APRIL 2003

LANCE CORPORAL
JAMES McCUE
30 APRIL 2003

PRIVATE
ANDREW KELLY
6 MAY 2003

GUNNER
DUNCAN PRITCHARD
8 MAY 2003

CORPORAL
DAVID SHEPHERD
19 MAY 2003

LEONARD HARVEY
22 MAY 2003

CORPORAL
RUSSELL ASTON
24 JUNE 2003

SERGEANT
SIMON HAMILTON-JEWELL
24 JUNE 2003

LANCE CORPORAL
BENJAMIN HYDE
24 JUNE 2003

LANCE CORPORAL
THOMAS KEYS
24 JUNE 2003

CORPORAL
PAUL LONG
24 JUNE 2003

CORPORAL
SIMON MILLER
24 JUNE 2003

CAPTAIN
JAMES LINTON
18 JULY 2003

PRIVATE
JASON SMITH
13 AUGUST 2003

CAPTAIN
DAVID JONES
14 AUGUST 2003

CORPORAL
DEWI PRITCHARD
23 AUGUST 2003

MAJOR
MATTHEW TITCHENER
23 AUGUST 2003

WARRANT OFFICER CLASS 2
COLIN WALL
23 AUGUST 2003

FUSILIER
RUSSELL BEESTON
27 AUGUST 2003

SERGEANT
JOHN NIGHTINGALE
23 SEPTEMBER 2003

CORPORAL
IAN PLANK
31 OCTOBER 2003

PRIVATE
RYAN THOMAS
6 NOVEMBER 2003

SERGEANT
NORMAN PATTERSON
1 JANUARY 2004

MAJOR
JAMES STENNER
1 JANUARY 2004

LANCE CORPORAL
ANDREW CRAW
7 JANUARY 2004

RIFLEMAN
VINCENT WINDSOR
21 JANUARY 2004

SAPPER
ROBERT THOMSON
31 JANUARY 2004

CORPORAL
RICHARD IVELL
12 FEBRUARY 2004

FUSILIER
GORDON GENTLE
28 JUNE 2004

FLIGHT LIEUTENANT
KRISTIAN GOVER
19 JULY 2004

PRIVATE
CHRISTOPHER RAYMENT
4 AUGUST 2004

PRIVATE
LEE O'CALLAGHAN
9 AUGUST 2004

PRIVATE
MARC FERNS
12 AUGUST 2004

LANCE CORPORAL
PAUL THOMAS
17 AUGUST 2004

FUSILIER
STEPHEN JONES
10 SEPTEMBER 2004

GUNNER
DAVID LAWRENCE
28 SEPTEMBER 2004

CORPORAL
MARC TAYLOR
28 SEPTEMBER 2004

PRIVATE
KEVIN MCHALE
29 OCTOBER 2004

STAFF SERGEANT
DENISE ROSE
31 OCTOBER 2004

SERGEANT
STUART GRAY
4 NOVEMBER 2004

PRIVATE
PAUL LOWE
4 NOVEMBER 2004

PRIVATE
SCOTT MCARDLE
4 NOVEMBER 2004

PRIVATE
PITA TUKUTUKUWAQA
8 NOVEMBER 2004

SERGEANT
PAUL CONNOLLY
26 DECEMBER 2004

CHIEF TECHNICIAN
RICHARD BROWN
30 JANUARY 2005

FLIGHT SERGEANT
MARK GIBSON
30 JANUARY 2005

ACTING LANCE CORPORAL
STEVEN JONES
30 JANUARY 2005

SQUADRON LEADER
PATRICK MARSHALL
30 JANUARY 2005

MASTER ENGINEER
GARY NICHOLSON
30 JANUARY 2005

SERGEANT
ROBERT O'CONNOR
30 JANUARY 2005

FLIGHT LIEUTENANT
PAUL PARDOEL
30 JANUARY 2005

FLIGHT LIEUTENANT
ANDREW SMITH
30 JANUARY 2005

FLIGHT LIEUTENANT
DAVID STEAD
30 JANUARY 2005

CORPORAL
DAVID WILLIAMS
30 JANUARY 2005

PRIVATE
MARK DOBSON
28 MARCH 2005

GUARDSMAN
ANTHONY WAKEFIELD
2 MAY 2005

LANCE CORPORAL
ALAN BRACKENBURY
29 MAY 2005

SIGNALLER
PAUL DIDSBURY
29 JUNE 2005

PRIVATE
PHILLIP HEWETT
16 JULY 2005

SECOND LIEUTENANT
RICHARD SHEARER
16 JULY 2005

PRIVATE
LEON SPICER
16 JULY 2005

FUSILIER
STEPHEN MANNING
5 SEPTEMBER 2005

FUSILIER
DONAL MEADE
5 SEPTEMBER 2005

MAJOR
MATTHEW BACON
11 SEPTEMBER 2005

CAPTAIN
KEN MASTERS
15 OCTOBER 2005

SERGEANT
CHRISTIAN HICKEY
18 OCTOBER 2005

SERGEANT
JOHN JONES
20 NOVEMBER 2005

LANCE CORPORAL
ALLAN DOUGLAS
30 JANUARY 2006

CORPORAL
GORDON PRITCHARD
31 JANUARY 2006

TROOPER
CARL SMITH
2 FEBRUARY 2006

PRIVATE
LEE ELLIS
28 FEBRUARY 2006

CAPTAIN
RICHARD HOLMES
28 FEBRUARY 2006

LIEUTENANT
RICHARD PALMER
15 APRIL 2006

LIEUTENANT COMMANDER
DARREN CHAPMAN
6 MAY 2006

MARINE
PAUL COLLINS
6 MAY 2006

WING COMMANDER
JOHN COXEN
6 MAY 2006

CAPTAIN
DAVID DOBSON
6 MAY 2006

FLIGHT LIEUTENANT
SARAH-JAYNE MULVIHILL
6 MAY 2006

PRIVATE
JOSEVA LEWAICEI
13 MAY 2006

PRIVATE
ADAM MORRIS
13 MAY 2006

LANCE CORPORAL
PAUL FARRELLY
28 MAY 2006

LIEUTENANT
TOM MILDINHALL
28 MAY 2006

CORPORAL
JOHN COSBY
16 JULY 2006

CORPORAL
MATTHEW CORNISH
1 AUGUST 2006

GUNNER
SAMUELA VANUA
4 SEPTEMBER 2006

GUNNER
STEPHEN WRIGHT
4 SEPTEMBER 2006

GUNNER
LEE THORNTON
7 SEPTEMBER 2006

LANCE CORPORAL
DENNIS BRADY
1 OCTOBER 2006

LIEUTENANT
TOM TANSWELL
27 OCTOBER 2006

KINGSMAN
JAMIE HANCOCK
6 NOVEMBER 2006

STAFF SERGEANT
SHARRON ELLIOTT
12 NOVEMBER 2006

WARRANT OFFICER CLASS 2
LEE HOPKINS
12 NOVEMBER 2006

MARINE
JASON HYLTON
12 NOVEMBER 2006

CORPORAL
BEN NOWAK
12 NOVEMBER 2006

SERGEANT
JONATHAN HOLLINGSWORTH
24 NOVEMBER 2006

SERGEANT
GRAHAM HESKETH
28 DECEMBER 2006

SERGEANT
WAYNE REES
7 JANUARY 2007

KINGSMAN
ALEXANDER GREEN
13 JANUARY 2007

PRIVATE
MICHAEL TENCH
21 JANUARY 2007

SECOND LIEUTENANT
JONATHAN BRACHO-COOKE
5 FEBRUARY 2007

PRIVATE
LUKE SIMPSON
9 FERUARY 2007

RIFLEMAN
DANIEL COFFEY
27 FEBRUARY 2007

PRIVATE
JOHNATHON WYSOCZAN
4 MARCH 2007

KINGSMAN
DANNY WILSON
1 APRIL 2007

RIFLEMAN
AARON LINCOLN
2 APRIL 2007

PRIVATE
ELEANOR DLUGOSZ
5 APRIL 2007

SECOND LIEUTENANT
JOANNA DYER
5 APRIL 2007

CORPORAL
KRIS O'NEILL
5 APRIL 2007

KINGSMAN
ADAM SMITH
5 APRIL 2007

SERGEANT
MARK MCLAREN
15 APRIL 2007

COLOUR SERGEANT
MARK POWELL
15 APRIL 2007

CORPORAL
BEN LEANING
19 APRIL 2007

TROOPER
KRISTEN TURTON
19 APRIL 2007

KINGSMAN
ALAN JONES
23 APRIL 2007

RIFLEMAN
PAUL DONNACHIE
29 APRIL 2007

MAJOR
NICK BATESON
1 MAY 2007

PRIVATE
KEVIN THOMPSON
6 MAY 2007

CORPORAL
JEREMY BROOKES
21 MAY 2007

CORPORAL
RODNEY WILSON
7 JUNE 2007

LANCE CORPORAL
JAMES CARTWRIGHT
16 JUNE 2007

MAJOR
PAUL HARDING
20 JUNE 2007

CORPORAL
JOHN RIGBY
22 JUNE 2007

CORPORAL
PAUL JOSZKO
28 JUNE 2007

PRIVATE
SCOTT KENNEDY
28 JUNE 2007

PRIVATE
JAMES KERR
28 JUNE 2007

RIFLEMAN
EDWARD VAKABUA
6 JULY 2007

CORPORAL
CHRISTOPHER READ
7 JULY 2007

LANCE CORPORAL
RYAN FRANCIS
7 JULY 2007

SENIOR AIRCRAFTMAN
MATTHEW CAULWELL
19 JULY 2007

SENIOR AIRCRAFTMAN
CHRISTOPHER DUNSMORE
19 JULY 2007

SENIOR AIRCRAFTMAN
PETER MCFERRAN
19 JULY 2007

LANCE CORPORAL
TIMOTHY FLOWERS
21 JULY 2007

CORPORAL
STEVE EDWARDS
31 JULY 2007

PRIVATE
CRAIG BARBER
6 AUGUST 2007

LEADING AIRCRAFTMAN
MARTIN BEARD
7 AUGUST 2007

LANCE SERGEANT
CHRIS CASEY
9 AUGUST 2007

LANCE CORPORAL
KIRK REDPATH
9 AUGUST 2007

SERGEANT
EDDIE COLLINS
5 SEPTEMBER 2007

SERGEANT
MARK STANSFIELD
21 SEPTEMBER 2007

LANCE CORPORAL
SARAH HOLMES
14 OCTOBER 2007

SERGEANT
JOHN BATTERSBY
20 NOVEMBER 2007

TROOPER
LEE FITZSIMMONS
20 NOVEMBER 2007

GUARDSMAN
STEPHEN FERGUSON
13 DECEMBER 2007

SERGEANT
DUANE BARWOOD
29 FEBRUARY 2008

NICHOLAS BROWN
26 MARCH 2008

masquerading as police officers was an open secret. Police chief General Hassan Suadi, an appointment of the Baghdad government with no links to the Islamists, said half of his force belonged to one or other of the militia groups.

All this had been for Captain Masters and his Royal Military Police colleagues to handle. He had served with The Royal Military Police since 1981 and had been commissioned from the ranks 20 years later. A Ministry of Defence statement confirmed his responsibility for 'all in-theatre serious incidents, plus investigations conducted by the General Police Duties element of the Theatre Investigations Group'.

18 November 2005

Basra

Sergeant Christian Hickey

Sergeant Christian Hickey had tried many jobs before enlisting at his local recruiting office. In his commanding officer's words, he was 'the epitome of a professional soldier'. When he had joined The Coldstream Guards, his mates in East Brierley, West Yorkshire, doubted he would last a week. But Hickey found himself in the army – and his wife Gemma in a nightclub near his training base at Catterick, North Yorkshire.

As his friend Robert Spence recalled, 'I never thought he would make it in the army. I thought he would be back. But when he passed out, he was one of the best new recruits and won an award. The army was always pushing him to do something else. They'd marked him out for better things. He was a professional soldier. He went where he was told. Outside the army, Gemma was his life.'

On 18 October 2005, Sergeant Hickey stepped out of a Snatch Land Rover to examine the road ahead as a roadside bomb was activated. Suspicion fell upon the Iraqi police: four of its officers had been seen acting suspiciously just fifty metres from where the blast had gone off in Basra. After six months in theatre,

Sergeant Hickey had been due to return to Britain. His mother said that he had used his brother's birthday present of £100 to buy his own desert boots.

Gemma Hickey's one comfort was that 'Chris will always be loved and remembered, which cannot be said for the cowards who killed him'.

Lieutenant Colonel Nick Henderson, Sergeant Hickey's commanding officer, said, 'Chris joined The Coldstream Guards in 1993, immediately making his mark as a capable and reliable individual. He was to maintain this impression throughout his service in the regiment as he promoted through the ranks, always displaying great commitment and efficiency in everything he did. In so doing, he set a fine example to those of all ranks who served with him.

'It is significant that at the time of his death he was, as ever, leading his men from the front. A bright future in the army beckoned, and he would undoubtedly have gone far in the profession that he had chosen and that he loved. He was the epitome of a professional soldier. But Chris was more than just this. He was a fun-loving and warm-hearted character who always displayed an irrepressible cheerfulness. However bad things were, Chris could always raise a smile. He had a certain spark that brought out the best in people, and this coupled with his infectious sense of humour could be relied on to lighten any situation. To him, things were always good, or, as he would put it, "canny".'

Lieutenant Colonel Nick Henderson later resigned after voicing concerns about the lack of effectively armoured vehicles – Fusilier Manning and Fusilier Meade had also been under his command. The inadequacy of the Snatch Land Rovers was widely considered an example of criminal incompetence by the government – a national disgrace, even – from which it repeatedly sought absolution.

20 November 2005

Basra

Sergeant John Jones

On 20 November 2005, a similar fate befell Sergeant John Jones when his Land Rover was hit by a roadside bomb in northern Basra. Sergeant Jones of the 1st Battalion, The Royal Regiment of Fusiliers, was on his second tour, having taken part in the invasion of Iraq.

His wife Nickie said, '"Jonah" was a real all-round sportsman. He boxed, played football and was passionate about Aston Villa. He loved being a soldier and was very proud of his regiment. But most of all he was a fantastic dad and loving husband. I would ask the media to respect the privacy of my family at this time as we try to come to terms with our terrible loss.'

Lieutenant Colonel Simon Marr said, 'The explosion hit the leading vehicle of a two-vehicle Land Rover patrol. Sergeant John Jones, the patrol commander, received a fatal wound, and despite the best possible efforts of the medical staff at the scene he could not be saved. Sergeant Jones was a much-loved and highly popular member of our battalion, brimming with energy, a love of soldiering, and an endearing sense of humour and compassion for his men. Whether it was on operations or during training with the soldiers he led so ably, or on the sports field or in the boxing ring, he showed remarkable qualities of professionalism, grit and absolute determination. In the short period of this tour, he and his patrol had already established an excellent rapport with the local population, and he was enjoying the challenges of his role. Sergeant Jones was an outstanding soldier, a wonderful husband and a loving father, who always found time to speak to and encourage those around him. We are left remembering his drive, his courage, his humour and his typically understated contribution to the battalion. Our thoughts and prayers are now with his wife Nickie and his young son Jack.'

Sergeant Jones's mother Carol joined forces with Roger Bacon and handed Defence Secretary Des Browne a report from a serving officer seriously injured in a similar blast. The wounded soldier's testimony described the Snatches as 'extremely vulnerable'. The Ministry of Defence maintained the vehicles were quicker, better suited to the terrain and less intimidating than alternative vehicles.

❖ ❖ ❖

Jones was the 98th British fatality. Blair's critics circled in anticipation of the 100th, the milestone everyone dreaded. To boost morale before Christmas 2005, the prime minister met serving soldiers, including Corporal Gordon Pritchard of The Royal Scots Dragoon Guards. The premier and the father of three posed happily for a photograph. Corporal Pritchard's father had been stationed in Germany, and his brother Peter had been one of the first British troops to enter Umm Qasr in March 2003. All three Pritchard men served with The Scots Cavalry, as The Royal Scots Dragoon Guards were also known.

At the time of his visit to Basra, Blair was buoyed by the increase in the numbers of Sunnis participating in the political process. Having snubbed the 30 January 2005 poll, one million had registered to vote in the recent constitutional referendum. While the vast majority had voted against, the result had been almost irrelevant. As a US Congressional report noted:

> The 15 October referendum represents another milestone for the democratic process regardless of its outcome. Recent State Department polls indicate high voter turnout across all communities, including Sunni Arabs, thus strengthening the political process and further isolating the violent extremists.

Sunni participation rose further in time for the 15 December 2005 elections, which saw a 77 per cent voter turnout nationwide. In the Sunni al-Anbar province, the increase was from 2 per cent in January to 86 per cent in December. While the United Nations declared the elections 'transparent and credible', no single party received sufficient support to form a government.

In late 2005, Iraq was gradually reintegrating itself into the world economy, and the benefits of billions of dollars of loans and donations were taking effect. In November, the World Bank approved its first loan to Iraq in 30 years – Saddam Hussein's international debts of $125 billion having precluded borrowing.

The failure to meet oil-production targets was blamed on insurgent attacks. The country's electricity infrastructure suffered similarly, reaching a peak of just 25 per cent of pre-war electricity generation. Demand for electricity outstripped production. Iraqis bought satellite dishes, air conditioning, fridges, mobile phones and laptops, only to find there was no energy to run them. The disgruntled residents of southern Iraq took out their frustrations on British soldiers. Although 2005 was a bloody year, 2006 was to be more costly still.

2006

30 January 2006
Al-Amarah

Lance Corporal Allan Douglas

On 30 January 2006, Lance Corporal Allan Douglas of The Highlanders was shot by a sniper in al-Amarah as he and Lance Corporal Colin Meikle erected a radio mast. At the time, their commanding officer was holding a meeting in the police station below. The pair were dismantling their equipment when Lance Corporal Meikle heard a rifle crack and looked up to hear a 'thump' as a round passed. Lance Corporal Douglas fell backwards and landed on the ground. He seemed to lift his head before slipping into unconsciousness. He was airlifted to hospital in Basra, where he died later that day.

In accordance with his family's wishes, his funeral in Aberdeen passed without the traditional eight-gun salute. His mother, Diane Douglas, said, 'It wasn't his war. But as he said, he was in the army. It was his job. He came home at Christmas for a fortnight, and he did not want to go back. He had seen enough the first time he was over there. He said it was a waste of time people being there. He just really didn't like it at all.'

31 January 2006
Umm Qasr

Corporal Gordon Pritchard

Early the following morning, 31-year-old Corporal Gordon Pritchard was on top-cover duty as a three-vehicle convoy drove through Umm Qasr on a routine 'rations and water' run. At 0834, insurgents detonated a roadside bomb, killing Corporal Pritchard and wounding three other soldiers, one seriously. The prime minister was 'deeply saddened' by the news, while George Galloway pointed out that nobody was counting the number of Iraqi fatalities so precisely. While *The Independent* remarked that the 100th fatality was no more tragic than the preceding 99 had been, other newspapers were not so restrained, with the *Daily Mail* asking how many more soldiers had to die to 'save the Prime Minister's face and justify his lies?' Vigils were held across Scotland, where opposition to the war was vehement. The Edinburgh-educated prime minister had dragged the country into a war of which only a minority of its people approved. Blair's rejoinder that 'the very forces that are creating this violence are those that are doing it in order to destroy the hope of that country and its people' was rejected by the vast majority of people north of the border. The beneficiary was the Scottish National Party, which had opposed the war from its outset.

One hundred white flowers were thrown into the River Clyde at a ceremony in Glasgow, while Lance Corporal Douglas's family attended a similar ceremony in Aberdeen. Corporal Pritchard's funeral, at St Nicholas's Church, Radstock, Somerset, was attended by 250 family members, friends and colleagues.

Of the 100 deaths, 77 were killed in action (including those killed by roadside bombs) and 23 from non-combat injuries, accidents, suicides or unknown causes. The figure did not include soldiers who committed suicide on their return from Iraq. While such a poignant milestone renewed calls for troops to be withdrawn, the latest victim's family disappointed those hoping to heap more blame at Blair's door. Jenny and Bill Pritchard described their son as an outstanding modern, professional soldier who was 'extremely proud' of his regiment. The soldier's father said, 'I joined up in the 1960s, Gordon's older brother was in the regiment and Gordon was proud to be, too. That's 40 years of family tradition which has abruptly come to an end. Gordon served in Kosovo and Bosnia, but this was his first time in Iraq. He wanted to go. He had done all the training and was happy to go. We were aware of the risks, and so was he. Other families don't talk about it, but we did, and we knew exactly what to expect and discussed it all, even down to the funeral arrangements.'

While they did not want his memory sullied with political sentiment, it was noted that he had died in Umm Qasr, where his brother had served, and where 3 Commando Brigade had fought to establish Britain's beachhead. The location added a sad symmetry. Meanwhile, to some people the occupation appeared as palpable a demonstration of failure as the invasion had been a military success.

◈ ◈ ◈

Corporal Pritchard's death made no waves in Washington DC, where the US death tally of more than 2,000 and rising took precedence. At the time, British-controlled provinces were barely visible on graphs measuring the numbers of attacks per day on Coalition Forces. While four provinces (Baghdad, al-Anbar, Salah ad Din and Ninawa) saw 85 per cent of the violence, Basra and Maysan belonged to a group of eleven that averaged one or fewer attacks per day – this was to change for the worse. Yet Basra languished among the provinces showing the least readiness, capability and numbers of Iraqi security forces to enforce law and order.

Al-Qaeda's response to Sunni participation in elections was a terrorist atrocity intended to trigger civil war. At 0700 hours on 22 February 2006, twelve terrorists disguised as police entered the al-Askari shrine, one of the most revered Shia sites in Iraq, where two of the twelve imams were buried, and handcuffed its guards. The bomb they left behind collapsed the famous golden dome. In response, Shia militia flooded onto the streets, letting off rocket-propelled grenades and bursts of small-arms fire randomly towards Sunni mosques – 27 were targeted that day in the capital. In Basra, British Forces were called to protect two Sunni mosques but could not prevent the killing of a Sunni imam and an attack on the headquarters of the main Sunni party.

To topple the newly elected government, Sunni and Shia insurgents required the passive acquiescence of their communities, if not their active support. Insurgent attacks rose through 2006 to peak in November. The death of every single British serviceman or woman, however he or she met his or her end, heaped further pressure on Tony Blair.

2 February 2006

Basra

Trooper Carl Smith

On 2 February 2006, Trooper Carl Smith of the 9th/12th Royal Lancers became the 101st UK serviceman to lose his life. The father of one from Kettering, Northamptonshire, was only eleven days into his tour when his Land Rover overturned as the driver negotiated a tight bend at high speed. Trooper Smith, who was in the top-cover position, was crushed when the vehicle crashed in the Abu al-Khasib district of Basra. His friend Trooper Christopher Carter lay on the rough ground talking to him as his pulse slowly faded.

Trooper Smith's parents, Paul and Dee Smith, his sister Katherine and partner Carly fully supported his decision to pursue an army career. He was proud to serve his country and was doing a job he loved, they stressed. Lieutenant Colonel Charles Crewdson, the deceased's commanding officer, added that despite only having served for a short time, Trooper Smith had earned a reputation as a hard worker among his fellow soldiers. An ardent Liverpool supporter, 'You'll Never Walk Alone', the club's adopted anthem, was sung at his funeral, which was attended by his three-year-old son Lewis and hundreds of mourners.

28 February 2006

Al-Amarah

Private Lee Ellis, Captain Richard Holmes

Paratroopers Captain Richard Holmes and Private Lee Ellis were killed on a routine patrol of al-Amarah on 28 February 2006. Just hours earlier, the officer, who was due to be posted as an instructor to the Royal Military Academy Sandhurst, had been filmed showing BBC reporter Jane Corbin around the city. Captain Holmes, from Winchester, Hampshire, was on his second tour of Iraq and had married Kate in October 2005. Corbin said the situation on the streets had been hard to read. 'Some people were throwing stones, a few people acknowledged me, but many were actively hostile,' she said.

Private Ellis, from Wythenshawe, Manchester, was a former professional footballer. He was survived by his fiancée Sarah and their daughter Courtney. His commanding officer, Lieutenant Colonel James Chiswell, said that Private Ellis had displayed all the qualities of a first-class paratrooper: 'His strength of character and dedication were exemplary. He was also a natural team player, who always looked out for others and who was always upbeat and focused. Above all else, he was a total professional, dedicated to his task. He made a genuine difference in Iraq.'

The explosive device was hidden inside a car and was triggered as the soldiers approached. Another paratrooper was wounded. A mob stoned British soldiers when they arrived to secure the scene and recover the bodies. A video taken afterwards showed locals hurling rocks at troops. The men from D Company, 2nd Battalion, The Parachute Regiment, were serving as part of The Royal Scots Dragoon Guards battle group based at Camp Abu Naji. Relations between inhabitants and locals had been strained following the release of a film recorded in the city in 2004 when members of 1st Battalion, The Light Infantry, beat local youths after a riot. Stills from the film, shot by a British soldier, were spread across newspapers and the footage broadcast globally.

❖ ❖ ❖

The number of recorded attacks on British Forces was on the rise. There were 36 in January, 41 in February, 57 in March and 103 in April, when Defence Secretary John Reid announced a reduction in troop numbers of 800 to 7,000.

15 April 2006

Ad Dayr

Lieutenant Richard Palmer

I n the wake of his son's death, Brigadier John Palmer told opponents of the war that the vast majority of Iraqis were better off as a result of the efforts of his son and others. Lieutenant Richard Palmer had died in Ad Dayr on 15 April 2006. 'Richard believed that what they were doing, and they were doing it very professionally, was making a difference,' Brigadier Palmer, who had served for 30 years, said. 'Little by little, it was happening. Clearly, there were those who did not want him to be there, but most were better off. He knew how dangerous it was out there, and he was doing a job he wanted to do and one which was worthwhile. That is a worthwhile memory: that if he had to go, he went doing something that he really believed in. I can't imagine him ever being unfair. I can't imagine him doing something because it would benefit him rather than anybody else. I'm sorry, it's probably just rose-tinted glasses, but his mother and I think the world of him. He was enormously proud to be a soldier and in particular to be a member of The Royal Scots Dragoon Guards.'

Lieutenant Palmer's commanding officer said that his regiment had lost a 'great ambassador. He was an intelligent, charming, talented yet incredibly modest individual.' According to Lieutenant Colonel Ben Edwards, Lieutenant Palmer, from Ware, Hertfordshire, had been regarded as a star of the future. Lieutenant Palmer, a Durham University graduate, had been commissioned in 2004 and was said to have demonstrated a natural flair for commanding tanks.

◈ ◈ ◈

By May 2006, order in Basra was disintegrating, with one person being assassinated every hour, according to the Iraqi Defence Ministry, while the number of violent deaths was said to be approaching the level of Baghdad. Spokesman Majid al-

Sari suggested that the militias were the real authority in the city, not the British or Iraqi armies. When the effectiveness of improvised explosive devices restricted the mobility of British Forces, Warriors were preferred to Land Rovers and greater responsibility placed upon the Joint Helicopter Force to transport personnel and update the intelligence picture. The symbolism of downing a British aircraft was not lost on the Madhi Army.

6 May 2006

Basra

Lieutenant Commander Darren Chapman, Marine Paul Collins, Wing Commander John Coxen, Captain David Dobson, Flight Lieutenant Sarah-Jayne Mulvihill

On 6 May 2006, the Joint Helicopter Force commander in Basra cancelled an appointment to show the city from the air to the newly arrived Lieutenant Commander Darren Chapman of 847 Naval Air Squadron when he realised it clashed with a visit to the city by the captain of the USS *Ronald Reagan*. Instead, the officer entrusted the airborne familiarisation recce to his adjutant Flight Lieutenant Sarah-Jayne Mulvihill and Wing Commander John Coxen.

After three months in Iraq, Flight Lieutenant Mulvihill was due to return to RAF Benson, Oxfordshire. Almost ten years had passed since she joined The Royal Air Force as an airwoman. In October 2001, she was selected for officer training and commissioned into The Royal Air Force's air traffic control branch. She then trained as a flight operations officer at RAF Shawbury, Shropshire. Her progress in the service said much for her character: Flight Lieutenant Mulvihill had left school in Kent with few qualifications, and most of her fellow officers were men, which made life easier for them. They also had A levels and degrees. She had married her first husband Simon, a kitchen fitter, as a teenager. Her second husband was also in The Royal Air Force.

On the recce, particular attention was to be paid to the helicopter landing sites used by the Joint Helicopter Force. Flight Lieutenant Mulvihill, Wing Commander Coxen and father-of-three Lieutenant Commander Chapman were joined aboard the Lynx Mk7 by Captain David Dobson of the Army Air Corps and Royal Marine Paul Collins.

Captain Dobson, from Devizes, Wiltshire, came from a military family. They had moved to South Africa when he was eight, but Captain Dobson returned to Britain after university to train as a military pilot. His brother Matthew served as an officer in The Scots Guards in Northern Ireland. Like Lieutenant Commander Chapman, Captain Dobson belonged to 847 Naval Air Squadron based at Yeovilton, Somerset.

Captain Dobson acted as handling pilot and secured himself in the right-hand front seat with his guest on his left. Marine Collins, the air-door gunner, strapped himself into his dispatcher's harness on the port-side door and prepared his General Purpose Machine Gun. Flight Lieutenant Mulvihill and Wing Commander Coxen sat behind the crew. At 1331, the weather was good, with a light north-westerly surface wind and broken clouds at high level. Visibility was 20 kilometres and the temperature 35 degrees Celsius.

The helicopter had recently undergone significant maintenance work. A Mobile Aircraft Support Unit had been deployed from the UK to repair its cracked stringer and refit the tail boom. Both engines had been replaced. The Lynx, which had already been modified in order to meet the requirements of service in Iraq, was then cleared to fly. Its specifications included sand filters, Missile Approach Warning Systems and beyond-line-of-sight communications, as well as flare and chaff capability. The Lynx was considered to have one of the most effective defensive aids suites of all the UK helicopter assets in theatre. The defensive aids were operated using a master armament safety switch located at the top of Captain Dobson's dashboard. A key was used to switch the master armament safety switch to its live setting. The on–off switch of his infrared jammer, designed to disable remote-controlled missiles, was situated on the pilot's centre console. The chaff and flare dispenser units were mounted onto the rear of the aircraft's skids, with two bins on each side.

Before take-off, the crew received a briefing that included the latest intelligence and threat summaries. There were no last-minute changes to the regular advice given to crews. The main threat was posed by surface-to-air fire and personnel should remain alert to the possibility of an attack at all times.

The Lynx took off at 1331 and was observed 'in the hover' at the Shatt al-Arab Hotel before flying south towards Basra Palace. They passed to the east of the palace before conducting a right-hand turn that took them above the palace's helicopter landing site. They hovered above the helicopter landing site for one minute before departing at low level in a north-westerly direction and climbing to a medium altitude, in accordance with the security guidance, maintaining a westerly course for two kilometres.

At 1347, British personnel stationed at the Old State Building heard a 'whoosh' followed by a 'pop'. Private Stuart Drummond told an inquest that he saw a 'yellow object going towards the helicopter. I thought it was a missile.' The Lynx was an easy target, the firer having a clear view of the helicopter against an uncluttered background.

'Just before it was hit, the helicopter lifted as though it was trying to move out of the way. It sort of jerked,' said Private Drummond. That was all Captain Dobson could do before his aircraft was struck in mid-air on its starboard rear quarter between its fuselage and tail pylon, in the area of its rear electrical bay. The blast partially severed the helicopter's tail cone, leaving it loosely attached to the fuselage.

'The helicopter exploded,' continued Private Drummond. 'It was engulfed in flames and went down.' The Lynx descended in an uncontrolled manner, crashing onto the flat, steel-reinforced roof of a three-storey building approximately 500 metres south of the Old State Building. At the moment of impact, the cockpit severed and fell two floors down into a narrow, enclosed alleyway. The rotors had either stopped or had been rotating very slowly at the point of impact and were later seen partially intact. The three crew and two passengers were fatally injured, and the crash was categorised as beyond survivable. The wreckage left a 1.2-metre-deep crater in the concrete roof.

The explosion was heard at Basra Palace and a quick-reaction force deployed. The soldiers were met at the scene by a 300-strong mob armed with AK-47s, chanting 'We are all soldiers of al-Sayed [Moqtada al-Sadr]'. They engaged the rescue party, and further British casualties were taken. Fire was returned, killing five Iraqis and wounding twenty-eight others. While the newly appointed Defence Secretary Des Browne told MPs that the city remained calm, Sunni vice president of Iraq Adil Abdul-Mahdi's response was more fitting: 'We are following this situation closely, not because other parts of Iraq are violence-free, but because of the importance of the city with regard to the security of the south as a whole and the economy of Iraq.' Concerns had also been heightened by the provincial governor's sacking of the chief of the Basra police.

Captain Dobson's brother Matthew said, 'He was an extrovert character who really celebrated his life. He could get on with anyone and everyone loved him. David followed a family tradition when he joined the army to be a pilot. One of our grandfathers was in the South African Air Force and the other was in The Royal Artillery.'

Flight Lieutenant Mulvihill was remembered at a moving ceremony. Her family followed her coffin into Canterbury Cathedral. She was the first woman to be killed in action in Iraq and the first British servicewoman killed by enemy action since The Ulster Defence Regiment's Corporal Heather Kerrigan was killed by an IRA landmine in County Tyrone, Northern Ireland, in July 1984.

Flight Lieutenant Mulvihill's husband Lee, a Royal Air Force sergeant, said, 'Sarah was my best friend and my most beloved wife. She was also an adored daughter and sister, highly loved and respected by all who had the pleasure of knowing her. Her love of sport and outdoor activities was only outshone by her commitment to The Royal Air Force, of which she and I are extremely proud to be part. Her loss has greatly affected and impacted on more people than anyone can comprehend. On behalf of her close family and friends, we would like to express our gratitude and heartfelt thanks to all those people who have expressed their sympathy at this most difficult of times, whilst also wishing to thank all at the MoD, at every level, for their most gracious respect.'

Group Captain Duncan Welham said, 'Sarah-Jayne was one of The Royal Air Force's finest: courageous, upbeat and unselfish. She was a dedicated officer who will be missed by us all. Whilst at Benson, Sarah-Jayne's lively character and commitment to colleagues and friends made her extremely popular, both in the workplace and across the wider station community. There was nothing that she would not tackle, and her contribution to all aspects of life and work was actively sought, valued and appreciated. She was a keen sportswoman who enjoyed running, rowing and football.'

Marine Collins began recruit training at CTCRM Lympstone, Devon, in June 2003. His first posting was to M Company, 42 Commando, based at Bickleigh Barracks, Plymouth, before transferring to 847 Naval Air Squadron in September 2005 and training as an air-door gunner. Two hundred mourners attended his funeral service at CTCRM Lympstone. They were led by his mother and father. His father Michael was a former Royal Marine, while his mother Deborah saw service with the Wrens. Marine Collins was survived by his brother Mark, a Royal Electrical and Mechanical Engineer.

Deborah and Michael Collins said, 'Paul was a wonderful young man, so full of potential and zest for life. He was physically and mentally strong, though this was tempered by an intelligent, thoughtful and caring nature. He loved outdoor pursuits, and from the early age of ten had wanted to be a Royal Marine. This dream was nearly spoiled due to injuries sustained in a motorcycle accident. However, he fought back, recovered and fulfilled his dream, passing out from Commando Training Centre on 13 February 2004. Though his time with the corps was only short, he made many good friends and was never happier than being with his brothers in arms. Paul was a much-loved son and brother to Mark who will be missed greatly by all his family and friends.'

A guard of honour of 12 Royal Marines lined the road outside the church as a mark of respect. After the service, a Royal Marines bugler sounded the last post, and a minute's silence was observed. A single Lynx helicopter from Marine Collins's 847 Naval Air Squadron flew overhead. A private cremation followed.

Colonel John McCardle said, 'Paul was the epitome of what
The Royal Marines represent. A fit, intelligent young man, he was
totally professional in everything he did and enjoyed life to the full.
He was an extremely popular member of both his squadron and
throughout the Commando Helicopter Force. He had an ambition
to fly in helicopters. He was with us for a tragically short time.'

Lieutenant Commander Chapman's family said, 'We are
deeply shocked and devastated at the untimely and tragic loss
of Darren. He was a fantastic father, husband, son and friend,
who was deeply committed to family life. Always there for
those who needed him, nothing was ever too much trouble.
Outgoing, gregarious and always joking, he was the consummate
entertainer, and he touched and enriched many people's lives.
Equally committed to his life as an officer in the Fleet Air Arm,
he adored flying in the service, and we can rest assured that he
died doing the job that he so loved. Our thanks go to all for the
kind thoughts and messages we have received.'

His daughter Georgina, nine, addressed those gathered for
the unveiling of the Armed Forces memorial at Alrewas, near
Lichfield, Staffordshire. She said, 'Dear Daddy, I hope that you
and Barney [the recently deceased family Labrador] are OK
together. We are OK, so you have to be the same as us. I am having
fun with my friends, enjoying school and looking forward to a
Royal Navy helicopter trip to London. Lots of love, Georgina.'

Wing Commander Coxen was the most senior British officer
to lose his life in Iraq. He gave 23 years' service to his country
as a pilot, instructor and military strategist, winning plaudits in
every position he held.

Group Captain Duncan Welham said, 'John's reputation across
the Support Helicopter Force and Royal Air Force was second to
none. He was a unique individual, humble and courageous. The
world will be a sadder place without him. A true professional at
work in all that he touched, he was outwardly quiet but always
had a twinkle in his eye that gave away a mischievous and dry
sense of humour. He could always see the fun in any situation.
A truly devoted husband, John enjoyed family life to the full
with his wife Agnes and will be sadly missed.'

❖ ❖ ❖

The next deaths came in pairs and brought the total number of fatalities for May 2006 to nine, all inflicted by the Basra militias. Almost inevitably, it was an improvised explosive device that killed Private Joseva Lewaicei and Private Adam Morris of the 2nd Battalion, The Royal Anglian Regiment, on 13 May 2006, while another roadside bomb killed Lieutenant Tom Mildinhall and Lance Corporal Paul Farrelly a fortnight later. In between the blasts, the Iraqi National Government was sworn in, with Nouri al-Maliki appointed prime minister.

13 May 2006

Basra

Private Joseva Lewaicei, Private Adam Morris

Private Lewaicei had been hoping to play professional rugby on his return from Iraq. He and Private Morris, from Leicester, were travelling in a Snatch when a command wire triggered a device placed near a bridge, shattering the Land Rover's composite-fibreglass chassis. Private Morris's leadership potential had surprised his officers, who had begun to predict great things for the former army cadet. He displayed a love of soldiering and tactical awareness, and knew when to and when not to play the clown. Private Lewaicei, who was survived by his seven-year-old daughter, boxed for The Anglians and was described as the 'soul of his platoon'. He was almost unbeatable at arm-wrestling. A third soldier was wounded and taken to Shaibah Logistics Base for medical treatment.

Private Joseva Lewaicei, one of the 1,800 Fijian soldiers in the British Army, served for five years, including tours of Northern Ireland and Afghanistan.

Lieutenant Colonel Des O'Driscoll said, 'Private Lewaicei was a valued and well-regarded member of C Company and was known as a fun-loving and exuberant character. Immensely strong, his colleagues will remember with some glee the day he was finally beaten in an arm-wrestle by their platoon sergeant, although he always maintained he let him win. Our sympathy goes out to his family at this terrible time. We are deeply saddened at his tragic loss. He will be sorely missed by his friends and the wider regimental family.'

Scores of villagers lined the streets of Measham as Private Morris's coffin passed by en route to St Laurence's Church, near his family home. Mourners at his funeral heard that he fulfilled a lifelong dream when he enlisted and joined his regiment.

His parents Nigel and Lyn said, 'Adam was a much-loved and adored son, brother and brother-in-law. His one goal in life was to join the army. It had been his ambition since the age of three. He was a member of the Army Cadet Force and went on to join the army when he was 17. In late 2005, Adam broke his ankle, but he pushed and pushed himself to get fit, because he was determined to go on operations in Iraq with his regiment. He was always on the go, doing everything at speed, living life in the fast lane, so much so that he was told off by his doctors for going too fast on his crutches. But that was Adam. His prime objective was to get his ankle better. He couldn't bear the thought of his friends going to Iraq without him. He will be greatly missed by us all. His loss has torn our world apart, and no words can describe the pain that we are experiencing.'

Lieutenant Colonel Des O'Driscoll said, 'Adam rapidly made his mark as an energetic and thoroughly professional young soldier. He was one of our most promising young soldiers. Always one of the keenest and most attentive soldiers in the company, he stood out from many of his peers. At times teased for his military knowledge, he had an enquiring mind and a desire to learn. Always army barmy, he even found a camouflage cover for the cast on his leg. Adam's loss has touched and saddened all of us who had the honour to know him.'

28 May 2006

Gizayza

Lance Corporal Paul Farrelly, Lieutenant Tom Mildinhall

> This is an ordeal I would not wish any mother or father to endure. For those parents who have lost sons and daughters in this way, we are with them now. We have lost a beautiful, talented and loving son for ever. Our world is in pieces, and our country has again lost one of its best.
>
> The parents of Lieutenant Tom Mildinhall

Lieutenant Tom Mildinhall, from Battersea, London, and Lance Corporal Paul Farrelly, from Runcorn, Cheshire, were killed while conducting a routine vehicle patrol through Gizayza, to the north-west of Basra. Their deaths came on the day colleagues from The Queen's Dragoon Guards discovered a huge weapons cache and sufficient explosives to make several such roadside bombs. Two other soldiers were injured when the device was activated at 2130 local time on 28 May 2006.

Lieutenant Mildinhall was a skilled skier and rower, father-of-three Lance Corporal Farrelly a keen footballer and a champion recruit during his basic training. 'Faz', who had been on his third tour of Iraq, was survived by his wife Natalie and their children Reece, Morgan and Brooke. His father said at his funeral, 'Paul, I love you, and I am really proud of you. I'll never forget you. Goodnight and God bless.' The service began with Reece, eight, lighting a candle for his father.

His mother Lyn Hurst, from Rhosneigr, Anglesey, said, 'Paul was taken from us too young and too soon. Words cannot express how I feel at the loss of a dear son, brother, father, husband and uncle. He was a very special and loving person in all our lives. We're devastated but extremely proud of Paul. He loved his wife, his children and his family very much. He will for ever be in our hearts.'

Lieutenant Colonel Anthony Pittman, Lance Corporal

Farrelly's commanding officer, said, 'Lance Corporal Farrelly was widely acknowledged as one of the most competent lance corporals in the regiment. He was knowledgeable, quick-thinking and tough. He stood out amongst his peers as a natural leader – level-headed and utterly dependable. His wealth of experience combined with his ability to identify quickly the critical path meant that his contribution was way beyond that commensurate with his rank. He was marked out for early promotion. He embodied much of what is best about soldiers in the British Army: selfless, determined, humorous and steadfast in the face of adversity.'

Artificial-intelligence and computer-science graduate Lieutenant Mildinhall was praised by his commanding officer as 'thoroughly capable, intelligent and determined'. Lieutenant Colonel Anthony Pittman of the Osnabruck-based Queen's Dragoon Guards added that the subaltern's soldiers had responded positively to his leadership by example and entrusted their lives in his command.

Company commander Major Richard Head totted up that his Light Infantry soldiers had faced 170 attacks in 200 days while stationed in Basra that year.

16 July 2006

Garmat Ali

Corporal John Cosby

Belfast-born Corporal John Cosby was three months into his six-month tour when he was shot by one of his own men. The accident occurred on 16 July 2006 during an operation to arrest a key militia leader in the Garmat Ali area, north of Basra. An inquest heard that Corporal Dean Newark of The Royal Anglian Regiment had fired five shots at a figure in the distance after he himself was fired upon. As Corporal Newark targeted insurgents, Corporal Cosby was caught in the crossfire and collapsed from a head wound.

Corporal Cosby, the patrol commander, was treated at the scene by Lance Corporal Nicholas Coleman, from Plymouth, who was awarded a Military Cross after insurgents attempted to pull Corporal Cosby and another wounded soldier from the back of a military vehicle. His citation read:

> By leading an ad-hoc team on a daring counter-attack and by fighting quite literally hand to hand to achieve extraction, spoke volumes for this man's courage, tenacity and sense of duty. His instinctive leadership, often with men considerably senior to him, is all the more remarkable when one considers he had only been a lance corporal for eight months and was only twenty years of age.

Lance Corporal Coleman said, 'We heard shooting and grenades going off quite close to us. When John and Andy were shot, I just acted on instinct. It was the first time I had treated bullet wounds. I knew it was dangerous, because the sand was flying around me as the bullets landed. But I just kept going.'

Corporal Cosby, who was held in great affection by his colleagues in the Brigade Surveillance Company, was airlifted to a field hospital where he died. Lieutenant Colonel Toffer Beattie, his commanding officer, described him as a 'monumental battalion personality', who put his friends and subordinates' safety before his own. A few weeks before his death, Corporal Cosby had said, 'As long as my team goes home safely, my job is done.'

His mother Jean, from Exeter, added, 'He was a great and loving family man and an amazing son, brother, uncle and nephew. His sense of humour and bubbly personality will be missed by all of his family and everyone who knew him. His memory will live in all our hearts for ever.'

1 August 2006

Basra

Corporal Matthew Cornish

Father-of-two Corporal Matthew Cornish was killed during a mortar attack in Basra on 1 August 2006. Known as 'Pastie', he had joined the army aged 18, served in Sierra Leone and Northern Ireland, and was on his third tour of Iraq. He was stationed in Germany with The Light Infantry and was preparing to take his exams for promotion to sergeant. His fifth wedding anniversary was only a couple of weeks away when the blast occurred.

Corporal Cornish's letters home to his father captured the intensity of daily life in Basra, the city where he was killed:

> Don't know if you saw anything on the news about a fire fight in southern Iraq, but I was there and I am fine. It was absolutely mental. Some bloke fired a shot at the OC's [officer commanding] rover group, who chased him into a building where they found loads of weapons and arrested him. We were on quick-reaction-force duty and were tasked to go and help with the arrest. We had to wait for the bomb disposal people to arrive, so we set up a cordon. A small crowd started to appear and it grew to 200. At this point, someone saw a gunman. He ran into a local police station and fired a full magazine at the chasers, who shot him and the other man who tried picking up the rifle to return fire. The police then threw grenades at the four soldiers. I was walking to one of our Land Rovers when a rocket-propelled grenade was fired at it. The RPG firer was then shot. Two of my lads were pinned down with fire landing all around them. We were holed up there waiting for two and half hours for the Warriors to come down. It was probably the scariest thing I've ever been involved in.

His father Robin, from Pool-in-Wharfedale, West Yorkshire, expressed how much his son was missing his children: 'He just adored his kids. He lived for them and his wife. He joined the army, and wherever they went he went. He was just doing the job he was paid to do. I am proud that he died a brave soldier.'

Lieutenant Colonel Johnny Bowron, the deceased's commanding officer, added that Corporal Cornish was 'a great soldier, a fine friend and a great character. Pastie could always be relied upon to give his opinion on any subject, whether it was wanted or not. His true passion, though, was for his family.'

A proud Yorkshireman, he died on Yorkshire Day.

❖ ❖ ❖

The handing back of responsibility for Muthanna and Dhi Qar provinces paved the way for a reduction in the number of Multinational Division troops in the south. In spite of this ray of hope, it was a hard sell for Lieutenant General Robert Fry of The Royal Marines, serving in Baghdad as deputy commander of the multinational force, to convince journalists that Iraq was not experiencing a civil war. Given his experience in the Balkans and Northern Ireland, he believed that he knew the difference between sectarian conflict and civil war. As he argued it, a civil war typically saw the collapse of the central institutions of government, which was not the case in post-war Iraq. Neither were the state's instruments of security breaking down.

Asked if there was anything from the British experience in Basra that could be applied to security plans for Baghdad, Lieutenant General Fry responded on 22 August, 'I think that the applicability of techniques is more appropriate from Baghdad down to Basra. If I'm to draw comparisons overall, it seems to me that Basra has more to learn from Baghdad than the other way around.'

The deaths of three British soldiers in early September darkened the mood further and took away any sense of progression stemming from the withdrawal of British forces from Camp Abu Naji – a prequel to the handing over of Maysan Province to the Iraqi security forces in early 2007.

4 September 2006

Ad Dayr

Gunner Samuela Vanua, Gunner Stephen Wright

Gunner Samuela Vanua and Gunner Stephen Wright were killed by a roadside bomb in Ad Dayr, near Basra, on 4 September 2006. They were returning to base in a Land Rover when the device was detonated. Gunner Vanua and Gunner Wright had been training the Iraqi police that day.

The 27-year-old Fijian, who belonged to 12 Regiment, Royal Artillery, was described by Lieutenant Colonel Jon Campbell as 'tough, hard-working and resourceful'. The commanding officer added that Gunner Vanua was 'one of the best Fijians in my regiment. His professionalism was a credit to his country, and I was impressed by his excellent attitude, infectious cheerfulness and confidence.'

Gunner Wright, from Leyland, Lancashire, was nicknamed 'Trigger' and joined the army aged 16. He had been selected to attend a promotional course on his return.

Gunner Wright's family said, 'Stephen's death has come as a massive shock to his family, who are still grieving the death of his mother Elaine, who died suddenly ten months ago. Stephen had since made his home, when on leave, with his grandparents Robert and Shirley Wright, of Leyland. Stephen attended Wellfield High School. On leaving school, he had a short time in the cadets before joining the army. He spent an enjoyable 12 months at the Army Foundation College in Harrogate before being posted to Germany and then to Iraq. Stephen was a quiet, happy young man who enjoyed nothing more than spending time with his friends and family. A few weeks ago, he spent time at home with his grandparents on R & R before returning to Iraq. He was looking forward to going back to finish his duties. Stephen loved the army life. It was all he wanted to do. The whole family is very proud of him.'

7 September 2006

Al-Qurna

Gunner Lee Thornton

G unner Lee Thornton of 12 Regiment, Royal Artillery, wrote
in his war diary, 'I hate this place. I really do. It is just not
worth dying for. I wish Tony Blair could see that. I don't trust the
Iraqi Army, the Iraqi police or the people. This is pointless.'

Gunner Thornton was left angry after being stranded for
several hours in great danger when his patrol's armoured vehicles
broke down. He added, 'Dear Tony [Blair]. Give the army better
equipment and stop putting our lives at risk. Thanks, Thorny.'

In the wake of his colleagues' deaths, Gunner Thornton, from
Blackpool, volunteered to participate in the next patrol. When it
came under fire in al-Qurna, north of Basra, Gunner Thornton
suffered a single gunshot wound. The shots were fired from a
building used to plan the reconstruction of the town.

Lieutenant Colonel Jon Campbell said that it was typical of
Thornton to put himself forward: 'He showed no hesitation in
driving out of the security of Shaibah Logistics Base and facing
the ever-present threat. It was his gesture of defiance in what
was a very sad week for the battery.'

Gunner Thornton was flown to Germany for treatment. His
mother Karen and father Mick were on holiday when they learnt
of their son's fate. They flew to Germany to be at his bedside.
Karen said, 'He was our hero, doing the job he loved. We are
very proud of him and will never forget him. The army made
him the man he was. He was tough when he first went out to
Iraq, but when he came back he was very much a family man
and put his fiancée and us before anyone. We were immensely
proud of Lee's achievements. He lived life to the full and packed
a lot in during his short time. Through the army, he managed
to fulfil many of his goals in life. He was a great sportsman and
an avid supporter of Blackpool Football Club. Lee leaves behind
his loving fiancée Helen and three younger brothers, Ryan, Sean
and Jake.'

His fiancée Helen O'Pray released his next-of-kin letter:

Hi Babe,

I don't know why I am writing this because I really hope that this letter never gets to you, because if it does, it means I am dead. It also means I never had time to show you just how much I really love you. You have shown me what love is and what it feels like to be loved.

Just because I have passed away does not mean I am not with you. I'll always be there looking over you, keeping you safe. So whenever you feel lonely just close your eyes and I'll be there by your side.

Love always and for ever,

Lee

❖ ❖ ❖

Operation Sinbad saw 1,000 British and Danish personnel working with 2,300 Iraqis to clean up Basra, cordoning off areas of the city one by one, taking over police stations infiltrated by rogue elements and starting 'immediate action projects', such as fixing street lighting, improving water systems and cleaning the streets. The most pressing problem remained the stranglehold of the militias and the fact that the most powerful criminal gangs enjoyed the protection of city officials, religious leaders and corrupt police officers. To combat their influence, Royal Military Police teams were to embed at Basra police stations for 30 days at a time. However, Dr Toby Dodge, an Iraq expert at Queen Mary College, London, regretted that 'Britain has never had the forces needed to make a sustained difference to law and order, and meaningful reconstruction is almost non-existent. Their role is a minor one, and the question is whether it justifies the casualties and the cost.'

Operation Sinbad was the main task for 19 Light Brigade, led by Brigadier Tim Evans. It was intended to increase security and accelerate the reconstruction of Basra. The soldiers' back-breaking efforts gained little publicity but the thanks from the vast majority of locals. The endeavours were overshadowed, however, by the candid or careless comments of General Sir

Richard Dannatt, the chief of the general staff, who said in October 2006, 'Let's face it, the military campaign we fought in 2003 effectively kicked the door in. Whatever consent we may have had in the first place has largely turned to intolerance. I don't say that the difficulties we are experiencing around the world are caused by our presence in Iraq, but undoubtedly our presence exacerbates them.'

What was supposed to be a soft feature with the *Daily Mail* covering all aspects of military life, including the service of Princes William and Harry, became the most outspoken commentary on government policy by a serving general anyone could remember. Serving soldiers were shocked to hear their commander say that they should 'get out some time soon', as their presence was supposedly making matters worse. At the very least, General Dannatt's comments were divisive. 'Thanks for nothing, sir,' said some soldiers. 'Thanks for listening,' said others.

It is unlikely that the comments were pre-planned or that they represented a courageous foray into political territory, as many sections of the media were eager to conclude. General Dannatt hastened to clarify himself on the *Today* programme the following morning. Only two months into office, the intellectual and evangelical general revealed himself to be less than comfortable in the public arena. 'It was not my intention to have this hoo-ha,' he told presenter Jim Naughtie.

1 October 2006

Basra

Lance Corporal Dennis Brady

As General Dannatt was interviewed in a Radio 4 studio, his men laid electrical cables, mended burst water pipes, repaired schools and continued to meet resistance from those who profited from the mayhem. Reservist medic Lance Corporal Dennis Brady died on 1 October 2006. Lance Corporal Brady, from Cumbria, was killed when a mortar round struck the Shatt al-Arab Hotel in northern Basra while he was serving with 1st Battalion, The Light Infantry.

A veteran of Kosovo, Bosnia and Afghanistan, Lance Corporal Brady was also on his second tour of Iraq after deploying with The Royal Gurkha Rifles in 2003. He was survived by his wife Zoe. A funeral service with full military honours was held at St George's Church, Barrow.

Lieutenant Colonel Johnny Bowron said, 'In the relatively short time he had been with us, he had become a full and trusted member of the battalion, admired by all he met and with that rare gift of universal popularity. He will be remembered for his calm and unflappable nature, whatever the circumstance. This approach, coupled with a high level of medical competence, allowed the soldiers of D Company to carry out their duties secure in the knowledge that if the worst was to happen, they were in safe hands. His loss will be keenly felt, and the battalion has lost a trusted member and a real friend. Lance Corporal Brady was armed with a dry sense of humour and was always ready with a barrage of friendly banter, as well as always being prepared to offer brutally honest advice regardless of the recipient's rank – advice that was nearly always correct.'

27 October 2006

Shaibah Logistics Base

Lieutenant Tom Tanswell

Lieutenant Tom Tanswell of 12 Regiment, Royal Artillery, was killed in a road accident outside Shaibah Logistics Base when his Land Rover collided with a civilian vehicle on 27 October 2006. Three other soldiers were injured.

His sister Kate said that he died 'leading from the front and doing a job he loved. He was a wonderful brother, son, soldier and friend.'

Ryan Cairns, one of Lieutenant Tanswell's former soldiers,

said, 'Mr T, as we used to call him, was a superb leader, and he was my commander in Iraq. He was always there for the lads in his team. We gave him a lot of stick, but he gave it back just as much. He will be fairly missed.'

Lieutenant Tanswell's commanding officer, Major Marcus Tivey, said, 'Tom was an immensely enthusiastic young officer, who embraced life with a vigour which inspired those around him. He was full of ideas and launched himself into everything he did. He was a jack of all trades and was due to be promoted early next year. Professionally, Tom was a fine officer who always looked out for his men. Prior to deploying to Iraq, Tom had been praised by his superiors on numerous exercises, and while on operations he had made his mark as a rising star. His friends and colleagues appreciated his easy, laid-back demeanour. The mark of the man was his boundless energy and infectious sense of humour. Tom was an unforgettable character who we were privileged to have served with. The army and the regiment have lost a fine young man, and the battery has lost a good friend. All who knew Tom were touched by his zest for life. It is tragic that he should have died so close to the end of his tour.'

❖ ❖ ❖

November 2006 saw the peak of insurgent activity and increased sectarian violence across Iraq, despite negotiations between tribal and religious leaders. The *Measuring Stability and Security in Iraq* report to the US Congress made grave reading:

> Concrete actions by the government of Iraq to implement national reconciliation have not been successful. For the past three months the total number of attacks has increased by 22 per cent. Coalition Forces remained the target of the majority (68 per cent) of attacks but the overwhelming majority of casualties were suffered by Iraqis. Violence in Iraq was divided along ethnic, religious and tribal lines, and political factions within these groups. The violence in Iraq poses a grave threat to political progress. Personal loyalties to various sub-national groups, such as tribe, sect or political party, are often stronger than loyalty to Iraq as a nation state. In

addition, Iraq's political parties are often unwilling or unable to resolve conflicts through compromise. Further, some Iraqis have joined the political process but condone or maintain support for violent means as a source of political leverage. The conflict in Basra, al-Amarah and the south was characterised by tribal rivalry, increasing intra-Shia competition and attacks on Coalition Forces operating in the region.

The hawks in Bush's administration were being forced to listen to doves such as James Baker, who suggested that the country's neighbours be brought into the picture and the issue of regional stability be given greater attention. Reluctantly, the State Department moved to facilitate negotiations with Iraq's neighbours: Iran, Jordan, Kuwait, Saudi Arabia, Syria and Turkey. These were to discuss 'contentious trans-national issues'.

6 November 2006

Basra

Kingsman Jamie Hancock

Kingsman Jamie Hancock, described as a 'born soldier', died from gunshot wounds on 6 November 2006. The teenager was on sentry duty at the Old State Building, Basra, when a sniper struck. His parents received his last letter home just before his death. He wrote that many insurgents had been killed attempting to attack his base and that his camp was mortared most nights. Kingsman Hancock, who lived with his soldier brother in Wigan, Greater Manchester, kept a picture of the Queen in his wallet. His company commander in the 2nd Battalion, The Duke of Lancaster's Regiment, described him as an 'energetic and enthusiastic individual who lived for the army'. His battalion belonged to 19 Light Brigade, and he had only been in Iraq for a matter of weeks when he was killed.

His father Tony said, 'We are deeply shocked at the loss of our much-loved son. We are and always will be very proud of him and all that he achieved.'

His family released the contents of Kingsman Hancock's last letter home, which read:

> Just writing to you to let you know I am fine. Not been blown up yet!! I got to Basra tonight. Last night the whole camp got attacked. A lot of Iraqi insurgents died. We lost nobody. But the place I am going gets attacked most nights and gets mortared a lot.

Major Chris Job said, 'Kingsman Hancock was an energetic and enthusiastic individual who lived for the army and had a very promising career ahead of him. Proud to be a kingsman, he was determined to do as well as he possibly could. His enthusiasm was boundless, and the fearless spirit with which he lived was amply demonstrated by his decision to volunteer for this Iraq tour. Although young and new to the army, he appeared older and more experienced than his 19 years. As a Warrior driver, he was considered to be one of the best, despite only recently passing his test. He was a magnet for his peers, who were drawn by his infectious sense of fun and all-embracing nature. Always at the centre of practical jokes, he lived life to the full. We will best remember him for creating, whilst going through pre-deployment training, his recent "Hammer Time" dance, in which he cajoled his mates to dance with only a field helmet covering their pride. He will be sorely missed by his many friends and the wider regimental family.'

12 November 2006

Basra

Staff Sergeant Sharron Elliott, Warrant Officer Class 2 Lee Hopkins, Marine Jason Hylton, Corporal Ben Nowak

Staff Sergeant Sharron Elliott had been serving in Cyprus when she redeployed to Iraq to fill a temporary post. She had served across the world with the army. In the aftermath of the death of her soldier fiancé in a motorcycle accident ten years earlier, she had devoted herself to the profession they shared. They had first met on a course to repair helicopters. His death had come only a short time before they had been due to marry.

Staff Sergeant Elliott, a warm, compassionate woman from Ipswich, had acquired four step-brothers when her mother remarried and acted as 'best man' for one of them at his wedding. Two of her step-brothers were also in the services.

On Remembrance Sunday, Staff Sergeant Elliott of the Intelligence Corps travelled to the Shatt al-Arab Hotel in a three-boat convoy. Also on board with her were Warrant Officer Lee Hopkins of the Royal Corps of Signals, Corporal Ben Nowak from 45 Commando, Royal Marines, Marine Jason Hylton from 539 Assault Squadron and Marine Richard Turner.

It was the job of Captain Richard Morris of 539 Assault Squadron to assess the various threats and plan the route accordingly. He later recalled, 'Boats were the favoured way of moving along the waterway, because at the time boats had never been targeted. It was perceived to be the safest means of travel.' His only concern was a narrow gap at a pontoon bridge. Insurgents knew that boats needed to slow down to pass this point, and they often fired shots at it. On the morning in question, the bridge should ideally have been secured in advance, but no personnel were available. It was also hoped that the electronic countermeasures fitted to two of the three boats in the convoy would detect any improvised explosive devices attached to the bridge.

At 1250, the first boat passed safely beneath the pontoon. Staff Sergeant Elliott and her colleagues were on the second craft. Marine Turner saw a flash and heard a loud bang. Disorientated by the cloud of thick smoke that enveloped him, he shook his head and remembered his crew members. He looked to his left to see Marine Hylton's body slumped in his seat. Only then did Marine Turner realise that he too was in bad shape. Blood was spurting from his arm and his face hurt. Staff Sergeant Elliott, Warrant Officer Hopkins, Corporal Nowak and Marine Hylton were dead. Marine Turner and two other passengers on the boat survived. Warrant Officer Hopkins was a father of three, Marine Hylton a father of two. Insurgents recorded the moment on video camera, and the footage was broadcast on Iraqi TV. As an inquest heard, it was also, unwittingly, broadcast by Sky TV in Iraq.

Coroner Andrew Walker was surprised that basic procedures such as searching the bridge prior to British personnel passing beneath and the equipping of all boats with electronic countermeasures had not been followed. Evidence was also put before the Oxford court that a warning had been received by email around the time of the attack, suggesting that British movements on that stretch of the waterway 'might be targeted'. Giving evidence, Captain Morris stated that this had been sent after the attack, and that it was 'vague' in content and insufficient to lead to alterations in route patterns and plans.

'So, it takes four people to lose their lives before this can happen?' asked Walker.

'Sadly, yes, that's right,' replied Captain Morris.

Walker concluded, 'This amounted to a really serious failure to follow basic procedure. This was an entirely avoidable incident if the basic principles had been followed. A vulnerable point, in this case the bridge, should not have been crossed unless a search of the point had been carried out. There was no search of the area, as required by basic training, and the bridge should not have been negotiated. The protective measures available, carried on two of the three boats, did not prevent the explosion. Had all the boats carried such measures, it is more likely than not that the explosion would have not occurred.'

Jill Hylton, Marine Hylton's sister-in-law, responded, 'It was a surprise to hear the deaths were preventable. We were not expecting that. Hindsight is a wonderful thing, and all the parties were acting with the best intentions. It is just unfortunate what happened that day.'

Corporal Nowak's father James was less philosophical: 'Not enough was done. Not enough thought was given to this. The Royal Marines are an elite force. At the end of the day, they made a cock-up.'

After becoming the first woman to qualify as an aircraft technician, Staff Sergeant Elliott had transferred to the

Intelligence Corps in search of variety and adventure. She had also served in Kosovo and Northern Ireland. Her commanding officer, Major Nick Tuppen, described her as a no-nonsense, professional soldier who 'would be remembered for her steel and determination, her calmness, considered words and her smile'.

Her grandmother Maureen Holland added, 'I never knew anyone who spoke ill of her. This is such a shock because I had not realised she was in Iraq.'

Marine Hylton's girlfriend, Sasha Martin, said that something had seemed wrong the night before the incident: 'He did not seem his usual self. I had spoken to him every single day of the week, but on Saturday he was not his happy self. He sounded like he knew something bad was going to happen. He had just moved to Basra Palace and was being shot at. I am very angry and upset. All I want is for him to come home again so I can see his smile.'

As Marine Hylton's coffin was carried into St George and St Mary Church, in Church Gresley, the sound of 'Everybody Hurts' by REM filtered through the Tannoy. Hundreds of friends, family, Royal Marine comrades, veterans and civic dignitaries crowded into the village church to pay their respects.

His childhood friend, Mark Young, tearfully told mourners, 'Jason always had a bed for me and never had a wrong word to say about anyone. We'd been together as friends since I came from Derby 25 years ago. We went from Pennine Way School up to Pingle, and we were a pair of buggers together. Many Wednesday nights we would have a detention, but we always told our parents we were playing football so we wouldn't get into trouble. After Pingle, we moved on to the Bretby Coal Board, and we never stopped laughing while we were there. We were together all the way, mate, until you went to the Marines. We all love and miss you and your smile. You will always be with us. God bless.'

Major Nathan Hale said, 'He was a bright and enthusiastic man, who, although joining The Royal Marines older than most recruits, had quickly made his mark within the service and had a promising career ahead of him. His unswerving loyalty led him to volunteer for this Iraq tour so soon after joining 539 Assault Squadron, Royal Marines, from his recent deployment to the Middle East with HMS *Bulwark*. In only his second year as a specialist in the Landing Craft Branch, Marine Jay Hylton's ability and professionalism belied his experience. An intelligent man, he adapted exceptionally well to his duties as a coxswain with a level of aptitude far in excess of his peers. We will best remember him for his infectious smile and for the constant cheerfulness. He epitomised the true commando spirit. Our sympathy and thoughts go out to his family, particularly his young children, at this awful time. He will be sorely missed by his many friends in the squadron and the wider Royal Marines family with whom he served.'

Warrant Officer Hopkins, who was airborne trained, was survived by his wife and three children. He joined the army in 1988 and served in Northern Ireland, Kosovo and Iraq, all with The Royal Corps of Signals. He was described as 'highly professional' and 'a dedicated family man'. His commanding officer, Lieutenant Colonel Andrew Park, said, 'He would always make time to pass on the benefit of his knowledge to the newer members of the unit. He won the respect of all who met him for his leadership, enthusiasm and dedication. Fit and ambitious, he was a shining example to all. He led from the front, was comfortable in the presence of all ranks and selfless. His keen sense of humour and sociable character made him very popular. He was great fun to be around. My thoughts and that of the unit are with his family and friends at this very difficult time. We have lost a trusted and valued colleague who will be sorely missed by all. He was also a loving husband and devoted father.'

❖ ❖ ❖

On 22 November 2006, Foreign Secretary Margaret Beckett came close to setting out a timetable for withdrawal when she said that she was confident control of the remaining provinces in the British sector could be returned in spring 2007. The Ministry of Defence clarified that the 7,000 troops would first be withdrawn from the streets and held at Basra Air Station, and that the numbers of service personnel in theatre would be reduced incrementally. British commander Major General Richard Shirreff suggested a 'reasonable reduction' in troop numbers at the completion of Operation Sinbad in late February 2007.

24 November 2006

Basra

Sergeant Jonathan Hollingsworth

Two days after Beckett's announcement, decorated Special Air Service hero Sergeant Jonathan Hollingsworth became the regiment's first combat fatality in Iraq when he was killed during a raid in Basra. The former paratrooper and member of G Squadron had been awarded the Conspicuous Gallantry Cross and Queen's Gallantry Medal for previous operations. He was shot in the neck a week before his death but volunteered to remain in theatre. On 24 November 2006, he was shot by a British bullet, fired either by a non-SAS soldier in a cordon around the house in Basra as the elite anti-terrorist operatives raided the building, or by an insurgent using a weapon stolen from British Forces. Sergeant Hollingsworth, who was married with children, was understood to have been shot in the ribs moments before he intended to throw a grenade. He was evacuated to a military hospital, where he died of his wounds.

Defence Secretary Des Browne said, 'The death of Sergeant Hollingsworth is a terrible loss, and my heartfelt sympathy goes out to his family, friends and comrades. Sergeant Hollingsworth was killed on a successful operation to detain those who were known to attack both civilian and military personnel. He did not die in vain.'

❖ ❖ ❖

British Forces chose Christmas Day to blow up the al-Jamiat police station, where two of Sergeant Hollingsworth's Special Forces colleagues had been held by anti-coalition elements in September 2005. This dramatic gesture formed part of Operation Thyme, to curtail the activities of the 400-strong Serious Crimes Unit. Around 1,000 troops, including infantry, stormed the police station at 0200. Many of the inmates had been falsely imprisoned. The Royal Engineers used bar mines and plastic explosives to reduce the building to rubble.

28 December 2006

Basra

Sergeant Graham Hesketh

The death of Sergeant Graham Hesketh on 28 December 2006 took the number of British fatalities to 127. The thirty-five-year-old father of two from The Duke of Lancaster's Regiment was killed by an improvised explosive device in Basra. His fiancée Rebecca Barnes, a serving army technician, had last seen him on Boxing Day. She said, 'He was everything to me. I just wish he had taken me with him. I've nothing to live for any more.'

His final letter to her read:

> Hi Bec,
>
> I'm just sat in the back of a Warrior waiting to come back to see you. I really love you and am missing you like mad and it's you babe. I never want to be away from you again. I want to spend the rest of my life with you. I so want us to be together till the day I die. You are in my world and I am so glad I met you. I want us to have a family of our own. You do me proud. I know I have met my soul mate and I never want to lose you. I will sign off now and hopefully I will see you when I get back.
> All my love,
> Graham.

The passing of Sergeant Hesketh, an Everton supporter, was acknowledged with a minute's silence at Goodison Park before his team's FA Cup match against Blackburn Rovers on Sunday, 7 January 2007. His beloved Toffees were knocked out by four goals to one.

Sergeant Hesketh was survived by a son and a daughter from a previous relationship. His father Kevin, who held a two-day candlelit vigil for his son at his house in Runcorn, said, 'Graham was a lovely child, enthusiastic, getting involved in sporting activities, including football, athletics and swimming. He also served as an altar boy at Our Lady's Parish Church. Graham had always had it in mind to join the army, enrolling at Catterick Garrison as a junior, aged 17. He went on to serve three years in the tank regiment and served in Germany, Northern Ireland and Cyprus. After three years, Graham left the army but could not settle. Aged 22, he re-enlisted and was promoted to sergeant in 2005. He will be remembered by his father, daughter and son, aunts, uncles and the many friends he made during his lifetime.'

Lieutenant Colonel Simon Hutchinson, Sergeant Hesketh's commanding officer, added, 'Graham cared deeply about his profession, about the men in his charge and about his job here in Iraq. He was part of the backbone of this battalion. We are proud to have known him. He is a great loss to the battalion and will be deeply missed by all who had the pleasure to serve with him. Our thoughts are with his family, particularly his son and daughter, and also with his fiancée.'

2007

The year began with Lieutenant General Graeme Lamb bemoaning the British media: 'The average citizens in Iraq want jobs, electricity and streets where their children can play without fear. There is certainly more of this than a glance over the [British] newspapers would portray.' It also became the accepted wisdom that the British public was not only tired of Iraq and its troubles, but also less caring towards the fate of the troops. While a government study group was set up to find ways to improve public recognition of the forces, affection for soldiers was best demonstrated at a microcosmic level. On the occasion of service funerals, silence fell over the streets, strangers bowed their heads and shopkeepers closed for business. Such spontaneous, heartfelt gestures disproved the notion that disillusioned civilians had turned their backs on those dying in their name. There was perhaps something patronising about the government's suggestion that the public needed help to show their gratitude, no matter how much it was deserved by the servicemen and women.

7 January 2007

Maysan Province

Sergeant Wayne Rees

On 7 January 2007, Sergeant Wayne Rees was killed and two other soldiers injured when a Scimitar armoured vehicle lost control and tumbled off the road in Maysan Province. The wrong brake fluid had been put in the vehicle. A coroner concluded that the vehicle should have been taken out of service for the parts to be replaced. Instead, the liquid was merely flushed out and the error documented.

Driver George Rowlands told the inquest that Sergeant Rees had shouted 'Brake! Brake!' as the Scimitar veered off-course in wet conditions.

'I'm braking, I'm braking!' Rowlands had replied.

Sergeant Rees, a married father of two from Worksop, suffered acute asphyxia when he drowned in a ditch. The commanding officer of The Queen's Royal Lancers, Lieutenant Colonel Richard Nixon-Eckersall, described him as a 'consummate professional'.

Family, friends and comrades attended his funeral at St Ann's Church, Worksop. Reverend Simon Cash told mourners, 'The one thing that sticks out above all else is his dedication both to his family and to his job. He was the sort of fella who loved to come back to his home town and spend time with his family and his friends. But he was also greatly respected by his work colleagues – not only as a work colleague, but as a true friend to them, as well.'

Major Martin Todd said, 'In Sergeant Wayne Rees, we lost not only a charismatic and wholly professional soldier, but also one of the regiment's most ebullient and best-loved characters. He was a natural leader, setting the very highest of personal standards and inspiring others to achieve the same. He could lighten the darkest moments with his mischievous sense of humour. And there was something irrepressible about his optimism and verve for life.

'He cared deeply, not only for his family and many friends, but also for the soldiers for whom he was responsible. He carefully nurtured those who struggled to enter the military fold and took immense pride in their subsequent successes. He has left an indelible stamp on them and on the troop of soldiers that he helped shape and train for this operation. We will continue in our task saddened without him, but inspired by his example and remembering always a staunch comrade in arms and the very best of friends. Our thoughts and prayers are with those whose loss is greater than ours: his fiancée Jayne and his children, Charlotte and Elliott.'

13 January 2007

Basra

Kingsman Alexander Green

A ccording to Kingsman Alexander Green's relatives, his 'single ambition' had been to serve in the British Army. He also proved himself an excellent soldier. On 13 January 2007, Kingsman Green climbed out of a Warrior vehicle to join a cordon protecting a 60-vehicle re-supply convoy through Basra and was struck by a sniper's bullet. His colleagues from the 2nd Battalion, The Duke of Lancaster's Regiment, dragged him into cover, provided first aid and sent a radio message to Basra Palace for the trauma reception area to be prepared. 'Stay with us,' Kingsman Green was urged as stretcher-bearers carried him inside. Embedded journalists reported that a soldier standing nearby was heard to utter, 'Why the f*** are we here?'

Kingsman Green received emergency treatment before being flown by helicopter to Basra Air Station. He was operated on for 90 minutes but lost the struggle for his life. Lieutenant Colonel Simon Hutchinson, Kingsman Green's commanding officer, said, 'If you could capture in one man all that a kingsman could hope to be, you would struggle to come closer to the mark than him.'

Kingsman Green belonged to Chindit Company and was survived by two-year-old son Bradley, who cried out 'Daddy' as pall-bearers carried his father's coffin into St Elphin's Church, Warrington. Mystified Bradley held a red heart-shaped balloon and cried as his father was carried in front of him.

The Reverend Michael Finlay told the hundreds of family members, friends and colleagues, 'He was a devoted father and a much loved brother, son and friend. He also loved the army, and according to his officers was a good soldier with good prospects, a professional and reliable colleague.'

In accordance with Kingsman Green's wishes, mourners listened to the Pink Floyd song 'Comfortably Numb' while his comrades from The Duke of Lancaster's Regiment formed a firing party at the private burial.

His half-brother Nick Owen, a Royal Marine, said, 'Alex was an amazing man both professionally and in his private life. He was honest and respectful, and he was always the first to offer his chair to somebody. He was so proud of his little boy Bradley. No one wants him to grow up not knowing his dad. We just hope when he is older we can explain to him – I know he will be proud of his dad.'

21 January 2007

Basra

Private Michael Tench

Private Michael Tench, from Sunderland, deployed to Iraq in December 2006. On 21 January 2007, he was killed by a roadside bomb while on patrol with the 2nd Battalion, The Light Infantry, in northern Basra. Private Tench was thrown forward, and his helmet struck Lance Corporal Rory Mackenzie's jaw, knocking the latter unconscious. Lance Corporal Mackenzie, who also lost a leg in the blast, said, 'Before the bomb went off, I had just woken up, and I put my safety goggles on. I looked over at Michael, and he was fast asleep. To the best of my knowledge, he didn't wake up. It felt as if the Warrior reared up, and I was lifted forward and flung back down. Michael was flung forward, and I got knocked out.'

Corporal David Lovell ran from another vehicle to find a large entry wound in Private Tench's chest where his armour had been penetrated. He was dead.

A horse-drawn carriage brought Private Tench's body from his family home in Carley Hill to the steps of Holy Trinity Church, Sunderland, for his funeral. Elderly residents of a local nursing home stood dressed in black as the cortege passed, while six of Private Tench's colleagues formed a guard of honour and carried his coffin, draped in the Union Jack, inside the church. Five hundred mourners attended the service, which was followed by a private burial at Southwick Cemetery. Private Tench was described as a soldier who was 'always happy' and 'liked a laugh'.

His commanding officer, Lieutenant Colonel Ted Shields of the Light Infantry, told those present, 'When news of Michael's death reached us, there was widespread shock, disbelief, immense sadness and, yes, anger. The untimely death of anyone, let alone a soldier, causes such emotions, but especially so with Michael, "Tenchy" to all those who knew him. Michael was one of those men who make the regiment the finest regiment in the British Army. He was a total enthusiast who loved his job.'

His friend, Private Craig Swan, said, 'Tenchy was a good friend not only to me, but to all the lads in the company. He was always happy and enjoyed having a laugh with his mates – he was a bit of a joker. He often spoke about his family and how he was happy that he had joined the army and made something of himself. We will all miss him very much as a friend and workmate, and my heart goes out to all his family and friends at home.'

Private Dean Graham added, 'Tenchy was a great friend who always helped out his mates. He was always up for laugh and a joke. He was a good and enthusiastic boxer, and he would always help people out in the gym. One of the best things I remember about him and will never forget is that he loved to dance when we went out for a drink. It has hit us all hard in A Company, but we will never forget him and feel for his family. It's a real shame that we never got to go away on holiday after the tour like he planned.'

5 February 2007

Basra

Second Lieutenant Jonathan Bracho-Cooke

The 2nd Battalion, The Duke of Lancaster's Regiment, suffered another fatality on 5 February 2007 when Second Lieutenant Jonathan Bracho-Cooke was killed by a roadside bomb in the As Sarraji district of Basra, close to the US Consulate. The subaltern from Hove, Sussex, had recently become engaged to

Laura Bottomley, and in his final email to her wrote that he loved her 'more than pizza and ice cream'. They had been due to marry that August on his return from Iraq.

'B.C.', as his friends knew him, had deployed to Iraq in January 2007. Second Lieutenant Bracho-Cooke's fellow officer Second Lieutenant Chris Ibbotson said that his colleague was 'faultless' and 'the nicest guy you could hope to meet'.

Second Lieutenant Bracho-Cooke's commanding officer, Lieutenant Colonel Simon Hutchinson, echoed his parents' assertion that he had an acute sense of duty and maturity beyond his years: 'He was a fine platoon commander, who quickly established himself under very difficult conditions. He stood out as a bright, enthusiastic and charismatic officer. We were proud he chose to be one of us and are desperately sad to have lost him.'

After visiting a war cemetery in Burma in 2006, Second Lieutenant Bracho-Cooke had told his friends that, should the worst happen, he wished to be buried alongside fellow soldiers. His family successfully appealed to the Commonwealth Graves Commission to overturn a ruling that spaces in the military section of Hove Cemetery were reserved for casualties from the Second World War.

❖ ❖ ❖

Statistics showed the militia's weapon of choice to be roadside explosive projectiles. Armed with ever more sophisticated devices, they were, according to British officers, determined to capitalise on the reduction in British troop numbers and see the 'occupiers' bombed out of Basra. With only 5,500 UK troops on the ground – 2,500 fewer than at the same period of 2006 – options were limited to respond offensively to this new challenge.

9 February 2007

Basra Province

Private Luke Simpson

On 9 February 2007, Private Luke Simpson, from Howden, East Yorkshire, was driving his colleagues back to base when a bomb went off beneath their Land Rover. Private Simpson suffered blast wounds to his pelvis and lower limbs but managed to steer the vehicle to a halt by the roadside before slumping across the front seats. Three of his passengers were also wounded: Captain Ibrar Ali's right hand and Private Christopher Herbert's lower right leg had been blown off, while Private Paul Davey required surgery to remove shrapnel from both legs. Those unscathed dragged Private Simpson into cover and administered first aid. Forty-five minutes after the blast, and with a further delay expected before a helicopter arrived to extract the wounded, Private Simpson complained that he was finding it hard to breathe. He slipped in and out of consciousness as his distraught friends from The Yorkshire Regiment looked on. Cardiopulmonary resuscitation failed to save his life. A post-mortem examination found that he died from blood loss.

Private Simpson had joined the army aged 16 and served in Northern Ireland and Bosnia before deployment to Iraq in November 2006. His father was a former sergeant major in the same battalion. He was known as 'Boob' to his colleagues, who relished his humour and positive attitude.

His six-year-old sister Hannah read a personal tribute to her brother at his funeral. She said, 'I love Luke. He used to ice skate with me. He used to play with me and throw snowballs with me. He used to play football with me. He used to push the sledge for me. I love my brother Luke.'

Private Simpson's mother Anita Hughes carried a single white rose as she and other family members followed her son's coffin into Howden Minster. Reverend James Little referred to a photograph of Private Simpson on duty in Bosnia. He had given his helmet to a local child to wear.

Major Toby Wilson, the officer commanding the battalion's rear party, told mourners, 'The regiment is absolutely devastated. He was one of the company's and the battalion's characters. Without a doubt, he was an awesome soldier and a lovely guy.'

Private Cameron Pierre said, 'He was always sticking up two fingers behind the boss's back and waving them around wildly. The boss would catch him now and again, but Boob could get away with that. The boss loved him.'

❖ ❖ ❖

On 14 February 2007, the United States launched Operation Fardh al-Qanoon. 'The Surge', as it became known, saw 22,000 additional US troops deployed to militia hot spots and a doubling in the strength of Provincial Reconstruction Teams. Some observers were of the opinion that US and British approaches to similar problems were polarised and that the British withdrawal was indicative of defeat. British commander Major General Jonathan Shaw insisted otherwise: 'If you take the attacks on the coalition out of the equation, what you are left with is actually a very low level of residual violence compared to anywhere else across Iraq. It is particularly the problems of gangsterism and criminality, Shia on Shia between competing parties. This is nothing like what you are seeing on the streets of Baghdad, and this is not a war zone. You have got to ask the question: what is the most appropriate force or capability to deal with this problem? I would argue that a foreign army is particularly ill-suited to resolving these kinds of societal problems. Far better the Iraqi Army and the Iraqi Police Force.'

While The Surge was followed by a reduction in sectarian violence, fewer civilian murders and increased resistance to al-Qaeda, academics such as Christopher Hitchens suggested that the impetus for the rejection of al-Qaeda and Wahhabism came from within militant Sunni communities and was not US-led. An unwanted consequence of The Surge was the knock-on impact on the British-controlled provinces. A US Congressional report revealed:

> Some JAM [Mahdi Army] members relocated to the south in response to FAQ [Operation Fardh al-Qanoon]

in Baghdad, further empowering JAM in confrontations with the Badr Organisation and provincial authorities. This intra-Shia violence has contributed to a significant increase in attacks against Coalition Forces in Basra and an observed greater hostility towards coalition presence.

Between 80 and 90 per cent of the violence in Basra was directed towards British troops. The simple solution was to leave: but how and at what pace? To pull out before the Iraqi Army was ready to take over responsibility for security would have been disastrous. The fear stemmed from to whom the British were handing over control. General Sir Michael Rose drew comparison with Aden in 1967: 'Basically, we handed over to two competing militias, just as we will be doing in Basra.'

British Forces were effectively camped on the slopes of a volcano, which, after three years of emitting smoke, was due to erupt. Iraq possessed the world's third-largest known oil reserves. The fact that Basra was the hub for petroleum exportation also exacerbated the turf war between the militias.

27 February 2007

Basra

Rifleman Daniel Coffey

Rifleman Daniel Coffey completed a seven-month tour with The Devon and Dorsets before volunteering two months later to redeploy with The Rifles to Basra. His brave decision came as no surprise to his family, who had witnessed his transition from youth to man since joining the army. On 27 February 2007, Rifleman Coffey, from Cullompton, Devon, was on top-cover when two gunmen ambushed his Land Rover as it returned to base in Basra. Rifleman Coffey was fatally injured by gunfire and died in hospital.

His funeral at St Andrew's Church, Cullompton, was attended by comrades who flew to Devon. He was buried in the town cemetery with full military honours. Rifleman Coffey was one of seven brothers and stepbrothers, all of whom were 'devastated'. According to his family, he joined the army to make them proud of him. To them, he died a hero.

His grandfather David Godfrey, a paper-mill worker from Cullompton, said, 'This hit us very hard. We are very, very proud of Daniel. He had a wonderful, caring heart. When Daniel joined the army, he changed immeasurably, almost overnight, or so it seemed to me. He changed from being a youthful teenager to a full-grown man, with full-grown beliefs to match. I am so proud of him and his achievements. He lived and died for the service he loved. He died protecting his comrades, and that is the most honourable duty of any soldier.'

His platoon commander, Lieutenant Aaron West, said, 'He was a good bloke for everyone, one of the best soldiers you can get. He was fit, motivated and enthusiastic about what he did. But not only that, he was a character behind the scenes and was able to raise morale, which was very important.'

4 March 2007

Died in UK Hospital After Attack in Basra

Private Johnathon Wysoczan

A week later, Private Johnathon Wysoczan was fatally wounded by a sniper. He had been in Iraq for two months with the 1st Battalion, The Staffordshire Regiment, when his patrol was attacked. In the first week of March, The Staffords hit back with Operation Phoenix, striking buildings used by the militias to launch attacks.

Private Wysoczan had joined the army in April 2006 and had been posted to Iraq on Boxing Day. A memorial service was held in his honour at St Mark's Church, Hanley, Stoke-on-Trent. His death came as his 300-year-old regiment prepared to merge with The Cheshire Regiment to become 1st Battalion, The Mercians.

His father Dany said, 'Johnathon was his own man, and it was his decision to be a soldier. We are all very proud of him for doing what he wanted to do. He was looking forward to his brother Jason joining him in B Company, 1 Staffords. He was a brave young man, nothing ever fazed him and he was happy to be on active service.'

Private Robert Tagg said, 'Johnathon was well respected by everyone who knew him. No matter what he was doing he always had time for his mates. He was a big football fan and supported Manchester United. He could always be found in the pub, with a beer in his hand, when they were playing. He also loved music. Every time I walked past his room, I could hear his music booming out. I can still picture his face when he passed out of training – he couldn't stop grinning. He was a great friend and will never be forgotten.'

Major Dominic Rutherford, Private Wysoczan's company commander, added, 'Private Wysoczan was a professional, enthusiastic and reliable soldier with a bright future. He arrived like an extra Christmas present on Boxing Day. He quickly fitted into the company, winning everyone's respect. Johnathon was always seen to have a smile on his face. He was a very confident soldier; indeed, the very first time I met him he jumped in before I could call him by his name and told me how to pronounce it or to call him A to Z, as it was easier. Private Wysoczan will always be remembered for his cheeky smile, which seemed to permanently adorn his face, even when he was doing something wrong. Even in the few months that he had served with us, Private Wysoczan had made his mark. It was an honour to lead and serve with such a brave, enthusiastic soldier.'

❖ ❖ ❖

The handing over of Shaibah Logistics Base, the Old State Building, the Shatt al-Arab Hotel and the al-Faw Security Base to local forces in the spring of 2007 left Basra Palace as a lone fortress in the city. It was bombed and mortared daily, sometimes hourly. Regimental Sergeant Major Jon Allen spoke for all British personnel: 'We could not just sit there and take the hits. We had to take the fight to the insurgents. We had to go toe to toe every time we went out. They had to understand that the British were not going to take the attacks lying down.'

Basra Palace was defended heroically and at great human cost: on one occasion Rifleman Alan Gormley, from Mansfield, was forced to use cooking oil to free his machine gun after it seized up from the sheer volume of rounds fired. 'By the end of one attack, we had used up nearly all our ammo,' Rifleman Gormley said. 'They were firing at us from all directions and giving us everything they had. It was really scary, but we just got on with what we had been trained to do. We had a really good feeling that we had done a good job.'

1 April 2007

Basra

Kingsman Danny Wilson

On 1 April 2007, Kingsman Danny Wilson was hit by a sniper just 500 metres from Basra Palace. He was the first of six British soldiers to be killed by the same weapon and type of ammunition. Kingsman Wilson's colleagues heard just one crack as the round pierced his left side and caused massive internal bleeding. Ten minutes earlier, Kingsman Wilson had been photographed smiling and wrapping his arms around his colleagues in the back of a Warrior armoured personnel carrier.

Kingsman Colin Thompson, from Carlisle, recalled, 'We had patrolled up the road for about 30 metres to check for roadside bombs near the palace. The pattern of life was normal, and there were Iraqis going about their business. We were on our knees, looking down the road, when the shot echoed and Danny was struck in the chest. I remember seeing Iraqis jumping to the floor for cover. Me and another soldier dragged Danny into the back of the vehicle, and a medic tried to save him. We sat outside the medical centre waiting for news of him. I was very angry when our company sergeant major came out and told us he had died. It was a bad day for our platoon, as we had already lost two soldiers in similar circumstances. Danny was a good lad. It did not really sink in that he had died until the night-time when his kit was boxed up and his bed-space and personal belongings packed up. It was hard for everyone. People dealt with it in their own way, but everyone was thinking, "Why the hell are we here, and what are we achieving?" It was not worth it, not on the money we were paid. You could work in a factory and earn the same. It seems pointless. It's Britain's Vietnam.'

Kingsman Wilson, from Workington, Cumbria, was survived by his wife Tracey and two-year-old son Leo. He was the third generation of his family to serve their country.

His mother Paulina McDowell, also from Workington, said, 'It is not possible to describe the grief of losing a son. It is unimaginable what you go through. You see and hear the television news, but you never think it is going to happen to you. Danny's widow Tracey made the decision to get Danny the forms to join the regular army. She has no regrets and neither do we. He served in the army like his father and his grandfather, and he has paid the ultimate price. My son loved the life, and he died doing what he wanted to do. He knew and appreciated the risks, and so did we. But that doesn't ease the pain of losing him. It was Tracey who came and told us in person that Danny was dead. She is a very brave and remarkable lady. We have been touched by the number of people who have wanted to share our grief, and we want to say thanks to them all.'

Kingsman Wilson's commanding officer, Lieutenant Colonel Mark Kenyon, said, 'Danny Wilson was the sort of kingsman with whom it is a privilege to serve alongside. Selfless, committed and always ready to look on the bright side, he will be sorely missed.'

2 April 2007

Basra

Rifleman Aaron Lincoln

On 2 April 2007, the same weapon and ammunition that were used to kill Kingsman Wilson were also used to kill Rifleman Aaron Lincoln in the al-Ashar district of Basra. A single bullet to the head smashed through Rifleman Lincoln's protective glasses and helmet. Another soldier, also from the 2nd Battalion, The Rifles, was wounded by small-arms fire. Rifleman Lincoln, from Durham, had gone to a house used by gunmen to stage attacks on British Forces when he was hit. Ballistics tests found that the sniper's high-velocity 5.56-millimetre rounds were manufactured in the United States. The weapon was thought to be either a British SA80 Mk2 or a US standard issue M16 rifle.

His parents Peter and Karen were among the pall-bearers who carried their son's coffin into St Giles's Church, Durham. Seven hundred mourners stood in silence as the service began. It was followed by a private ceremony at Belmont Cemetery.

His uncle Arthur Lincoln said, 'He left school aged 17 and went straight into the army. He lived for the army. It was all he wanted to do all his life. We are all proud of him. He had been in Iraq for three months and had recently been home on a week's leave. Private Lincoln was the 105th soldier to die in the conflict.'

Lieutenant Colonel Justin Maciejewski, Rifleman Lincoln's commanding officer, said, 'Rifleman Lincoln loved soldiering and was very good at it. He represents a tradition of soldiering that has very deep roots in County Durham. He lived a life of courage, loyalty and selfless commitment to others. Ultimately, he sacrificed his life for his friends. He died following up an attack on one of his platoon in which a fellow rifleman was wounded.'

5 April 2007

Basra

Private Eleanor Dlugosz, Second Lieutenant Joanna Dyer,
Corporal Kris O'Neill, Kingsman Adam Smith

Only three more days passed before further lives were lost. Four British soldiers, including two women, were killed by an improvised explosive device in Basra. The deaths of Second Lieutenant Joanna Dyer, a personal friend of Prince William from their time at the Royal Military Academy Sandhurst, and Private Eleanor Dlugosz coincided with the parading on Iranian television of the captured Leading Seaman Faye Turney. While women remained barred, at least officially, from roles in which they might be expected to kill the enemy, they were most certainly serving on the front line. (Women also serve in combat roles with the Special Reconnaissance Regiment, although this is not discussed by the Ministry of Defence.) The opinions of recent chiefs of the defence staff varied as to whether or not the battlefield was an appropriate place for a woman. Admiral Sir Michael Boyce was markedly more comfortable with the idea than his predecessor General Sir Charles Guthrie, who famously remarked, 'We are not yet ready for women on the front line, and maybe we will never be ready.'

Private Dlugosz, from Swanmore, Hampshire, had looked forward to her tour of Iraq and told her family just days before her death how proud she was to serve on operations. As her mother Sally Veck remembered, 'She was an extremely independent young lady and was well aware of the dangers in what she was doing. Nothing could have stopped her. She was doing exactly what she wanted.'

The 19 year old was killed alongside fellow Royal Army Medical Corps volunteer Corporal Kris O'Neill, Lieutenant Dyer of The Intelligence Corps and Kingsman Adam Smith of The Duke of Lancaster's Regiment. An Iraqi interpreter also died and another soldier was injured when the Warrior armoured vehicle was targeted in the early hours of 5 April 2007 en route to Basra Air Station after a mission to find arms caches. The vehicle was fitted with measures to detect explosives, but these proved ineffective.

Corporal Michael Carr was the only survivor. He remembered the flames and debris, and shouting, 'Is everyone all right?' There was no reply. 'I looked across for the female officer, Lieutenant Dyer, but she was no longer there.'

Second Lieutenant Dyer, an Oxford University graduate from near Yeovil in Somerset, was described as 'bright, ballsy and an absolute credit to the army'. She was attached to The Duke of Lancaster's Regiment as the infantry battalion's intelligence, surveillance, target acquisition and reconnaissance officer. Both her parents had served in uniform; her sister, a fellow Intelligence Corps officer, was at home on leave from Iraq.

The commanding officer of The Duke of Lancaster's Regiment, Lieutenant Colonel Mark Kenyon, said, 'From a very early stage, it was evident that Jo was a talented and very energetic officer, who was determined to make the most of her deployment to Iraq. Her enthusiasm was boundless, and her contribution to our operations, even in a few short weeks, was invaluable. We very quickly came to think of her as one of us.'

Colour Sergeant Paul Skelton was travelling in the vehicle behind. He saw a massive crater in the road and the heavy Warrior vehicle tilting at an angle. The improvised explosive device, which had been triggered by command wire, was found buried in the ground beneath the crater.

Combat medical technician Corporal Kris O'Neill told his family that his duties confined him to base. During his first tour of Iraq in 2003, his wife had announced that she was expecting twins. She gave birth to sons. Four years later, Tina O'Neill read on Teletext that two combat medical technicians were among those killed in a bomb blast. Her husband had only returned from leave to Iraq five days earlier. She said, 'As far as we knew, he was a medic, so we didn't think he was out there where the fighting was.'

Kingsman Smith was the latest loss for the soldiers of The Duke of Lancaster's Regiment – another young kingsman would lose his life two weeks later. Smith was born on the Isle of Man and raised in the Old Swan district of Liverpool. His inquest heard that the roof and sides of the Warrior were armour-plated, but there was no such protection below. He died instantly from blast wounds.

Known as 'Smudge', Kingsman Smith received praise from Captain Mike Peel, the commander of his reconnaissance platoon, for his 'cheerful nature which marked him out as a constant source of morale and strength in times of difficulty. He was thoroughly popular throughout the battalion and especially in the reconnaissance platoon. He will be sorely missed by all who had the honour to serve alongside him.'

A horse-drawn carriage brought his coffin, draped in the Union Jack, to All Saints Church, Broadgreen, Liverpool. Pall-bearers selected from his regiment carried the coffin into the church, where his girlfriend Terri Dunphy told the congregation that they spoke of getting married on his return from Iraq. The procession was led by his parents, Pam and Derek, and his teenage brother Mark. As Kingsman Smith was an avid Evertonian, his coffin passed the club's Goodison Park ground on his journey to Anfield Crematorium. He received full military honours, including a gun salute, two minutes' silence and the sounding of the last post.

His family said, 'This was the hardest thing we have ever had to do. It just doesn't seem real, and no amount of words can describe how much we are hurting. We keep thinking, hoping, it's not real and at any moment we will wake up from this nightmare. Adam was the most wonderful and beautiful person anyone could wish to meet. He always had a smile on his face and loved life so much. He had everything to live for. He was the most popular person you could ever know. Everyone loved him, and he has left so many broken hearts behind him. He was a loving son, brother and the best boyfriend in the whole world, and he will be missed more than words can say. He will for ever be in our hearts. Adam our hero, our star.'

15 April 2007

Baghdad

Sergeant Mark McLaren, Colour Sergeant Mark Powell

On 15 April 2007, two Royal Air Force helicopters collided, killing Colour Sergeant Mark Powell and Sergeant Mark McLaren. Enemy activity was not to blame.

Colour Sergeant Powell, a former paratrooper, was one of The Special Air Service's most experienced non-commissioned officers. A combat-hardened leader of men, he also enjoyed surfing off the coast of Porthcawl, South Wales. He was married with a young daughter and lived in Hereford, the home of The Special Air Service. His brother Darren, a businessman, said that he had died doing a job he loved and had been a soldier for 17 years. 'We lived near the beach and spent most of our time surfing,' said Darren. 'Mark would always meet up with his friends and head for the beach when he came home. I will always remember the good times we spent together.'

The two Puma helicopters were reportedly returning to base after a mission with US Special Forces when the mid-air crash occurred north of Baghdad. The cause of the crash was never confirmed by the Ministry of Defence.

Royal Air Force loadmaster Sergeant Mark McLaren was on the same helicopter as Colour Sergeant Powell. The pair died when the Puma hurtled to earth. At least two other servicemen suffered severe injuries. Father-of-two Sergeant McLaren, who was born in Ashington, Northumberland, deployed to Iraq as part of a detachment from RAF Benson. He had grown up in the county and attended Carterton Community College.

Wing Commander Chris Hunter paid tribute to his former colleague's positive attitude and self-motivation. 'It was a pleasure to fly with him, and he will be sadly missed,' he said. 'As an air loadmaster, he was a master of his trade, a consummate professional.'

Sergeant McLaren was on his fourth tour and was just days away from returning home to his wife Kerry and their twin boys, who were nine months old at the time of their father's death. His funeral at St George's Church, Brockworth, near Gloucester, was attended by more than 300 mourners, including family, friends and colleagues. Those in attendance witnessed a fly-past by two Royal Air Force Puma helicopters. The service included tributes and poems read out by Sergeant McLaren's widow Kerry and his best friend Nigel Lomas.

His father Stuart, a prison officer from Wallingford, Oxfordshire, said, 'It was a moving, dignified service. As an ex-serviceman, I have been to too many than I care to remember, but it is different when it is for your family. Mark was the hero of our family. He was a loving son and will be sadly missed. He has gone too soon. I was proud to be his father. He was the joker in the squadron, and he was just a lovely lad. We were frustrated about the fact that he was out in Iraq for so long, but he enjoyed his job, and he always knew there was a likelihood that he could go to war. Mark enjoyed the air force and enjoyed what he was doing, but I disagree with why he was there.'

His sister Sarah added, 'You certainly didn't forget Mark if you met him. We will all miss him.'

❖ ❖ ❖

For several months, British operations in Maysan had been restricted to long-range reconnaissance patrols and operations to secure the Iranian border. On 18 April 2007, a ceremony was held at Camp Sparrowhawk to mark the return of Maysan to provincial control. Soldiers from the Iraqi 10th Division marched past dignitaries in their American-style uniforms and waved the national flag – a 'moment of optimism', according to Major General Jonathan Shaw, the officer commanding the Multinational Division in southern Iraq.

19 April 2007

Maysan

Corporal Ben Leaning, Trooper Kristen Turton

Given that the British government habitually stressed that provinces were only handed over once they were secure, it was a tragic irony that two British soldiers were killed in Maysan by a roadside bomb just hours after the ceremony. At the time, Prince Harry was preparing to deploy to Iraq to fulfil a similar role to the two fallen servicemen. The media suggested that the attack on The Queen's Royal Lancers convoy was a dry run for an attack on the prince.

At 1119 on 19 April 2007, The Lancers' commanding officer, Lieutenant Colonel Richard Nixon-Eckersall, led 50 of his men towards a river crossing. This was known to insurgents to be one of the few positions where British soldiers, their Land Rovers and their Scimitar-tracked reconnaissance vehicles could cross the waterway. Insurgents had been spotted using mobile phones and outriders on motorbikes to track the progress of The Lancers, who, with just a few days of their tour remaining, were looking forward to going home.

Lieutenant Colonel Nixon-Eckersall saw and heard a blast and moved up to the front of the convoy as a black cloud rose from one of the leading vehicles. The projectile had pierced the Scimitar's armour. Although its electronic countermeasures were functioning, they had failed to protect the soldiers. Two were already dead, and three were badly wounded.

The vehicle's commander, Corporal Ben Leaning, and its driver, Trooper Kristen Turton, had also been wearing helmets and body armour inside the Scimitar. Their injuries were described as 'not compatible with life'. Their deaths led Buckingham Palace, Clarence House and General Sir Richard Dannatt to reconsider the decision to send Prince Harry to Iraq.

Corporal Leaning, from Scunthorpe, was described as a natural leader and a fine soldier. Having joined the army in 1999, he had quickly risen through the ranks, and further promotions were expected.

Trooper Turton's funeral was held at St Mary's Church, Richmond, North Yorkshire. He was survived by his parents, Jenny and Alan, and his wife Sharon, who said, 'Kris always told me he lived for two things – me and the army. I am proud he has died doing something he loved so much. He was the most amazing person I have ever met, and I loved him with all my heart and soul as he loved me. He was kind, generous and was always able to make everyone smile with his brilliant sense of humour. He always walked with dignity, and he will never walk alone. He will always be remembered as a hero by all. When Kris joined the army and his regiment, The Queen's Royal Lancers, he became part of a larger family. The heartfelt messages from his friends and colleagues have shown me just how many lives he touched. By those who knew him personally, he will be remembered as an amazing friend, a true comrade and someone who could be relied upon, while I will remember him as my life, my world and my soulmate.'

The following year, Jenny Turton said, 'We are grieving deeply. The pain and sadness never goes away. He never leaves our thoughts. He left such a big hole in our lives, and he was our only son. Nearly a year on it does not get any better, and it never will. I have photographs of him, and I have got flowers for him, though it does not make it any better, and it does not bring him back. He was a young man, only 27 years old. We knew he was going to be promoted. We knew he was going to go a long way in the army. He had that determination, ambition and drive. It was so, so sad that it was all taken away from him and that his life was just stopped. That is what we find so very hard to accept and to come to terms with. There is just nothing we can do. I am sure Ben's [Corporal Leaning] mother must feel the same way.'

Lieutenant Colonel Nixon-Eckersall described both men as committed, selfless soldiers. He told an inquest that the enemy had invested heavily in this particular explosive device, which was 'very large and very deliberate'. 'There were only a very limited number of points that we could cross the river – only three,' he continued. 'The anti-Iraq forces knew this and where we had been operating in Maysan. They would not just have dug this device in and left it there. I imagine they would have manned the position at all times.'

23 April 2007

Basra

Kingsman Alan Jones

The Basra sniper was suspected of killing Kingsman Alan Jones on 23 April 2007. The soldier was on patrol in the al-Ashar district of Basra when he was struck down by a single shot. He was killed as British Forces mounted a fightback against the insurgents and launched raids on the Shia Flats on the city's western outskirts. A commander briefed reporters: 'We are prepared to go there in daylight and take whatever comes our way. We are not being bombed out or intimidated.'

The raids recovered hundreds of weapons used by the militia. Soldiers from the 2nd Battalion, The Duke of Lancaster's Regiment, and the 2nd Battalion, The Rifles, were to the fore.

Liverpool-born Kingsman Jones was on top-cover above a Warrior armoured vehicle when he was shot. His mother Julie had been against his joining the army and had torn up his application form when he requested her consent to enlist aged 16. When he deployed to Iraq, she repeatedly told him to be careful. He told her how he was giving food and water to the local children. She said, 'It was his choice, and it was what he wanted to do. He was so proud to be a soldier. He was a joker. He never had a straight face and was always flashing his white teeth.'

29 April 2007

Basra

Rifleman Paul Donnachie

The Basra sniper was also suspected of killing Rifleman Paul Donnachie six days after the death of Kingsman Jones. He too was struck down by a single shot when on patrol in the al-Ashar district of Basra.

Rifleman Donnachie showed remarkable courage for an 18 year old. Major Alex Baring, Rifleman Donnachie's company commander, paid tribute: 'He was one of those rare sorts who never complained whatever he was told to do. In fact, he used to volunteer to go out on patrols. He never wanted to be away from where the action was, and that was pretty impressive. He had already volunteered to go to Afghanistan, too, later this year. He loved the army, he loved The Rifles and he died protecting those around him, having got out of his vehicle to check the route ahead. He really was the best of British.'

Rifleman Donnachie, from Reading, Berkshire, was immediately evacuated to Basra Palace following the shooting but subsequently died of his injuries. He was the 12th and last soldier to die in April, a month when the British death rate was comparable to that suffered by US services in central and western Iraq.

1 May 2007

Basra

Major Nick Bateson

May began ominously on the first of the month when Major Nick Bateson was killed at Basra Air Station. One of the army's most talented endurance athletes, the 49-year-old Royal Signals officer was knocked off his bicycle at 0800 and died later in hospital. Major Bateson, a member of the army's triathlon and orienteering teams, had been serving in southern Iraq for three months on detachment from the Defence Information Integrated Project Team based at Corsham, Wiltshire. He was survived by his wife Angela.

Lieutenant Colonel Colin McGrory said, 'If you mention Nick Bateson to anyone from the Royal Signals of Nick's vintage, they will immediately picture certain things about him. He always had a great big grin on his face, very bandy legs, an eccentric approach to uniform, and wherever he was his workspace would expand gradually as bikes, bits of bike and running kit began to appear. Nick was a lovely guy who will be sorely missed. He was a real character in every way. A hugely fit, active man, he was somewhat uncomfortable in a desk environment but was always professional, and whether he enjoyed it or not he got on and did a professional job. A real people person, his wicked sense of humour and willingness to make cups of coffee and toast for his workmates made him a great guy to work near. We were all looking forward to having him back from Iraq in only a few short weeks. We all miss him greatly and extend our condolences to his wife Angela.'

❖ ❖ ❖

'Does this look like a defeated army? No, it's complete bollocks. We fought hard and could have stayed for as long as we wanted to. They threw everything at us. We left because it was the right thing to do.'

Lieutenant Colonel Patrick Sanders,
commanding officer, 4th Battalion, The Rifles

Were the insurgents right to continue their campaign against Lieutenant Colonel Sanders' men and Coalition Forces? General Sir Michael Rose thought so, as he told Jeremy Paxman on *Newsnight*: 'Yes, I do. As Lord Chatham said when he was speaking on the British presence in North America, "If I was an American, as I am an Englishman, as long as one Englishman remained on American native soil, I would never, never, never lay down my arms." The Iraqi insurgents feel exactly the same way. I understand them. I don't excuse them for some of the terrible things they do, but I understand why they are resisting. The war they [British soldiers] have been fighting is a hopeless war. They cannot possibly win it.'

General Rose's comments attracted more media attention than the heroic efforts of 19 Light Brigade to rebuild Basra. Their seven-month tour, which cost twenty-six service personnel their lives and resulted in one hundred and thirty wounded, saw two hundred kilometres of water pipes laid to seven thousand homes, eleven primary-healthcare centres and five electrical-distribution plants built, two hundred and fifty schools repaired, and twenty thousand jobs created. While their commander Brigadier Tim Evans conceded that it had been a 'very challenging tour', he was adamant that his men and women had not died in vain and their campaign had not been hopeless: 'The enemy were determined to make their mark, but we were never going to be beaten. We knew before we went it would not be easy, but as soldiers we do not get to choose our operations. The fact that the officers and soldiers never lost their direction or motivation was a testament to the standard of our people today. They could not have performed better.'

The 1st Mechanised Brigade, commanded by Brigadier James Bashall, an ex-Para, took over from 19 Light Brigade. Brigadier Bashall's brigade was 500 troops light on the 5,500 whom 1 Mech replaced – the fewer the troops who remained, the greater the vulnerability of those on the ground. Brigadier Bashall promised to 'stand by' ordinary Iraqis and insisted that the reduced British presence should not be misinterpreted: 'As the Iraqi security forces increasingly take the lead for security, the Multinational Force will adjust its force posture. Improvements to the security situation will encourage investment in Basra, and your economy will grow as a result.'

6 May 2007

Died in UK Hospital After Attack in Basra

Private Kevin Thompson

When Private Kevin Thompson of The Royal Logistic Corps returned to Britain on compassionate grounds to attend a family funeral, he made up his mind to leave the army. He returned to Iraq with his mind set on starting a carpentry course in Lancaster and a holiday to New York with his fiancée when his tour ended in a few weeks' time. His mother Theresa said, 'I was making the travel arrangements. He and Lucy were due to fly out on 26 June.' Private Thompson, whose brother Andrew was serving with the same unit, was still mourning his grandfather's loss from a heart attack as he prepared to patrol in Basra on 6 May 2007.

Private Thompson's vehicle was targeted by a roadside bomb. Severely wounded, he was flown back from Basra to the forces' wing at Selly Oak Hospital. Despite being expected to recover, Private Thompson's wounds caused a sudden brain haemorrhage. Lucy and his family were at his bedside when he died. Following his brother's death, Private Andrew Thompson also decided to quit the services.

'I could strangle Tony Blair,' said Private Thompson's father Mark. 'So many young men have died in Iraq when they shouldn't have been there in the first place. When Kevin was over for his grandfather's funeral, he said morale was very low. My only consolation is that he died a hero.'

❖ ❖ ❖

In late spring 2007, clashes between British troops and insurgents in Basra became more intense than at any time during the war, including the invasion phase, with more rounds expended and more lives lost. The newly arrived 4th Battalion, The Rifles, were hit hard almost immediately. The quick loss of two gallant, combat-hardened corporals, Corporal Jeremy Brookes and Corporal Rodney Wilson, and the wise and respected Major Paul Harding, was followed by the death of rising star Corporal John Rigby. Corporal Brookes and Corporal Wilson were killed in the heat of battle while putting the safety of their younger colleagues before their own. Their bravery was described as inspirational.

21 May 2007

Basra

Corporal Jeremy Brookes

On 21 May 2007, with his men pinned down, Corporal Brookes placed himself in jeopardy to lay down suppressing machine-gun fire. His gallantry allowed his section to take cover after insurgents ambushed a Bulldog armoured vehicle in Basra. Corporal Brookes' cousin, Lance Corporal Kevin Bagling, was caught in the same attack. As rocket-propelled grenades and small arms slammed into the armoured plating around The Rifles vehicles, Lance Corporal Bagling screamed out in pain. He had been wounded not by enemy fire, but by the red-hot empty bullet casings ejected from another soldier's weapon that had slid down the back of his body armour, scalding his spine. 'It was mayhem,' said Lance Corporal Bagling. 'I was just praying we made it back to base.' He did, only to be told that Corporal Brookes, from Kings Heath, Birmingham, was dead.

Lance Corporal Bagling later told the BBC, 'One of the lads told me my cousin died in the small-arms fire – he got shot in the head. It was a bad experience. You have to put it out of your mind, really, when you're over here. You can't get really emotional, because you've got a job to do.'

True to his word, Lance Corporal Bagling was straight back in the action and the following month was struck by a rocket-propelled grenade. Fifty-two pieces of shrapnel were embedded in his neck. 'I did not really feel it,' Lance Corporal Bagling insisted. 'It was just like a scratching sensation, and I touched my neck and just felt the blood. So I looked around and said to all the lads, "I've been hit." But then I returned fire some more and went back to camp. We didn't realise how serious the wound was until we got back here. One of the pieces of shrapnel was touching my jugular.'

Corporal Brookes was raised in Birmingham and attended St Martin de Pores Primary School and Kings Heath Boys. An ultra-marathon runner, he enlisted in February 2001 and served with The Royal Green Jackets before the regiment's amalgamation with three other historic units to form The Rifles. His funeral service with full military honours was held at All Saints Church, Kings Heath, and was attended by his family and girlfriend.

Reverend John Wilkinson told mourners, 'Jez was no conscript. He went into the army with his eyes wide open and found purpose and challenge. He took his orders and set about doing his duty while caring for the men under his command and developing his own strengths and capabilities. Every parent has at the back of their minds the dread of receiving sudden news that their child is dead, but how much more so for those whose grown-up sons or daughters are serving with Her Majesty's forces in a conflict. And so it was that an officer arrived on your doorstep to break the tragic news.'

Soldiers from The Rifles paid tribute. Corporal 'Rizzer' Smith said, 'Jez was my battle partner. We would cover each other and, no matter what, we would do our tasks together. He was always for his blokes.'

Rifleman Brett Campbell agreed: 'In this action, as ever, he thought of everyone else but himself. He told me and the top-cover sentries to get down into cover, covering us as we did so. His selfless commitment was legendary.'

Lieutenant Colonel Patrick Sanders described Corporal Brookes as 'one of the best corporals I have ever had the privilege of serving with. He was not always easy, but the best rarely are. What stood out was his amazing determination and zest for life. I don't think he wasted a single day of his life.'

7 June 2007

Basra

Corporal Rodney Wilson

Corporal Rodney Wilson was shot dead by the Basra sniper as he dragged a wounded colleague to safety on 7 June 2007, an action for which he was awarded a posthumous Mention in

Dispatches. Corporal Wilson had been rated in the top 2 per cent of corporals across the British Army after his recent performances in exams and practical exercises to determine his suitability for promotion on the Platoon Sergeants Battle Course.

On the day of Corporal Wilson's death, elements of the 4th Battalion, The Rifles, and the 2nd Battalion, The Royal Welsh Regiment, had been on patrol in the al-Atiyah district of Basra when Lance Corporal Jonathan 'Frenchie' LeGalloudec was shot in the back. 'As soon I was hit,' he said later, 'I knew I was going to be all right because Rodney would come and get me.'

When Corporal Wilson summoned Second Lieutenant Charles Kilner to assist him, the subaltern was also hit. 'The next thing I knew, I had been hit in my left arm, with which I was carrying Lance Corporal LeGalloudec,' said Second Lieutenant Kilner. 'At that point, I looked over and Corporal Wilson was already on the floor. I fell to my knees. I looked at Corporal Wilson again, and it appeared he had been shot in the neck.' Second Lieutenant Kilner and Lance Corporal LeGalloudec survived, but Wilson, so often their inspiration, was fatally wounded.

'Where Corporal Wilson led, others followed,' said Lieutenant Colonel Saunders. 'He was, in the words of his own riflemen, "a legend".'

Corporal Wilson's father Richard, from Fareham, Hampshire, added, 'It is no surprise to me that Rodney did what he did. I wish he had not done it, but if he had not, he would not have been the man I knew. I am hugely proud of him. I am just incredulous that I played a part in producing a lad like him.'

❖ ❖ ❖

The operation that cost Corporal Wilson his life found the biggest cache of ammunition and weapons to date in southern Iraq and resulted in the arrest of five suspected insurgents. For all the American talk of the British being defeated militarily, there was no question of them declining to patrol certain neighbourhoods because they belonged to the militias.

16 June 2007

Basra

Lance Corporal James Cartwright

The death of Lance Corporal James Cartwright passed relatively unnoticed. As Major General Julian Thompson noted, the public had passed its threshold for news of Iraq received through the media, not that they had stopped caring. The Royal Marines commander during the Falklands War added that he had seen this before with the response to the deaths of soldiers in Northern Ireland. 'The public may well be fed up with what is going on in Iraq,' he said. 'But it would be a great shame if we forgot what our forces are facing out there on a daily basis. Taking an interest in them does not mean supporting the war. It means acknowledging that they are there in our name.'

Lance Corporal Cartwright of the 2nd Royal Tank Regiment died when his Warrior armoured vehicle rolled off a bridge near Basra and landed in water. Two other soldiers were also injured in the accident. No enemy forces were involved.

The soldier from Battersea had served for four years and was described by his commanding officer as a 'committed tankie'. His father Gerald said that his son had always been destined to be a soldier: 'He always played soldiers as a boy. He wanted to do his bit in Iraq. He was bubbly, friendly, everyone liked him and he had very close friends. He had just finished his first month when this terrible accident occurred.' Lance Corporal Cartwright had hoped to retire from the army and start a new career as a fireman in Leicestershire with his fiancée Natalie Richardson.

His funeral took place at St Luke's Church, London. Colleagues from The Royal Tank Regiment acted as pall-bearers. He received full military honours and a piper played 'Amazing Grace'.

20 June 2007

Basra

Major Paul Harding

Major Paul Harding, aged 48, had risen from the rank of rifleman through regimental sergeant major in the then Royal Green Jackets to his last appointment as officer commanding of the 4th Battalion, The Rifles, Fire Support Company. Major Harding, from Winchester, had been in Basra only a short while when Lieutenant Colonel Patrick Sanders posted him to become chief of staff at the 110-strong Provincial Joint Coordination Centre and deputy to the commander of the base, Lieutenant Colonel Bob Fram. A few days after his arrival, Major Harding's men expended 9,000 rounds in a rearguard action.

At just before 0300 on 20 June 2007, Major Harding was crouched in the front sangar (fortified guard post) supervising the unloading of supply trucks when the Provincial Joint Coordination Centre was mortared. Major Harding knew that his position was dangerous but refused to delegate manning the sangar to a junior soldier. He was killed instantly when a mortar shell – probably a 60-millimetre calibre – landed immediately in front of him.

Such was the esteem in which Major Harding was held that Brigadier James Bashall later admitted he had slipped briefly into a state of disbelief when woken with the news. Brigadier Bashall had known what a blow Major Harding's death would be to morale and battalion strength. Afterwards, Lieutenant Colonel Fram described Major Harding as 'simply irreplaceable'.

Brigadier Bashall forced himself to return to focusing on the tasks at hand – as Harding would have wanted. He described his fellow officer as 'a legend in The Rifles, a wonderful man and an outstanding soldier. I had come to know him personally, and only last week I saw at first hand the impact of his leadership at an isolated base in the centre of Basra [the Provincial Joint Coordination Centre]. He was a rock around which others took strength.'

A memorial service was held in Major Harding's honour at Winchester Cathedral. The 800 mourners were led by his wife Paula and their sons, Christopher and Jake. The hymns chosen for his funeral were apposite: 'Onward Christian Soldiers' and 'I Vow to Thee My Country'. His coffin, draped in the Union Jack and with his regimental cap, sword and belt resting on top of it, was carried to the altar on the shoulders of six of his comrades.

Major Nick Haddock noted pertinently, 'He touched so many lives and died where he was always to be found: leading from the front.'

Major Harding's commanding officer, Lieutenant Colonel Sanders, gave perhaps the most moving eulogy of any serviceman or woman killed in Iraq: 'It may seem strange to talk of love between soldiers, but the very best officers and soldiers inspire extraordinary love, devotion and loyalty in their fellow men. He loved his riflemen as a father and they loved him back.'

22 June 2007

Basra

Corporal John Rigby

Only two days passed before the same battalion mourned a soldier who, had he not been undermined by fate, might have emulated Major Harding's achievements. Aged 24, Corporal John Rigby was a sergeant in waiting and would have taken his third stripe in September. Lieutenant Colonel Sanders described him as 'the most talented corporal of his generation', while his colleagues in the junior ranks nicknamed him 'Goldenballs' as the David Beckham of the squaddies.

Corporal Rigby, from Rye, East Sussex, was accompanied on operations in Basra by his twin brother Will, each serving in the 4th Battalion, The Rifles. On 22 June 2007, Corporal Rigby was on top-cover duty when an improvised explosive device struck his vehicle. Rifleman William Long later recalled, 'I had ducked my head down. Then there was dust and debris everywhere. I looked around and saw "Riggers" drop his weapon. He fell down straight away. I was tapping him on the cheek, but I got no response. Then I saw blood coming down his forehead.'

The wire-controlled explosive device ripped through the Bulldog vehicle. Lieutenant Thomas Knight said, 'The force broke the tracking on the right-hand side, destroying the steering.'

Corporal Rigby was airlifted to military hospital, suffering from serious head wounds. A thin piece of shrapnel had pierced his helmet and penetrated his skull.

His twin brother Will was awoken at 0700. 'I packed a few things and went straight to the battalion headquarters to be addressed by the colonel and the doctor who dealt with John at the scene,' he said. He was then taken to his twin's bedside, where he spent the next ten hours holding his hand, reminiscing and joking. 'I'm certain he was hearing what I was saying.'

Every half hour, Will rang their father Doug at home in the UK with updates. Once he saw CAT scans, however, he knew that his brother had only a few hours to live.

Will found it a great comfort to be at his brother's bedside on their 24th birthday. 'I came into this world with John, and 24 years to the day, he left us,' he said. After a short period of compassionate leave, he returned to Iraq to complete his tour: 'It had become very apparent to me and John the good that British soldiers were doing. I am a serving soldier. Where they say I go, I go.'

Corporal Rigby and his twin's family said that since the age of four it had been their joint ambition to be soldiers. They both joined aged 16 and were swiftly promoted. A cherry tree was planted in Corporal Rigby's memory at Robertsbridge Community College. Anne Pope, the school's governor, said that it was important to remember John, as he was popular among staff and pupils and achieved so much.

A family statement read:

> John was a cherished and devoted son and brother, and a talented, hard-working and successful soldier, popular with his peers and across all ranks alike. He was due to be promoted to sergeant in September and had a very

bright future ahead of him, which included plans to undertake higher education. He will be accompanied back to England by his twin brother William, who is also serving in Iraq with The Rifles and who was with him at his bedside at Basra Military Hospital when he died. The army have been tremendously helpful and supportive to us at this difficult time, but we are understandably devastated at his loss.

Major John Wakelin said, 'Corporal Rigby was quite simply unique. He was a free-thinking, independent and bright young corporal who approached life with vigour. Life was out there for the taking for Corporal Rigby, and he was going to get all that he could from it. Professionally, he stood out. His style of soldiering was not only about professionalism and getting the basics right – although he did. His approach was more human, and his relationship with his men, and his love for them, defined him. He has blistered his way through the ranks and was recently awarded early promotion to sergeant. Typically, there was little or no fanfare but a quiet knock at my door. "Sir," he said. "I'm not sure about this. Section commanding is where I want to be. I love my job and do not want to leave my boys just yet." Nobody interfered with Corporal Rigby's section, and they were brilliantly trained and utterly effective under his leadership. He had longed to take his section on operations, and no stone was left unturned in his drive for excellence.'

❖ ❖ ❖

Basra Palace stood alone, the presence of British soldiers a defiant stance against the insurgents. Its continued use put at risk the lives of everyone there, as well as the lives of those who drove and protected the re-supply convoys. In order to defend the palace and take the fight to the Madhi Army, British soldiers were now being killed at a proportionally greater rate than US soldiers – a watershed in the battle for southern Iraq. Professor Sheila Bird of the Royal Statistical Society found that roadside bombs were killing more soldiers than any other weapon or form of attack – Lieutenant Colonel James Swift, the commanding officer of the 2nd Battalion, The Royal Regiment of Wales, agreed: 'It would not be unusual during one trip to Basra to be confronted by a dozen roadside bombs. We faced over 70 roadside bombs as a battle group in our first few months.'

28 June 2007

Basra

Corporal Paul Joszko, Private Scott Kennedy, Private James Kerr

At 0100 on 28 June 2007, Corporal Paul Joszko of the 2nd Battalion, The Royal Regiment of Wales, and Private Scott Kennedy and Private James Kerr of The Black Watch were making their way back to Basra Air Station after another re-supply run to the palace. The soldiers had dismounted in the al-Antahiya district when an improvised explosive device was detonated, blowing a three-metre crater in the road. Corporal Joszko, from Abercynon, South Wales, who was standing just an arm's length from the centre of the blast, was killed instantly. Survivors watched in horror as he was engulfed in orange flame. Private Kennedy died of multiple blast injuries at the scene, while Private Kerr died shortly afterwards.

The deaths occurred on Gordon Brown's first day in office. Among his first official duties as prime minister was to pay tribute to the soldiers in the House of Commons. One of the deceased was from his own constituency. Private James Kerr's mother Pauline, from Cowdenbeath, Fife, received a personal telephone call in which Brown passed on his condolences. Her son had been in Iraq for seven weeks. When she had heard the news of the deaths of three soldiers, Pauline had left a message on her son's webpage that read, 'Please get in touch asap.'

Corporal Joszko's partner Kayleigh gave birth to their second child six months after his death on what would have been his 29th birthday. 'It was as if it was meant to be,' she said. 'And that he was a boy. He was due four days earlier, but he held on.' Corporal Joszko's commanding officer, Lieutenant Colonel James

Swift, said, 'He was particularly strong in the field and a very strong contender for promotion for sergeant. He always looked scruffy, and had a cheeky smile and a cigarette in his hand, but he never failed to deliver the goods. He was doggedly loyal.'

Private Kennedy joined the army from Queen Anne High School and was known affectionately as 'Casper'. He was looking forward to becoming a father for the first time, and his girlfriend Vicki brought their baby daughter Jessica-Lee to his memorial service, which was moved from a nearby church to the local school to accommodate the hundreds of mourners wishing to pay their respects. The congregation was shown pictures of Private Kennedy through his young life and heard one of his favourite songs, 'The Impossible Dream'.

His family said, 'We are devastated by the loss of our son Scott. Even as a child, he was determined to join the army and was a very proud soldier. His grandfather, who served with The Black Watch in Korea, was a great influence on him, and we also supported him in following his dream. Although we are heartbroken, we are comforted by the fact that he died doing the job he loved. Scott was a wonderful, happy-go-lucky, kind son who always had a smile on his face. He will be greatly missed by all of his family.'

Reverend Elizabeth Kenny told those gathered, 'Scott was keen to expand his skills as a soldier and volunteered to serve in Iraq. It was while serving there that Vicki shared with him the news that she had given birth to a daughter, whom he was destined not to see.'

Lieutenant Colonel James Swift said, 'Private Scott Kennedy was a young, enthusiastic soldier. He had volunteered to leave the peace in Northern Ireland, where his regiment is based, to reinforce The Royal Welsh for their operational tour in Iraq. He gave his life for his friends and his country. He had not been in the army long but was already a very competent soldier. He could appear shy, but he was not. He was his own man. He would do anything for anyone, and the blokes loved him. We will miss Scott very much. We will learn from his example, and we will honour his memory.'

Private Kerr joined The Black Watch in 2005 and volunteered to leave the battalion's barracks in Northern Ireland to serve in

Iraq. His mother Pauline Ward expressed her feelings on the Bebo website the day after she learned of her son's death. She wrote:

> I can't even begin to explain the pain I'm feeling right now or the emotional roller coaster that I've been on for the last 24 hours. My heart is breaking. I feel no pain, just numbness. I see no light at the end of the tunnel. My son, my action man, has been taken from me. I can't believe I will never see or hear from him ever again. I feel empty, sad and bitter. I keep asking myself, why him? God only takes the good ones, so I've been told, but this does not help to ease my pain and grief. All who knew him will cry a silent tear. His smile lit up every room he entered. My cheeky rogue, everyone loved him, you will be sorely missed. My family's life has been turned upside down, but we'll be strong. Gordon Brown phoned me today with his condolences – thank you. I just want to say always remembered, never forgotten, for ever and always you are in our thoughts, my hero.

A friend from Beath High School expressed his emotions just hours after learning that his school pal was dead. William Fisher said, 'I remember Jamie saying he would be back in October, and we should all go out and have a big weekend on the town in Perth. He was excited about it. He was making good money, and he wanted to come back and spend it, even buy a house. Jamie wanted to see the world. There's not much opportunity to do that in Cowdenbeath.'

❖ ❖ ❖

In July, Air Chief Marshal Jock Stirrup was right to acknowledge that any judgement on whether or not the British mission was a success depended on 'what your interpretation of the mission was in the first place. I am afraid people had, in many instances, unrealistic aspirations. The mission was to get the place and the people to a state where Iraqis could run this part of the country, if they chose to.'

6 July 2007

Basra Palace

Rifleman Edward Vakabua

On 6 July 2007, Rifleman Edward Vakabua died after one of his colleagues inadvertently shot him in the head at Basra Palace. The soldier, who later faced an investigation by the Army Prosecuting Authority, had no idea that the L96 high-velocity sniper rifle was loaded when he pointed it at his colleague's head and fired. Rifleman Vakabua, of the 4th Battalion, The Rifles, was described by colleagues as a 'shy and pleasant character'. His brother Joji was also serving in the British Army in Iraq at the time.

Rifleman Vakabua's platoon commander, Captain Will Peltor, said, 'Vaka's death yesterday hurt us all deeply. A friend, a cherished brother rifleman and a proud son of Fiji, one of whom Fiji can be proud, has been lost serving our country on active service. His faith, courage, selflessness and simple decency defined him and inspired all who knew him.'

Rifleman Vakabua's fellow countrymen sang traditional Fijian songs in tribute to him in a deeply moving ceremony. The soldier's family received letters of condolence from the Prince of Wales and Gordon Brown.

7 July 2007

Basra

Corporal Christopher Read

The following day, Corporal Christopher Read of the 3rd Regiment, Royal Military Police, was fatally wounded by small-arms fire. Corporal Read, from Poole, Dorset, was among 1,000 British troops taking part in the biggest operation of its kind in 2007. This was aimed at arresting insurgents believed to be responsible for the attack on the Provincial Joint Coordination Centre that had killed Major Harding. Coalition aircraft provided top-cover as troops withdrew. Following a series of house searches and arrests of militia suspects, British Forces had come under heavy attack in the Hay al-Mudhara district of Basra. The mission was launched hours after the office of Nouri al-Maliki announced to the world's press that the Iraqi prime minister had told Gordon Brown by telephone that he wanted Iraqi troops to assume sole control of Basra within three months.

Corporal Read inspired great affection from his friends, one of whom, Corporal Barry Key, wrote a poem in his honour:

> Chris recently told me with his signature smile on his face that his civilian friends thought he was mad,
>
> Who am I to disagree, as my opinion of him was the same they had.
>
> An unhealthy fascination with all things mechanical defined Chris's character –
>
> A young man obsessed with fast cars is what I will always remember.
>
> The last words I spoke to Chris were, 'You take care of yourself tonight' –
>
> I remember saying them clearly as he was drawing his weapon, appearing larger than life in the Basra daylight.
>
> My thoughts are now with his family and those close to him –
>
> For I am a religious man myself but can't help feeling that God's decision to take him so early is a sin.

Corporal James McIntyre said, 'Chris, whom I knew as "Readie", will always be remembered for his love of modified cars – he loved everything about them, including the cruising culture. He was often seen driving around various locations in the Bulford area in his not-to-everyone's-taste, in-your-face modified cars, which he loved. However, this was always to everyone's enjoyment, whether it be "Cool, look at that car" or "God, what is Readie driving now?" He was planning on buying his ultimate dream car, a Sierra Cosworth, on return from this tour. It was something he often talked about and always got really excited over. Unfortunately, it is a dream that he will now never live out.

'Readie was a gentle giant who would never have hurt a fly and who would do anything for anyone. He was a well-liked member of strike section and a big part of our family. I often used to lie in my room watching TV, listening to Readie's Frank Sinatra music being played from the room next door and him singing along at the top of his voice.'

7 July 2007

Basra

Lance Corporal Ryan Francis

Lance Corporal Francis, of the 2nd Battalion, The Royal Regiment of Wales, died when the armoured Warrior he was driving was hit by a roadside bomb during the same operation as Corporal Read.

Lance Corporal Francis's father Wyn paid tribute to his son, who was on his third tour of Iraq: 'Ryan was wonderful. I had three wonderful sons, now I've lost one of them.'

Lieutenant Colonel James Swift, Lance Corporal Francis's commanding officer, said, 'He was promoted to lance corporal on Christmas Day 2006 at lunch in front of the whole battalion – a very proud moment for him. He happily accepted this extra responsibility, had an easy leadership style and was developing into a very good junior leader. His strongest quality was that he was always a team player – he was the very centre of the team. In Iraq this time, he had been involved in almost all types of operation. His platoon is one of the best in the battle group, so it often finds itself with greater responsibility. Frankie thrived on this and was keen to get stuck in. He escorted convoys in order to make sure other soldiers had food to eat, he conducted successful cordon-and-search operations to arrest insurgents and make Basra safer, and he deployed over 100 kilometres to provide protection for another part of the battle group coming home from a difficult trip. He was always helping others.'

❖ ❖ ❖

Brigadier James Bashall laid blame for the increased attacks on British Forces in southern Iraq at Iran's door, suggesting that it was Tehran's intention to make it appear the British were being forced out. 'That is the whole strategy,' he stressed. 'Embarrass the West and make it look like they have bombed us out of Basra, out of Iraq, frankly. They [Iranians] are saying to these JAM [Madhi Army] guys, "Hey, look, I will give you money to fire rockets at the British," and they are providing training and technology. It makes our lives more difficult, as we are waging a proxy war against Iranian-backed secret cells, but it has not affected our military plan.'

Lieutenant Colonel Patrick Sanders agreed: 'There's no doubt Iranian support for the militias was pretty strong. They were providing weapons, ammunition and lethal aids. I think most of the training took place in Iran, but we certainly received a lot of intelligence reports of Iranians coming to Basra. Then we started to see mortar teams speaking Farsi in downtown Basra.'

19 July 2007

Basra Air Station

Senior Aircraftman Matthew Caulwell, Senior Aircraftman Christopher Dunsmore, Senior Aircraftman Peter McFerran

Royal Air Force personnel Senior Aircraftman Matthew Caulwell, Senior Aircraftman Christopher Dunsmore and Senior Aircraftman Peter McFerran were resting between repair shifts on 19 July 2007 when they were killed in a mortar attack on Basra Air Station.

Senior Aircraftman Dunsmore had been a part-time serviceman deployed to Iraq in late March, putting aside his commitments as a manager with a powder-coating business. His father Geoff hoped that his son's death would highlight the courage and commitment of the reserve forces, in particular those men and women from the Royal Auxiliary Air Force who received little media attention: 'People think of the auxiliary force as a bit of a Boy Scout force, but these people are well-trained and fight on the front line. Chris was trusted implicitly. He had served in Basra for almost four months, and on the evening he was killed was due home to start ten days' leave. During this period, he would have shared his 30th birthday with his family, friends and fiancée Donna.'

Senior Aircraftman McFerran's father received a letter from his son posted before he died to the family home in Connah's Quay, North Wales. His note included the words *Per Ardua*, Latin for 'Through Adversity', the motto of The Royal Air Force Regiment. His death came just a few weeks after a visit to North Wales on leave. He attended Mold Alyn High School and Deeside College before joining The Royal Air Force aged 21. He was due to complete his second tour of Iraq in September 2007. His funeral service with full military honours was held in St Mark's Church, Connah's Quay, followed by interment in Connah's Quay Cemetery. Parts of Deeside came to a halt as hundreds of people and Royal Air Force comrades paid their last respects. The coffin was draped in a Union Jack and was carried by six pall-bearers from The Queen's Colour Squadron, RAF Uxbridge, through a guard of honour.

His father Robert, a former Royal Air Force Regiment soldier and college lecturer, said, 'Peter was very, very fit. He joined The Royal Air Force at 21. It was always what he was going to do. We would go and see rugby together when we could. My son was brave and patriotic. He brought a laptop computer back that was broken and said it fell off his bed when a mortar fell outside the tent – that's the only way we knew they were getting close. There were a few attacks a week. We didn't know how many. Peter had more of a patrolling role. You always think they're safe in the airfield. It's the safest place compared to the army, who are out on the streets. The armed forces do look after each other as best they can. My argument has always been against the politicians.'

His mother Ann said, 'I haven't forgotten you, son, and I never will. You're always in my thoughts and always will be, my precious son.'

Senior Aircraftman Caulwell joined The Royal Air Force in 2001 and Number 1 Squadron, Royal Air Force Regiment, the following year. He was known as 'The Lip' for his ability to raise morale and had fought back from a serious ankle injury to remain on operational duty. More than 150 mourners paid tribute to him at a service at St Francis of Assisi Church, Bournville. He attended primary and secondary schools in the area and was an avid Birmingham City fan. Reverend Peter Babington described Senior Aircraftman Caulwell as 'everyone's friend'. He was survived by his parents, Judy and Steve, and his brothers Adam and Sean. 'Matthew was a loving son and brother, a devoted and tender godfather to three-year-old Olivia, and a loyal, caring friend to those he held close to him,' said Sean.

Squadron Leader Jason Sutton said, 'The loss of Senior Aircraftman Caulwell has been felt very deeply by all the squadron and by other members of 903 Expeditionary Air Wing. He rose to this new challenge magnificently, and the bearing and deportment of a junior non-commissioned officer came very naturally to him. His lads had the utmost respect for him and instinctively followed his example. Throughout all, his trademark good humour would keep up the spirits of his many friends.'

21 July 2007

Basra

Lance Corporal Timothy Flowers

On 21 July 2007, Lance Corporal Tim Flowers of The Royal Electrical and Mechanical Engineers died during an attack on Basra Palace that was similar to the one that had killed Senior Aircraftman Matthew Caulwell, Senior Aircraftman Christopher

Dunsmore and Senior Aircraftman Peter McFerran two days earlier. An inquest heard how the 25 year old from Londonderry, Northern Ireland, was repairing a Warrior vehicle when a shell landed a few metres from him as he went to fetch a generator. He was found face down wearing half-undone standard combat body armour. Soldiers were subsequently ordered to keep their vest fastened at all times.

Lance Corporal Flowers was described as a gifted mechanic, never happier than when he was in the tank park, spanner in hand. He had already resigned from the army, but Artifice Quartermaster Sergeant Lee attested that the lance corporal never let his impending departure affect his work: 'It is a testimony to the loyalty and courage of the man that he extended his service to see the job through with his friends, regardless of his personal situation. No job was too difficult or too much trouble. The diligent endeavour that he constantly displayed was as infectious as his cracking sense of humour.'

A former pupil of Condermott School, Waterside, Lance Corporal Flowers joined the army in 2003 after a period of service with The Royal Air Force. His mother Ann flew to RAF Lyneham to watch the repatriation of her son's body. His coffin, draped in a Union Jack, was carried by pall-bearers from a Hercules aircraft. At the time of his death, Lance Corporal Flowers was attached to 2nd Royal Tank Regiment, part of The Irish Guards battle group. Among those to comfort his mother was Rita Restorick, mother of Stephen Restorick, the last British soldier to be shot dead by the IRA in Northern Ireland. His funeral service was held at Burnside Presbyterian Church before his burial at Portstewart New Cemetery. A notice was placed in the family notices section of the *Belfast Telegraph*: 'Flowers, Timothy Darren (Lance Corporal), 21 July 2007 (suddenly), 51 Mill Road, Portstewart, dearly loved grandson of Granny Flowers, Lower Bennett Street, Londonderry.'

The commanding officer of The Irish Guards, Lieutenant Colonel Michael O'Dwyer, recalled an evening spent under the stars with Lance Corporal Flowers, listening to his views on life: 'He was bright, thoughtful and erudite, with intelligent opinions.'

31 July 2007

Basra

Corporal Steve Edwards

On 31 July 2007, Corporal Steve Edwards from the 2nd Royal Tank Regiment was on routine patrol in the Mustashfa district of Basra when his Warrior vehicle was struck by an improvised explosive device hidden by the roadside. Corporal Edwards had deployed to Iraq in May and was married to Gabriele. They had a young son, Ryan, and lived in Sutton Coldfield, West Midlands.

Lieutenant Colonel David Catmur, Corporal Edwards' commanding officer, said that the corporal's experience and kind-hearted nature were a great loss to his unit: 'Eddie epitomised all that is good about our soldiers and was an example to all.'

6 August 2007

Al-Fursi

Private Craig Barber

A week later, a freak ricochet cost Private Craig Barber his life. The enemy round was deflected through the window of the Welshman's Warrior and struck him fatally beneath the rim of his helmet. His colleagues from the 2nd Battalion, The Royal Welsh Regiment, could not at first understand why he was slumped across his seat. Platoon commander Second Lieutenant Oliver Pope told an inquest, 'The chances of that happening to someone in Craig's position were absolutely minute.'

Private Barber had been due to return home to Ogmore Vale, near Bridgend, on leave to celebrate his first wedding anniversary with wife Donna and their three-year-old son Bradley. He was on his second tour of Iraq when his battalion launched a night operation to counter direct-fire attacks on Basra Palace. His bed-space at the unit's base was decorated with pictures of his wife and child.

Private Barber's company commander, Major Steve Mannings, said, 'He was a huge physical presence in his platoon but was the epitome of the gentle giant. Always ready for a chat, always eager to please, he was an extremely popular young man. Craig died as he lived: working for others and helping to protect them.'

Private Barber's coffin was carried by horse and carriage through his home village on the day of his funeral, while shops on Ogmore High Street closed as a mark of respect and local residents in Blaengarw displayed Welsh flags in their windows. His funeral service was held at Coychurch Crematorium, Bridgend, and was attended by hundreds of family members, friends and service colleagues.

7 August 2007

Basra

Leading Aircraftman Martin Beard

On 7 August 2007, Leading Aircraftman Martin Beard of The Royal Air Force Regiment was fatally wounded by small-arms fire while on routine foot patrol through the al-Waki market north of Basra Air Station. According to colleagues, Leading Aircraftman Beard's quiet exterior hid a subtle sense of humour. The man from Rainworth, Nottinghamshire, had been serving with 1 Squadron, Royal Air Force Regiment, for a year. He was buried with full military honours at All Saints Church, Ripley, Derbyshire.

His family said, 'Martin was always incredibly loyal to his family, to his fiancée, to those privileged enough to know him as their friend and to The Royal Air Force Regiment. He will always be known for his fantastic and vibrant personality, and for his cheeky desire to be the centre of attention. The news of Martin's death has come as a huge shock to all of us, and his loss will create a huge gap in all our lives. To his sister Victoria, the memory of Martin giving her away at her wedding three months ago will always be the proudest moment of her life, a fact she knows would have instilled equal pride in their mother. Every time his fiancée Nic thinks of him, she always sees a picture of his smiling and happy face. She knows that although their future together is no longer possible, the happiness of the last four years will stay with her and keep her company for ever.'

Leading Aircraftman Matthew Brown, Leading Aircraftman Beard's long-standing friend, said, 'I first met "Beardy" on our basic training, when his confidence was obvious. He always found time to talk to you and cheer you up. He was a very happy, social person. I know he was very nervous about proposing to Nic, but when she said yes he could not wipe the smile off his face. A few weeks later, he was proudly giving away Victoria at her wedding and showing off in his uniform. But that was him: a poser on the sly. When I found out I was going to be on the same squadron, flight and fire team as him, and even be his battle buddy, I knew I would never get rid of him. He was a great soldier, never to be forgotten, and to be remembered for good things and good times.'

Squadron Leader Jason Sutton added that Leading Aircraftman Beard was 'strong, fit and an exceptionally gifted infantryman' with a bright future and high ambitions. 'He had set his sights on selection for Special Forces. I have no doubt whatsoever he would have succeeded in that as he did in all else. He was due to marry upon his return, and we all feel so deeply for his fiancée Nic.'

❖ ❖ ❖

While senior British Army officials continued to insist that the militias were not 'winning' in Basra, they were continuing to inflict heavy casualties and fatalities through their favoured method of engagement, the roadside improvised explosive device. The official line ran that the Madhi Army wanted to create, in the words of military spokesman Major Mike Shearer, a 'false impression' that the British were leaving because they were being pushed out.

9 August 2007

Rumaylah

Lance Sergeant Chris Casey, Lance Corporal Kirk Redpath

On 9 August 2007, two Irish guardsmen were killed. Lance Sergeant Chris Casey and Lance Corporal Kirk Redpath died when a device detonated beneath their Land Rover as they drove through the vicinity of the Rumaylah oil fields. The explosion caused the ammunition in the vehicle to 'cook off', engulfing the soldiers in flames. Both men were musicians from their regiment's pipe and drum band and were on their first escort duty in Iraq. Lance Corporal Redpath, from Romford, was not a regular on the vehicle crews. A member of the intelligence cell, he had volunteered for convoy duty to increase his local knowledge. He played the bugle. Lance Sergeant Casey, a married father of two from Aldershot, was a drummer who had performed at the Edinburgh Tattoo.

Lance Sergeant Casey's brother-in-law, Lance Sergeant Neil Nicholson, said, 'He was one of the finest musicians in The Irish Guards and the most professional soldier we have seen. Sadly, he leaves behind his wife Tanya, his son Kian and his daughter Ashlyn. He was a great family man, forever worrying about them and their well-being when he was away.'

A passage from Lance Corporal Redpath's next-of-kin letter was read out at his funeral:

> To my mum and dad, thank you for all your love and support over the many years, and also in the job that I love. To the rest of my family, don't be sad. To my many girlfriends in the legion and the lads: think of me when you have your wild parties out.

Lance Sergeant Lyttle, one of Lance Corporal 'Reders' Redpath's colleagues, said, 'If God spares me and I live long enough, I will look with great interest at any young men who aspire to join the army that show but half of Reders's quality. Only then will I advise them to make an application to join the "Fighting Micks". I am not ashamed to count my friend as among the finest of all Micks.'

An inquest heard that the soldiers' troop commander, Second Lieutenant Orlando Roberts, had asked for Mastiff vehicles to be employed on the convoy, as these offered greater protection than Land Rovers, but the Mastiffs had been prioritised for other missions.

Lance Corporal Redpath's father Colin said, 'We knew there were problems with equipment – we knew there was a shortage. It's the government's fault rather than the army's. The Irish Guards used the equipment they were given. Kirk did not die for Queen and country. He died for his regiment.'

5 September 2007

Baghdad

Sergeant Eddie Collins

On 1 September 2007, British Forces withdrew from Basra Palace. Four days later, Sergeant Eddie Collins became the seventh Special Forces fatality in Iraq when he was shot dead during a joint UK–US mission to target al-Qaeda in Baghdad.

The lack of reliable information about the circumstances of the shooting, and an abundance of speculation, highlighted the secrecy surrounding what was considered by many American commanders as Britain's biggest contribution to the conflict: the role of the UK's Special Forces. Hundreds of Special Air Service and Special Forces Support Group soldiers were fighting battles in and around the capital city. All the Ministry of Defence would say was that Sergeant Collins was killed while conducting a 'routine operation in support of coalition activity'.

According to his commanding officer, Sergeant Collins was a 'champion soldier, a proud and loving family man, and a great friend'.

21 September 2007

Died in UK Hospital After Accident at Basra Air Station

Sergeant Mark Stansfield

Sergeant Mark Stansfield of 32 Close Support Squadron, UK Logistic Battalion, was looking forward to becoming a father when he was killed in an accident involving a fork-lift truck at Basra Air Station on 21 September 2007. Sergeant Stansfield, from Bicester, Oxfordshire, was carrying out security checks when the accident occurred. He was operated on in theatre before being flown to Selly Oak Hospital, Birmingham, for further treatment. He had married his wife Joanne in St Lucia at Christmas the previous year and had joined the army aged 17. He died of his injuries in hospital in the UK.

His family said, 'Mark was a loving and devoted husband and he would have made a wonderful dad. Mark was also a loving son, brother and uncle. He was very much a family man. Mark will remain close in our hearts for always.'

His commanding officer, Lieutenant Colonel David Roberts, said, 'Sergeant Stansfield was a first-class soldier and a very fine senior non-commissioned officer, with an extremely bright career ahead of him. Mark had a wealth of experience from previous operational tours in the Balkans, Northern Ireland and Iraq, and his performance on Operation Telic had brimmed with his effervescent, enthusiastic and focused approach. He never shied from responsibility and was always keen to be in the thick of the action, never expecting anyone to do something he would not do himself. We will be much less in the future without Mark in our ranks. Our heartfelt thoughts and prayers are with Mark's wife Joanne, their unborn baby boy and their family.'

14 October 2007

Died in UK Hospital After Accident at Al-Udeid Airbase

Lance Corporal Sarah Holmes

Lance Corporal Sarah Holmes was working at the al-Udeid Airbase in Qatar on 14 October 2007 when the car in which she was a passenger collided with a truck. Lance Corporal Holmes, from Wantage, Oxfordshire, was flown back to Britain for treatment. She died from her injuries with her family at her bedside. She had deployed to the Gulf as part of 80 Postal and Courier Squadron, Royal Logistics Corps. Her death came shortly before her operational tour was due to end. Lance Corporal Holmes had previously served in Northern Ireland, the former Republic of Yugoslavia, Kenya and Poland.

Major Neil Blenkinsop of The Royal Logistics Corps said, 'She will forever be remembered as a first class "postie" and a true friend to all those who had the pleasure of knowing her. Having served alongside her at the British Forces Post Office in Basra, I fondly remember her quick wit and infectious sense of humour.'

20 November 2007

Baghdad

Sergeant John Battersby, Trooper Lee Fitzsimmons

Sergeant John Battersby and Trooper Lee Fitzsimmons died when the wreckage of a crashed Royal Air Force Lynx helicopter exploded in the Salman Pak district of Baghdad. Seconds earlier, their colleagues in the Special Air Service had attempted to free them from the downed aircraft. They were forced to withdraw because the helicopter was leaking fuel.

Twelve other injured personnel were dragged to safety. An inquest heard that the pilot lost control on landing when his rotor blades kicked up an enormous dust cloud. Sergeant Battersby, formerly of The Queen's Lancashire Regiment, and Trooper Fitzsimmons, formerly of The Royal Marines, belonged to A Squadron, 22 SAS, based in Hereford and had only recently passed Special Air Service selection.

Trooper Fitzsimmons's mother, Jacqui Arty, said, 'I cannot believe that it has happened and that I will never see or hold Lee again. It is some small comfort knowing that he loved his job, knew the risks and would not have had it any other way, but it does not make up for the aching loss I feel.' Trooper Fitzsimmons had joined the Royal Marines aged 17 and also saw action in Afghanistan.

At the time of the accident, the SAS were about to launch an operation to storm a compound used by insurgents. They pressed on in spite of the deaths and captured at least two terrorists.

13 December 2007

Died in UK Hospital After Accident in Basra

Guardsman Stephen Ferguson

Guardsman Stephen Ferguson was fatally wounded on 13 December 2007 when his Warrior vehicle slid into a canal during a night manoeuvre in Basra. His friends pulled him from the wreckage and gave him first aid. He was flown back to the UK but died at Selly Oak Hospital. The 31 year old from Motherwell had served in The Scots Guards for almost 12 years. A popular driver, he used to joke with the company mechanics about their vehicles: 'If you can fix them, I can break them.'

Guardsman Ferguson was the joker in his battalion. He wore daft hats and shaped his camouflage cream to craft a Groucho Marx-style moustache. His dying wish was to be buried in a Motherwell Football Club shirt, holding a bottle of whisky. The club donated a signed shirt, held a minute's applause before a home match in his honour, delivered a bouquet of flowers to his mother and offered his family the use of a private box at the stadium.

His family said he was a 'fantastic son, loved by all those who knew him'.

His friends Robert Kennedy and John Shilliday said, 'Stephen was the life and soul of the party. He had a love of life and was proud to serve his country. Being in the army was all he ever wanted to do, and if he was going to die, he would have liked to have died on active service. There's no anger towards anyone for causing his death – just a pride in the job he was doing.'

❖ ❖ ❖

A simple ceremony in a disused departure lounge at Basra International Airport marked Britain's formal handing over of control of Basra to the Iraqi government. Fittingly, it was one of the commanders of the initial invasion, Major General Graham Binns, who shook hands with local dignitaries and national security advisor Muwaffaq al-Rubaie. Major General Binns, who had commanded a brigade in 2003, said that he was 'handing the city back to its friends'. 'We are guests in your country,' he said, 'and we will act accordingly.'

2008

29 February 2008

Basra Air Station

Sergeant Duane Barwood

On 29 February 2008, insurgents pounded Basra Air Station with rockets and mortars. Thousands of machine-gun rounds fired into the sky took out most but not all of the rockets. Such an occurrence was far from unusual: on one day in February alone, 27 missiles were counted targeting the base. On this occasion, Sergeant Duane Barwood, attached to 903 Expeditionary Air Wing, was fatally wounded. He died ten days before he had been due to leave Iraq and was the first British serviceman to be lost to the enemy in southern Iraq for six months.

Sergeant Barwood had received a commendation for his bravery following a rocket attack on his position. Senior officers spoke of his 'strong judgement and exceptional courage' in the fulfilment of his duties as the airfield motor transport officer.

Sergeant Barwood, from Carterton, Oxfordshire, was survived by his wife Sharon and daughters Leanna and Rebecca. His family said that he was a much-loved husband, father and friend who would be greatly missed by all those who knew him: 'He was a very proud and dedicated member of The Royal Air Force, who gave his life for the job he loved. Baz lived life to the full and will never, ever be forgotten.'

Corporal Ed Way knew Sergeant Barwood for ten years. He added, 'He was the most professional, loyal and committed serviceman I ever met. His guidance to me and all those who were fortunate to work with him was second to none. He was a caring, honest and refreshingly genuine person who will always be remembered.'

Group Captain Malcolm Brecht, officer commanding RAF Brize Norton, said, 'He was a caring and diligent man with a larger-than-life personality. Sergeant Barwood was admired and respected.'

26 March 2008

Baghdad

Nicholas Brown

The last British soldier to die at the time of writing was Special Air Service volunteer Nicholas Brown. On 26 March 2008, he was killed in a fire fight with militias in central Iraq. His identity was revealed by the *Hereford Times*, his and the regiment's local newspaper, but his rank was not disclosed. He had grown up in the city.

Introduction to Postscript

The deaths of the Red Caps in Majar al-Kabir encompass many issues of the Iraq campaign. After five years of investigation, I am of the mind that the deceased were done an injustice when it was concluded officially that their deaths could not have been prevented. They deserve an acknowledgement to the contrary and a formal apology. Where there was negligence, it was neither criminal nor malicious. I do not favour legal action against military personnel.

The six Royal Military Policemen were executed at a police station that they visited on the morning of 24 June 2003 to train local officers, enquire as to why they had failed to intervene when the building was attacked two days previously and to deliver money so that the damage could be repaired. The following passages explain the background to these events and describe in 'real time' the events themselves. I regret the constraints of this book preclude other events being given similarly in-depth consideration.

This section is wholly factual and based upon lengthy research, evidence from a Board of Inquiry, an inquest and interviews with survivors, many of whom were not called to Oxford Coroners' Court. Dialogue and direct speech is based upon the protagonists' explicit recollections given on oath in official hearings and interviews. Timings are those used by the Board of Inquiry.

Mark Nicol
London, August 2008

Postscript

The Red Caps were led by Sergeant Simon Hamilton-Jewell, a 41-year-old single man from Chessington, Surrey. There was a darker, private side to this gregarious former Special Air Service reservist. As he explained in his next-of-kin letter, 'No one really knows every part of my life; some people know some things and other people know other things. No one person knows it all and the sum of everyone's knowledge is not a true reflection of my life.'

Known to everyone as 'H.J.', Sergeant Hamilton-Jewell never married but prior to his deployment spoke of proposing to Katie, who was 19 years old. He said that after speaking to her father he would take her to Paris.

Sergeant Hamilton-Jewell's letters rarely mentioned the inhumane heat and working conditions, topics which dominated his colleagues' missives. While Hamilton-Jewell was considered to be 'on permanent send', in the vernacular of military communications, his private writings revealed humility and natural intelligence. He saw the bigger picture, and realised the importance of the mission and of leading his colleagues, many of whom were half his age, by example.

His deputy in C Section was Corporal Russ Aston. The 30 year old from rural south Derbyshire was a lovable rogue whose company was widely enjoyed. He was married to Anna, and they had a daughter Paygan. The war got under Corporal Aston's sunburned skin. He suggested he had been bitten by every insect in Maysan Province and that he missed his local pub's 'flat beer and ugly women'. While he had spoken previously of leaving the army, he insisted that Anna should look into career options in the Prison Service on his behalf.

Lance Corporal Ben Hyde, from Northallerton, North Yorkshire, delighted in Coporal Aston's scorpion bites, reminding the handsome but vain former grenadier guardsman that he 'did not like anything messing with his precious face'. Lance Corporal Hyde was a proud, diligent Red Cap with something to prove, having left The Royal Marines after 16 weeks' training when his girlfriend gave him an ultimatum: her or military life. He left the Commando Training Centre, Lympstone, Devon, only for them to separate. Lance Corporal Hyde thought that he had let himself and his family down. He would not do so again. His grandfather was a Normandy Landings veteran, while his father John regretted not joining the services himself. When his son's application to join his local constabulary was declined, he enlisted with The Royal Military Police.

Suffering from desperation and boredom, Lance Corporal Hyde listed his priorities upon returning to Britain in a letter home:

> Have sex, get drunk, eat steak, have a bath, sleep in a bed, get up when I feel like it, have a shit in peace, have sex again, get drunk again, persuade Mum to buy me clothes from the catalogue, put on clean clothes, go to the supermarket, watch telly for a week.

Lance Corporal Thomas Keys was also showing the strain. His parents were stunned to hear he hated Arabs and thought Iraq a 'shitehole'.

In early May, all The Royal Military Police personnel attached to the 1st Battalion, The Parachute Regiment, battle group were hoping to avoid a 'spamming'. As Lance Corporal Keys wrote:

> Well, I've heard some dates . . . 4 to 14 June. Only one problem. They want a platoon strength of 25 people to stay behind for an extra month. As yet we don't know who those 25 people are. It is possible I could be one of them.

When I know for certain, I will give you a ring, but let's hope I'm not one of the ones to get spammed for staying behind.

As a teenage private soldier in the 1st Battalion, The Parachute Regiment, Lance Corporal Keys had taken part in Operation Barras to rescue members of The Royal Irish Regiment held by the West Side Boys in Sierra Leone. He was only a few weeks out of the training depot, and it did not cross his parents' minds as they watched footage of the operation that he would be taking part. 'They'll have sent seasoned Paras, Sally, not our Tom,' said Reg. Stunned to learn that his son had been one of those sprinting towards the terrorists, who were firing heavy machine guns, Reg suggested that he might consider joining a 'safer' unit. He transferred to The Royal Military Police.

To Lance Corporal Keys' chagrin, the Red Caps provided less stimulation. He wrote:

> I haven't seen an Iraqi soldier yet. We are right at the dud end of the action, so try not to worry too much. More people have been killed by accidents than enemy fire . . . No problems apart from being bored out of my mind. It's all chilled out, fighting pretty much stopped, now dealing with policing the towns and humanitarian aid, wearing floppy hats and no body armour . . . A bit of a holiday camp [here] at the moment! There isn't much for us to do at all. At the moment we are just offering advice to the local police to try and restore some normality here.

When he was chosen for the 'Stay Behind Party', Lance Corporal Keys was separated from his girlfriend, Lance Corporal Joanne Richardson, a fellow Red Cap. They planned to celebrate their reunion with a holiday in the United States.

The newly promoted Corporal Simon Miller was protective towards his fiancée Lance Corporal Emma Morris. Corporal Miller, from Washington, Tyne-and-Wear, wrote love notes to her as they worked together in 156 Provost Company headquarters.

Corporal Paul Long bemoaned his vacation with 'Bush and Blair Tours' and wrote, 'I will never go on holiday with this company again. The brochure promised state-of-the-art war, luxury hotels, two to a room. No murder mystery here. Bush did it. War? What war? Have I been to war?' Corporal Long likened the singing imams of al-Amarah to rap artists and renamed them 'DJ Az and Co'. Behind his aviator sunglasses, Corporal Long was a sensitive soul, devoted to Gemma and their baby. He could not wait to take tiny Benjamin to meet his mother in South Shields, Tyne-and-Wear, and eat her homemade cheese-and-onion pies. Corporal Long had joined the regular army after a stint as a reservist. According to his mother, he had dismissed the idea of joining the Metropolitan Police, as London was 'too dangerous'. As he counted down the days to his return, to die of boredom seemed the biggest threat to his life.

Sergeant Hamilton-Jewell's men were attached to C Company, 1 Para, commanded by Major Chris Kemp. The company consisted of three rifle platoons, numbered 7, 8 and 9. While the Red Caps sought to achieve their goals through mediation, the Paras' strategy was more assertive. C Company seldom took a backward step, as a couple of incidents that took place prior to 24 June 2003 demonstrated. Occasions when the Red Caps and Paras came face to face laid bare their differences.

On the evening of 26 May 2003, Sergeant Gordon Robertson led a 12-man patrol through the Hay Abu Romaneh district of al-Amarah. His interpreter Joseph had told him that criminal gangs were trading weapons there. Sergeant Robertson, from Ayrshire, held the world record for the military marathon, running twenty-six miles in boots and carrying a forty-pound pack in four hours forty minutes – a respectable time without such a burden. His second-in-command that evening was Corporal John Dolman, known as 'The Dolmanator'. Corporal Dolman, from Olleton, Nottinghamshire, was as formidable as his sobriquet suggested and often shouted 'Cuckoo', mocking those who thought him crazy. After an investigation cleared Corporal Dolman's shooting of a civilian protester in Pristina, Kosovo, there was no love lost between him and The Royal Military Police.

When Sergeant Robertson put his finger to his lips, his Paras fell silent. Joseph, an elderly Christian from Majar al-Kabir, sat beside him. 'Slow it down,' Robertson whispered to his driver, 'in case they've got dickers out.' The patrol continued with the vehicle lights off. 'OK,' Robertson said abruptly. 'Quick battle orders: John's [Dolman] boys, you get out here. The radios are crap, and we won't be able to speak to each other on them. So if you get into a contact, fire some tracer in the air. We'll see it and provide support.'

One of those to dismount was Private Freddie Ellis, a soldier with a dramatic part to play on 24 June 2003. Essex boy Private Ellis loved himself and his regiment, and had left a madcap life behind to enlist. His teeth were like a good fighting patrol: well spaced out. He had picked out his molars with a compass.

The Pinzgauer chugged away to leave Corporal Dolman, Private Ellis and two other private soldiers squeezed against an exterior wall. Wa'el Rahim Jabar, a baker working to support his mother, wife and two children, was strolling with two friends, Majed Jasem and Mu'taz 'Ati, along the same street with a Kalashnikov slung casually over his right shoulder. This was in breach of the British Army edict that weapons should be kept at home, a ruling some considered insensitive to local customs.

After spotting Jabar standing beside a car, Dolman scuttled forward to confront him. The car headlights flashed on, bathing him in white light and leaving him dangerously exposed. Jabar uncoiled his rifle and walked towards Corporal Dolman.

'Stop,' the corporal ordered. 'Put down your weapon, now.'

Jabar spoke as little English as Corporal Dolman spoke Arabic. Corporal Dolman repeated his command then dropped to one knee. When Jabar raised his rifle, Corporal Dolman fired three single shots. Jabar collapsed dead as his friends, who were unarmed, ran for their lives. The neighbourhood stirred. Dogs barked. Corporal Dolman stood over Jabar's body.

As a crowd gathered and fired shots in the air, Corporal Dolman ordered his colleagues to form a defensive cordon. The corporal fired tracer into the air to summon Sergeant Robertson.

He sounded almost apologetic when the sergeant arrived: 'We've had a contact.'

Sergeant Robertson gazed down at Jabar's body and back up at Corporal Dolman. There was a heavy pause. 'All right, John . . .'

'Hello, Robbo,' Corporal Dolman replied.

'I see youse have got another one . . . When are you going to grow up?'

'He was going to shoot me,' Corporal Dolman pleaded.

Sergeant Robertson's face cracked into a smile. 'Don't worry about it, John. You're not in trouble with me!'

'Thank f***. I thought you was going to give me shit.'

'We'll have to radio the ops room. Colonel Beckett [the commanding officer of 1 Para] and the RMPs will be down. You should know the drill well enough by now, eh?'

Senior officers congratulated Sergeant Robertson for his execution of a well-worked plan. Corporal Dolman was aggrieved not to get the credit, as 'it was me who slotted 'im'.

'Rank has its advantages, John,' Sergeant Robertson replied.

When two Royal Military Policemen approached Corporal Dolman to take his statement, he eyed them curiously. 'I know you from somewhere, don't I?'

'Do you?' replied one of the police officers as he flicked through his notebook.

'Yeah, that's right,' Corporal Dolman said. 'You were the monkey who dealt with me in Kosovo!'

While no charges were brought against Corporal Dolman – it was concluded that he had acted within the rules of engagement – officers visited Jabar's family to express their condolences. The family lodged a formal complaint, supported by Amnesty International. They claimed that he had been assigned by his local community as a security guard to stave off thieves.

Jabar's death was toasted at Camp Abu Naji as 'the first kill for the regiment'. An officer opened a fresh bottle of whisky and poured drams for Sergeant Robertson and Corporal Dolman.

'The regiment,' they responded in chorus.

Sergeant Hamilton-Jewell's men were frequent visitors to Majar al-Kabir, where 60,000 people squeezed into an urban space that measured just four kilometres from north to south and three kilometres from east to west. On its outskirts, sloping warehouse roofs knelt to meet the horizon. To the south, the River Majar parted into the Adil and Wadiya tributaries and the dried marshland area began. The town also enjoyed a quirky notoriety for *dhakar binta*, teenage boys hired to dance and entertain at weddings. Living conditions were basic, with regular power cuts, drinking water in short supply and little paid employment. The townsfolk did not like being dictated to or told how many weapons they were allowed – or when and where they could carry them. They also objected to weapons searches. On occasions when the Paras were too rough, Joseph would intervene, saying, 'No, no, Mr Robertson. No need for that.' The stoning of patrols was instigated by anti-coalition elements and Iranian factions. Claims were rife that British soldiers were conspiring with Saddam to steal oil. Israeli involvement in a petroleum conspiracy was suspected.

The Red Caps were often at the police station while Lieutenant Ross Kennedy, the commander of 8 Platoon, and Sergeant Robertson conducted patrols of the town. The Red Caps and Paras would bump into each other by chance, unaware of each other's presence. The Red Caps declined the Paras' offers to escort them to and from Majar al-Kabir, as they preferred not to be seen in such forceful company.

Sergeant Robertson arrived at the police station one day to find two members of C Section playing outside with water-pistols. Their casual attitude to security left him dismayed. When Sergeant Robertson visited the building, with its blood-stained walls, he deployed a young paratrooper on the roof armed with a heavy machine gun. In line with their soft posture, the Red Caps routinely left their rifles in their vehicles. While Sergeant Robertson's men were 'armed to the teeth', Sergeant Hamilton-Jewell and his colleagues had been reduced to 50 rounds per man. They were also short on numbers. While the two-thirds reduction in 156 Provo's strength was in line with the downscaling of other units, it placed a considerable burden on those who remained.

In spite of the Iraqi attitude towards women, several female Red Caps had been chosen to stay on, including Corporal Miller's fiancée Lance Corporal Morris. As one male Red Cap recalled,

'We had a couple of blonde girls in our section, and they were getting stoned. This one time, the villagers came out, stared and threw rocks at Lianne Fielding and Cath Berrows. The locals were doing that sort of thing all the time. After that stoning, there was only a couple of girls going out on the ground. They either wouldn't go or couldn't go because they weren't allowed. But it didn't make sense keeping so many of them out there, because it left more work for the rest of us.'

The 25-strong stay-behind party was supplemented by a new company sergeant major. Warrant Officer Matthew 'Bob' Marley observed a slippage in his colleagues' standards of personal administration. 'He [Marley] wasn't there for any of the build-up or the war-fighting,' one Red Cap recalled. 'By the time he came out, everyone was bollocksed. He wanted to put it on orders that people had to shave in the mornings, but we weren't getting any time to do it. Si Miller was in trouble for having a traffic accident. He crashed a Land Rover because he was knackered. It was simply down to fatigue. The hours we were doing were ridiculous. We couldn't admin ourselves up.'

Under the strain of operations, teamwork gave way to one-upmanship, with the misuse of a fridge causing friction. A Red Cap said, 'We'd be out on the ground grafting and all the rear echelon guys would nick them or put their names on the bottles so we'd have no water. They were taking the piss, and that's our own people, RMPs! That's what it's like when you're on ops. You learn who the real guys are and who the f***ers are.'

Lance Corporal Hyde was another vociferous complainant. He wrote to his father:

> Well, another boiling hot day over here. It's 11 p.m., and I couldn't be any wetter if I'd just been in the shower with my clothes on. Two 15-year sergeants signed off to get out of the army today. They are so disgusted with the way we are being treated. I can't sign off for another year, more is the pity. It's red hot, you get no food, no sleep, you can't wash properly and you get treated like shit. We're the hardest-working unit in the brigade by far.

In a letter to his mother, Corporal Long described himself as 'very hot, very sweaty, very dirty, very bored and pissed off'.

At a party staged to raise morale, Sergeant Hamilton-Jewell wore one of Lance Corporal Morris's black thongs as an eye-patch and presented Lance Corporal Keys with a cake made of congealed Mars bars in anticipation of his 21st birthday. The Red Caps forgot their troubles that night as tracer flashed across the night sky above Camp Abu Naji. They posed for photographs with their shirts off, holding cans of lager.

Sergeant Hamilton-Jewell had been raised by his mother Teresa and older step-brother Tony Fisher. The whereabouts of his father were unknown. Before his deployment, he was a doting step-parent to his girlfriend Katie's son Ollie.

As June 2003 progressed, he emailed his friend Lee:

> Hello, mate. Looks like I'm flying back on 12 July [2003], so I will be on the piss soon after. Katie will be out with me and no doubt will have to carry me home, having been dry for five months. I will be on leave until 1 September [2003] and will spend most of that time training hard and eating well. I have lost twenty-two pounds (ten kilos or a stone and a half). I'm pretty skinny, but there isn't an ounce of fat on me. Got a few photos and some amusing stories to tell. So keep your head down, and I will see you soon. H.

Major Kemp ordered Lieutenant Kennedy to Majar al-Kabir to 'smile at people' and collect but not search for weapons. On 22 June 2003, the soldiers of 8 Platoon began an intended 72-hour watch at the police station.

As he later told the inquest, Lieutenant Kennedy thought the townspeople fickle and impossible to please. They were hostile and on most days greeted his arrival with fingers pulled across their throats.

As his soldiers sunbathed naked, Lieutenant Kennedy's rooftop sentry observed scores of men chanting, pumping their fists and holding banners that read 'Death to Amerika'. Lieutenant Kennedy jumped from his mattress in an empty cell as his colleagues dressed hastily, and Lance Corporal Mark Weadon sprinted up the concrete stairs onto the roof. While Private Tim May and Private Richie Clement were posted on the front door, the Iraqi police officers, trained exhaustively by the Red Caps, cowered in the back of the station.

Lieutenant Kennedy heard shots fired from the roof. As the mob attacked the Paras' vehicles, Lance Corporal Weadon had taken it upon himself to fire live rounds above their heads. When Lieutenant Kennedy rebuked him, Lance Corporal Weadon insisted that it had been his 'mission command', or decision, in response to the protesters' actions. Lieutenant Kennedy disagreed, believing warning shots would exacerbate the situation. He thought most of the protesters would confuse the motive behind them. The stone-throwing intensified and more windows were broken. Two baton rounds (plastic bullets) were fired, one of which bounced off the ground and stuck a protester's head. Another was injured in unarmed combat.

When Lieutenant Kennedy made an emergency call to base, operations officer Captain Richard Todd's response suggested an agenda to 'occupy' the town. 'Ross, it's Toddy. Stay there if you can. We do not want to be seen to be forced out.'

'Toddy, we've got no chance of extracting. There's too many people. I hope someone can come and get us.'

'We'll crash out the QRF [quick-reaction force],' Captain Todd replied.

Abu Hateem, at the time one of the most influential men in Maysan, persuaded the crowd to disperse and promised to take up the locals' grievances with the British. The arrival of the quick-reaction force – a column of armoured vehicles and heavily armed open-top Land Rovers – hurried protesters on their way.

On 23 June, Major Kemp, Company Sergeant Major Grant Naylor and an officer from the 1st Battalion, The King's Own Scottish Borderers – who were due to replace the Paras – met elders and councillors. While a simple option was to make Majar al-Kabir a 'no go' area, if only temporarily, this had been prohibited by divisional commanders. Conscious of the need to generate goodwill, Major Kemp agreed an immediate suspension of weapon searches to allow for a 'joint approach to confiscation' to develop over the following months. He stressed that his soldiers would continue to patrol, on their own and with local militia units. The militia had played a key role in the self-liberation of Maysan Province and commanded greater respect than the police force.

Major Kemp signed a document written in Arabic and English. While this was intended to clarify the position between the 'two tribes', it was nonsensical and entirely confusing:

> The process of searching heavy weapons in al-Majar district to the Security Commission and the Foujer established inside the district and the province and there is no necessity that the Coalition and its different people be there – and according to the following strategical plan. Searching heavy weapons for two months, before that, a period of a week must be given to inform people to hand their heavy weapons including Dushka, mortars, heavy cannons and ground defence weapons against airplanes. We want to see results in one month.

Major Kemp ordered all 24 members of 8 Platoon back into the town on 24 June to 'show a presence'. The doubling of strength from 22 June, when only 12 soldiers were there, was a sign of intent. As he told Lieutenant Kennedy, 'Ross, this is your area of operations. Focus on Majar al-Kabir. You can settle it down. You should patrol through the market place.'

Sergeant Robertson later said that Major Kemp suggested he 'cut Ross some slack'. As was customary, the more experienced and able platoon sergeant had been taking the lead. Lieutenant Kennedy duly asserted his authority when he declined Sergeant Robertson's advice to notify Major Kemp of the shooting incident involving Lance Corporal Weadon. This decision returned to haunt the young officer. While his only intention had been to protect Lance Corporal Weadon, not to mislead army investigators, a Board of Inquiry condemned his failure to disclose the matter during interview. Lieutenant Kennedy's rebuke came after Lance Corporal Weadon admitted to Special Investigation Branch detectives that he had opened fire.

In preparation for the return to Majar al-Kabir, Sergeant Robertson requested additional rubber bullets. He was denied extra non-lethal rounds, as they were already boxed ready to be returned to Britain. This left him with thirteen, six of which he issued to Corporal Dolman.

Sergeant Hamilton-Jewell often got his way with his platoon commander Lieutenant Richard Phillips, who was a softly spoken subaltern and barely half the sergeant's age. As Lieutenant Phillips later conceded, he bowed to Sergeant Hamilton-Jewell's greater knowledge. Sergeant Hamilton-Jewell knew many officers at Majar al-Kabir by their first names, and his informality and humour played well with them. As the senior 156 Provo rank at Abu Naji, Lieutenant Phillips juggled various responsibilities and pressures. When he was asked to explain The Royal Military Police role, he said that it was to 'train policemen in all the local stations, write down incidents and control the towns with the consent of the local people'. He added that he expected his Royal Military Police officers to 'pass on basic knowledge and skills, using notebooks and implementing shift systems'. By his own admission, Lieutenant Phillips rarely visited the police station at Majar al-Kabir.

Late on 23 June, Lieutenant Phillips reminded Sergeant Hamilton-Jewell that his priority the following day was to reach al-Uzayr at lunchtime to meet Brigadier Jonathan Page, the commanding officer of 16 Air Assault Brigade. Sergeant Hamilton-Jewell agreed and confirmed that he would merely pass through Majar al-Kabir and Qalat Salih en route, spending approximately an hour in each town. He added that he would ask why the local police had failed to intervene during the attack on the station and hand over US dollars to pay for the necessary repairs. Sergeant Hamilton-Jewell should have been lying beside a swimming pool in Kuwait, rather than spending another long hot day on the road, but his promised rest-and-recreation break had been cancelled at short notice.

The sun's rays fanned upwards from beneath the horizon, and the sound of 'happy fire' from al-Amarah stirred the sleeping Red Caps. Lance Corporal Keys was so desperate to return home that most of his kit was already packed. His ankle was strapped following a strain during a football match.

Early that morning, Lieutenant Kennedy and Sergeant Robertson checked out through the operations room. Lieutenant

Kennedy's 'flap sheet' – a hand-sized piece of white paper – listed his soldiers' names, military numbers, blood groups and radio call-sign codes. He also listed the registration number of his platoon's DAF truck and two Pinzgauer open-topped personnel carriers. The flap sheet was placed on an A4-sized clipboard and the information transferred onto the current-situation, call-sign and location-status boards. Lieutenant Kennedy also signed for two satellite, or Iridium, phones, one each for the two equal-strength multiples, Alpha and Bravo. They also took VHF and HF radio equipment, even though the platoon commander considered the heavy kits 'absolutely ineffective'. Range, flat landscape, dry air and power lines in central Majar al-Kabir reduced the effectiveness of these communication channels. Although the batteries died at critical times and the phones directed soldiers' calls to answering machines at times of crisis, the satellite handsets were the primary communications asset. In order to preserve battery life, the phones were only switched on to make calls. Routine communications were made during 'time windows'. Alpha and Bravo's departure time was listed as 0900.

Sergeant Hamilton-Jewell visited the operations room to check out and print off name badges for the Iraqi policemen. According to his colleagues, he hoped that the labels would inspire a sense of corporate identity and encourage active, engaging policing. The local police were also awaiting delivery of uniforms. He told Warrant Officer Marley that he was only mildly concerned about the events of 22 June. As the warrant officer told an inquest, Sergeant Hamilton-Jewell did not think that he would have to alter his routine but would ask why the police did not protect the station or force back the mob. Lieutenant Phillips again reminded Sergeant Hamilton-Jewell of the importance of getting to al-Uzayr on time. 'You need to talk to C Company,' he added. 'Let them know what you're doing. Double check.'

Sergeant Hamilton-Jewell paced over to the C Company desk and Captain Jonathan Palmer. A few days previously, Sergeant Hamilton-Jewell's failure to notify him of his movements had earned a rebuke from the officer.

The Red Caps were given the radio call-sign '33J', and their times of departure and projected return were written onto a white board. When Sergeant Hamilton-Jewell bumped into Major Kemp, they too discussed the meeting in al-Uzayr. The conversation did not include reference to the Red Caps' visit to Majar al-Kabir. As the environment was considered benign, and the functions of C Company and 156 Provo were different, Major Kemp saw no need for mutual support.

Sergeant Hamilton-Jewell did not complete a full flap sheet, but in accordance with Royal Military Police standard practice provided an outline schedule without precise timings. He handed the sheet to Warrant Officer Marley, who placed a pin next to 'Majar al-Kabir' on the map that sat on a bird table. Sergeant Hamilton-Jewell's time of departure was listed as 0910. He did not take a satellite phone; the Red Caps did not use them.

The six Red Caps climbed into three Land Rovers and drove in convoy around Camp Abu Naji's one-way system, through the main gate and a further kilometre to a set of stone arches. The landmark at the junction with the Route 6 highway represented the boundary between two worlds: British and Iraqi; safe and unsafe.

At 0930, the Paras entered Majar al-Kabir, passing municipal buildings and the road leading to the police station on their left. Lieutenant Kennedy and Sergeant Robertson's men turned right, crossed the town's northern bridge and arrived at the headquarters of the civil militia, or 'Fawjer'. A few stones were thrown at the DAF.

The Red Caps arrived at the police station at 0940 to find their interpreter waiting and his rusty bicycle leaning against an exterior wall. Mr Ghazi worked at the State Sugar Company factory on the town's northern outskirts and was hired by police chief Abu Dhia Kadhim. The Red Caps introduced themselves, and Sergeant Hamilton-Jewell, Corporal Aston and Lance Corporal Hyde were ushered into the building. Ghazi was eager to ingratiate himself, and in a statement to investigators referred to the military policemen as 'beloved liberators' and 'lion-hearted Englishmen'. Corporal Long, Corporal Miller and Lance Corporal Keys remained with the vehicles, where their rifles and body armour were kept.

Lieutenant Kennedy set off on a foot patrol with the militia, while Sergeant Robertson remained at the Fawjer building. At

0955, Alpha moved out in staggered file, watching their arcs for threats. At 1005, a 4x4 vehicle drove at speed towards the patrol. Militia commander Talal Zubeida stuck his shaven head out the passenger window and barked at Lieutenant Kennedy. Joseph translated Zubeida's remarks: 'What are you doing? The British said no more searches.'

'We're not here to search,' Lieutenant Kennedy replied. 'We want to patrol with the militia. My sole aim is to be seen working with the militia – to patrol, not to search. Soft posture.'

'What are you doing with my men?' snapped Zubeida, seeing locals he recognised on patrol.

'These men were volunteers to come with us. We had to say no to others. Mr Zubeida,' Lieutenant Kennedy explained, 'we are here to patrol through the town, not to search.'

'If you continue on, you will come under some serious attack. Not safe.'

'Sorry?'

'Bad men in town today. There will be bloodshed. You will be attacked.'

Major Kemp's instruction to Lieutenant Kennedy had been explicit: to patrol through the marketplace, the beating heart of the town. 'What can we do to carry out our patrol?' Lieutenant Kennedy asked.

'Nothing.'

'What about in vehicles?'

A compromise was reached, with some adjustments to the intended route. Lieutenant Kennedy turned his patrol around.

As Sergeant Robertson later admitted, he reacted strongly to news of Lieutenant Kennedy's exchange with Zubeida. He recalled telling the subaltern at the time, 'We're not getting told what to do by those f***ers, Ross! You've had your shot. You stay here. I'll take John [Dolman] with me, and we'll go out in the Pinzes. We've got to show a presence – show we're not scared.'

Bravo set off with Joseph and the militia, driving south along the riverbank. Trouble began almost as soon as they entered the market. When youths attempted to block Lance Corporal Steve Oellerman's path, Sergeant Robertson ordered him to drive through the 500-strong crowd. Sergeant Robertson urged

279

his soldiers to 'stay switched on' and to identify any gunmen.

The chanting began: 'La, La Amerika. La, La Amerika.'

The locals were convinced that the Paras were there to conduct searches. Messages were broadcast via speakers on rooftops: 'They are coming for our weapons. We must not let them. Arm yourselves. They want to fight us.'

By 1020, the locals closed in. Meanwhile, there were at least 100 protesters throwing rocks outside the Fawjer building. The situation at the police station remained calm.

Back in the marketplace, fists punched the bonnets of Bravo's vehicles. Sergeant Robertson took action. 'OK, dismount!' He stood up. 'Form a cordon and walk the vehicles through. Push them back. We can't afford to go static.'

With the Paras' helmets and body armour aboard the Pinzes, stones hurt when the Iraqis scored direct hits. Sergeant Robertson and Corporal Dolman spoke on their personal radios: 'Robbo, I'm getting a lot of incoming [stones]. Permission to fire baton rounds?'

'If you see the need to fire them, John, then fire them.'

Locals delivered another volley of rocks, cracking Corporal Billy Brown's windscreen. Corporal Dolman identified a ringleader and slid the first dummy into the gun. The round left the chamber with a dull thud amid a plume of white smoke. Up to 50 metres, the gun caused internal injuries comparable with a golf ball driven at close range. The youth fell, and the crowd backed off.

'I'm going to fire another round, Robbo.'

'You crack on, John.'

Corporal Dolman put two youths on the ground, writhing in pain. The crowd surged, throwing kerbstones. Sergeant Robertson attempted to call the ops room on his satellite phone but could not get a signal. He tried the radio, also to no avail. As Corporal Dolman expended his stock, Sergeant Robertson fired his seven in quick succession, creating space for the vehicles to advance.

'Keep the momentum going, Steve.'

Sergeant Robertson looked back to see that the militia were absent; their courage had deserted them at the moment of truth. Corporal Dolman's vehicle remained under attack, forcing Corporal Brown to punch out his shattered windscreen. Sergeant Robertson jumped down and weaved through falling masonry.

'I'm still getting beasted here, mate!' Corporal Dolman told him.

Lance Corporal Oellerman radioed Sergeant Robertson from the front of the British column: 'We've got a vehicle in front of us, blocking our route.'

Sergeant Robertson advanced to see a white 4x4 parked across the carriageway, its driver standing defiantly against the chassis. Sergeant Robertson charged forward alone, clutching his rifle, which he stabbed into the man's face. Sergeant Robertson stared at him with ice-blue eyes. 'You get your f***ing vehicle out of here or I'll kill you,' he ordered. Terrified, the man remounted.

'Close in on me,' Sergeant Robertson said, beckoning to his men. 'We're going forward.'

The crowd was hard on the Paras' heels, with 300 protesters in tow. Sergeant Robertson told Corporal Dolman, 'John, we're getting big-time boulders, and we've got no more plastics.'

'Right,' responded Corporal Dolman. 'I'm going to fire a couple of live rounds over these c***s' heads!'

'Small burst, John. Three to five rounds,' Sergeant Robertson replied. As Sergeant Robertson had feared, firing warning shots was only a partial success. The use of lethal force was now almost inevitable. As a last resort, more bursts were fired, this time with machine guns, over the unarmed locals' heads. To them, the 'white tribe' had fired and missed. Sergeant Robertson directed his machine gunners, Private Serge Lynch and Private 'Smudge' Smith, to mount the rear Pinz and be ready to put down a burst of sustained fire.

A gunman appeared at a first-floor window and fired an AK-47. Sergeant Robertson and Corporal Dolman returned single shots that struck the Iraqi in the chest. He died instantly. As more armed youths appeared, the pair took cover behind a wall. Sergeant Robertson killed a youth wearing a bright yellow T-shirt as the boy dashed between parked cars. Corporal Dolman was struck in the mouth by secondary fragmentation when a round hit the wall. Sergeant Robertson took out another gunman before he and Corporal Dolman climbed onto the rear Pinzgauer.

The vehicles skidded away. A strafe from the machine gunners ensured no locals gave chase.

Alpha were by this time under constant stone fire at the Fawjer building. No warning shots were fired in return. The lieutenant favoured a more passive approach. He instructed Lance Corporal Weadon to get the men mounted on the DAF while he joined Private May in the cabin. One of Lieutenant Kennedy's men said that he could hear British weapons being fired and recognised the sharp pitch of the SA80 Mk2 personal rifle and the rattle of the General Purpose Machine Gun. Lieutenant Kennedy decided he would drive to wherever Sergeant Robertson was in contact to provide covering fire. He repeated his instruction to his men to fire only at armed targets.

The sound of gunfire prompted the adjournment of Sergeant Hamilton-Jewell's meeting at the police station. He led Corporal Aston and Lance Corporal Hyde as they filed out of the office and marched around the courtyard perimeter. The noise also awoke the Iraqi policemen, who were less inclined to leave the confines of the station.

Private May found second gear – he never put the wagon in first, as it stalled habitually – and the wagon chugged forwards under a hail of stones. As Sergeant Robertson sped north up the main road and crossed the junction, his vehicles were spotted by a member of Lieutenant Kennedy's multiple perched in the crow's nest of the DAF, 200 metres to Sergeant Robertson's west. Private May was ordered to 'follow that Pinzgauer'.

Alpha and Bravo then ended up chasing each other's tails, with each multiple assuming that the other required immediate assistance and risking life and limb to rescue them. Sergeant Robertson's plan was to find a position on the eastern riverbank, where his men could provide covering fire across the water towards the Fawjer building to assist Alpha's extraction. Unbeknown to Sergeant Robertson, Lieutenant Kennedy's men had left unaided. Hundreds of protesters streamed up the main street intent on exacting revenge and settling the blood feud.

When they reached the junction, Lieutenant Kennedy's men were attacked with rocket-propelled grenades and small arms. They jumped from the cargo hold and ran in all directions. Two

Paras asked if they could hide inside a house; the inhabitants refused. Lieutenant Kennedy stole a glance towards the police station. As Sergeant Hamilton-Jewell had ordered the Land Rovers to be driven inside the compound, Lieutenant Kennedy could not see any 'friendly' vehicles or personnel – only a large orange-coloured oil tanker and hundreds of protesters. Gunmen among them were using women and children as human shields. Lieutenant Kennedy later said in his submission to the inquest that had he known the Red Caps were at the police station – he was not told of their whereabouts or plans before he left Camp Abu Naji earlier that morning – he would have gone there. Together, the Paras and Red Caps would have been able to withstand the mob for a sufficient time for the quick-reaction force to arrive.

Sergeant Hamilton-Jewell used Ghazi to ask the head of the Iraqi police to bring his officers to stand against the advancing armed mob. They did, but only briefly.

Private May was helpless as gunmen took pot shots at him. A rocket-propelled grenade fizzed over his cabin and exploded at the roadside. He pulled in, yanked open the driver's door and jumped from the cabin in search of somewhere to hide. At least the local custom of sawing off the barrels of AK-47s ensured that rounds were sprayed erratically.

It was 1030. The Paras were only 200 metres from the police station and in search of shelter. Approximately 800 metres away, Sergeant Robertson and his men 'de-bussed' from their Pinzgauers and dived into ditches for cover. The sergeant looked east across the river, towards the Fawjer building, in search of his young platoon commander. Instead, he saw matchstick figures scuttling along the riverbank and preparing to fire at his positions. He was to come under fire from the east, west and south.

On the crossroads, Lieutenant Kennedy's men regrouped. 'Tim,' said Lieutenant Kennedy, 'get in the cabin. You've got to drive us out of here.'

'It won't start, boss,' replied Private May. 'It'll never start from neutral first time.'

Lieutenant Kennedy's men formed a scrum and pushed as Private May turned the key in the ignition, put the wagon in second gear and suppressed the clutch. The truck crept forward at first, without generating sufficient momentum to assist the engine. Inches became feet before he pressed hard on the accelerator and engaged the handbrake. On its release, the DAF shot forward. Private May spotted figures moving towards him from an alleyway. He saw both were armed. A volley of fire from the cargo hold did for the two gunmen.

For weeks, Sergeant Hamilton-Jewell had borne the failings of the police trainees with patience. Now the local recruits shuffled backwards. Some turned on their heels and fled, taking with them Sergeant Hamilton-Jewell's hopes of demonstrating control over such a hostile crowd. The policemen ran inside and across the courtyard to rooms where they pulled window frames from hinges, climbed through and sprinted for their lives. Outside, gunmen fired over the Red Caps' heads.

For Lance Corporal Keys, the experience of being at what he described as the 'dud end of the action' must have been stranger than for most military policemen. Of the six Red Caps in Majar al-Kabir that day, only he knew what it was like to storm a terrorist camp in the West African jungle. Lance Corporal Keys had returned from Sierra Leone a hero. When he posed for photographs in his back garden, the cameraman's lens captured his pride and the fear in his parents' eyes.

Sergeant Hamilton-Jewell would have drawn upon the steadfastness and courage he had inherited from his mother. Teresa's 80th birthday pub lunch in Esher, Surrey, had been the last family occasion he had attended before deploying to Iraq. She had beamed with pride as she held his hand. Asked by his sister-in-law if he was scared, Sergeant Hamilton-Jewell took a long sip of stout. 'It's what I do,' he said. 'I'm just looking forward to getting out there. We've got an important job to do.'

To flee went against the grain. Sergeant Hamilton-Jewell no more wanted to be forced out of the town than Sergeant Robertson. This was Sergeant Hamilton-Jewell's Rorke's Drift moment. For him and his men to simply jump in their Land Rovers and scoot off would have signalled defeat for the British mission to establish order in Majar al-Kabir. Sergeant Hamilton-Jewell was also morally committed to the ethos of military policing, which preached conflict resolution through peaceful means. With only 50 rounds each, it made sense for the Red Caps to play for time.

The only position in the ops room where the satellite phone received a signal was on a window ledge. Even then the strained ringtone was barely audible. Countless calls were missed. This time the caller got through and shouted, 'It's Sergeant Robertson. I'm in Majar al-Kabir! I've been in contact for 20 minutes!'

Gunfire sounded in the earpiece as the phone was passed to Lieutenant Lawrence Knighton. The duty watchkeeper spoke to Sergeant Robertson briefly before updating the log: '1037 hours. Contact. Two times enemy dead. 150 Rounds fired. No FF [Friendly] casualties.'

The phone was then handed to Captain Todd, the operations officer. As the severity of the situation hit, he ordered all non-essential personnel to leave the ops room. Warrant Officer Marley dispatched a runner to The Royal Military Police accommodation.

'There's been an incident in Majar al-Kabir,' the runner said.

'Oh?' The messenger startled Lieutenant Phillips.

'One or two Iraqi civilians have been shot.'

In Lieutenant Phillips' mind, the shooting of Iraqi civilians by British soldiers was a mere civilian criminal issue, similar to the incident involving Corporal Dolman in al-Amarah. There was no indication that Royal Military Policemen were involved. He returned with the runner to discuss developments with Warrant Officer Marley. Lieutenant Phillips believed Sergeant Hamilton-Jewell was able to deal with any criminal situation and establish a crime scene – if he was still in the town. Warrant Officer Marley suggested to Lieutenant Phillips he should deploy.

Major Stuart Tootal, the wiry, intense, battalion second-in-command, appeared. 'Sir,' Captain Todd began, 'a Para call-sign has been involved in a contact and Iraqi civilians have been shot. The Para call-sign is running out of ammunition and needs immediate assistance.'

Warrant Officer Marley interrupted, 'I might have men in there, but I cannot be sure. I don't want to say they've left, but I cannot say they are there either.'

Captain Todd sought confirmation from Captain Palmer: 'Do you know if we have RMP call-signs in the town?'

'Well, there might be. I haven't been told exactly what time they are going through.'

Major Kemp tapped Lieutenant Phillips on the shoulder. 'I think it would be best if you come with me,' he said. 'There may be forensic issues [at the crime scene].'

Lieutenant Phillips was accompanied by Royal Military Policeman Sergeant Nigel Turnbull, who had driven hundreds of kilometres overnight from Kuwait. 'Get your kit ready,' said Warrant Officer Marley. 'You'll have to go down with Lieutenant Phillips. All the other sections are out. Secure the scene, and start an investigation. Bring the camera for when you're there. There's a helicopter going down. See if you can get down on that.'

Lieutenant Knighton briefed the commander of the airborne-reaction force. Sergeant Jason Rogers was told, 'There's a C Company call-sign in contact in Majar al-Kabir. We're unsure of their exact location in the town, but we know they are running out of ammunition, so bring as much additional ammo as you can. You'll need to get down there fast by Chinook.'

The female helicopter pilot asked for a 'drop-off grid'.

'I can't give you one,' Captain Todd replied. 'I don't have their precise locations on the ground. There's lots of firing going on. Once you've made the journey down, I suggest you drop the troops off short, out of immediate danger. Oh, and there may be Royal Military Policemen in the town. We're not sure.'

The police chief was reluctant to leave without the Red Caps: 'Please, Mr Hamilton-Jewell, leave with us.'

'It is our duty to stay,' Sergeant Hamilton-Jewell replied.

'You'll be safe with us.'

'No.'

Meanwhile, rocket-propelled grenades slammed into Sergeant Robertson's Pinzgauers on the riverbank. He put his hand on Joseph's shoulder. 'Can you find us somewhere to hide?' he asked. 'We need to lie low for a while.'

After regrouping outside the town and calling the ops room, Lieutenant Kennedy's men were ordered back in Majar al-Kabir and soon came under fire. Rounds passed over the heads of those Paras ducking for cover in the cargo hold. A round cracked the windscreen, followed closely by another that smashed an indicator light. When they dismounted, rounds deflected off masonry inches from Lieutenant Kennedy's head as he huddled behind a pile of rubble.

Back at the police station, Ghazi watched as what he later described as a 'deafening bomb' – probably a rocket-propelled grenade – struck a Land Rover. Sergeant Hamilton-Jewell's only forms of radio communications were mounted on the dashboards. He granted Ghazi's wish to leave, with one request: to call the police station at Qalat Salih. As Ghazi later told British investigators, Sergeant Hamilton-Jewell instructed him to 'get himself to a safer place'. Ghazi left by the rear of the station as the last of the Iraqi police officers slid through an open window and climbed over the back fence. Ghazi reported a 'grave situation' at Majar al-Kabir and that British officers were, in his words, 'besieged by a big mob'.

Back at Abu Naji, Lieutenant Phillips and Sergeant Turnbull climbed into another Royal Military Police Land Rover and drove out of the camp gates. They believed that they were going to begin a routine investigation into a one-off shooting, similar to the incident in al-Amarah with Wa'el Rahim Jabar.

In Majar al-Kabir, Sergeant Robertson gave his orders: 'Shut up, split into pairs and move as quietly as you can.'

Sergeant Robertson stopped at a house. After checking its perimeter for gunmen, he burst inside. Women screamed as they were thrown against walls and searched. When the Paras' eyes flashed across the darkened, dusty room, they caught a man trying to escape. He was pulled back and a torch flashed in his eyes. 'Tell him, Joseph,' said Sergeant Robertson, 'that if he tries that again, he will be shot.'

Sergeant Robertson then used Joseph to identify the house elder. 'The British will not hurt you or your family, but you must cooperate,' Joseph said. 'He [Sergeant Robertson] wants you to go outside to check if there are any gunmen following us or if they have found where we are. Please do it. Go to where the vehicles are burning. It is not far. Come back and tell us what you see. Nobody else is to leave this room. Anyone who tries will be shot.'

'Oh, Joseph.' Sergeant Robertson pointed his rifle at a woman's head. 'If he's not back in five minutes, I'll kill his family.' The man scuttled away.

Sergeant Robertson used his satellite phone again to speak to Captain Palmer. 'Where's my QRF? Where's my ARF [airborne reaction force]?'

'The ARF has not left yet. The QRF is on its way.'

Sergeant Robertson could not hold it back for long. 'For f***'s sake,' he exploded. 'We're up shit creek here with no ammo!'

'Can't you go back to your vehicles?' Captain Palmer was significantly senior to Sergeant Robertson, a company second-in-command on detachment from The Irish Guards.

'Are your ears painted on?' Sergeant Robertson asked incredulously. 'I told you before. They got blown up!'

At Camp Abu Naji, Sergeant Rogers found his quick-reaction-force colleagues standing beside vehicles and awaiting his briefing. He suggested that on landing they burst out of their Chinook and separate into two teams of six, led by him and his second-in-command, Corporal Steve Thurtle. They were driven to the helicopter landing site to find two Chinooks, one of which had just arrived from Basra, its rotors still spinning. The soldiers were directed to the other helicopter, with its rotors tied to the ground. It was due to be flown by the female Royal Air Force pilot. She realised time would be saved if the newly arrived helicopter was used. She asked its pilot, Wing Commander Guy van den Berg, if she could borrow his helicopter. Instead, he suggested that the soldiers should transfer from her helicopter to his. They sprinted across the tarmac and charged up the ramp into the hot, sticky cargo hold. Amid a crescendo of banging, the pumped-up Paras found seats. Lance Corporal Gary McMahon squeezed into a seat on the starboard side alongside Lance Corporal Dan Marsh, Private Phil 'Tubs' Johnson, Private 'Ruby' Murray, Private Paul 'Jingles' Chambers and Lance Corporal Del Aspinall. Corporal Thurtle, Squadron Leader Gavin McCallum, a Royal Air Force medic, Sergeant Rogers and Corporal Robbie Cormie sat opposite as translation lift began. Flying time to Majar al-Kabir was approximately eight minutes. It was 1105.

As the helicopter flew over Major Kemp's 'rover group' on

Highway 6, the officer gazed up at the aircraft, its twin rotors turning in apparent slow motion. As he later recalled, Major Kemp realised at that moment that the situation in the town was much worse than previously thought.

Lieutenant Phillips and Sergeant Turnbull chugged along behind. With no more success than before, Lieutenant Phillips attempted to use the radio.

Back in the operations room, Warrant Officer Marley came under pressure from Major Tootal: 'Can you confirm there are RMPs in the town?'

'Sir, I cannot confirm. Because they are scheduled to meet the brigadier, they could have left. I don't know.'

Major Tootal stiffened. This was not what he expected or hoped to hear from The Royal Military Police representative in a busy ops room at a time of crisis. 'Well, are you trying to get in touch with them?'

'Yes, sir. I've been doing that.'

'Have they got an Iridium phone?'

'No, sir.'

Major Tootal had assumed that Royal Military Police call-signs were taking satellite phones in accordance with stated battle-group orders. 'Why not?'

'There weren't enough available in the company.'

To some in the ops room it seemed typical that at such a critical time The Royal Military Police 'might' be somewhere, yet even their own desk was unsure and nobody could get hold of them. Major Tootal was still frowning as he walked back to the map of Maysan Province, protected by see-through plastic sheeting, into which Sergeant Hamilton-Jewell's pin and others were stuck. 'Take simple decisions ... Focus on certainty,' he told himself. While he could not ignore the possible predicament of the Red Caps, focusing on certainty meant that they could not be afforded equal priority to Alpha and Bravo.

'Two minutes.'

'Two minutes.' The pre-landing warning was passed from man to man. The tension was upped and men gripped their weapons more tightly. The Chinook dipped violently, jolting its passengers forward. When the turbulence settled, a Royal Air Force crew member scribbled three letters onto a notepad, which he held up: 'RPG'.

The Chinook was soon to be visible from Bravo's hiding place, Alpha's trenches and the police station. A soldier peered through a port hole to see a vehicle on fire – one of Sergeant Robertson's Pinzgauers, perhaps, or one of the Red Caps' Land Rovers. Rotor blades slapped the air as Wing Commander van den Berg leaned into a bend. His arrival distracted those keeping Lieutenant Kennedy and his men pinned down. They dashed to find better cover. The most Alpha could achieve was to hold off local gunmen until the 'road move' arrived. There was no chance of advancing to assist Bravo.

Back at the house, the elder reported gunmen circling the smouldering wreckages of Sergeant Robertson's vehicles. Sergeant Robertson's thoughts returned to the Chinook. He knew the use of flares to signal his whereabouts would invite hundreds of gunmen to surround the house and yard.

When Corporal Dolman spoke to the pilot of a Gazelle helicopter circling the town, he confirmed the numbers of protesters swarming the streets in his vicinity. 'Gaz 1' also cast an eye at the police station, but his priority was to assist Sergeant Robertson's multiple.

Sergeant Robertson spoke to Corporal Pat Grainger on the C Company desk: 'Pat, we're in deep shit and have got f*** all ammo left. It's a house on the eastern side of the river with wastelands to the north of us.'

Sergeant Robertson removed the plastic covering from his mini-flares. When Corporal Dolman reported the crowd closing in, Sergeant Robertson psyched himself up: 'F***ing hell, Robbo, you've got to be strong now. You're fighting for your boys!' Everything stopped. It was all about him. Any tactical error on his part would cost their lives.

'Right, boys,' he said. 'The Chinook's inbound. We're out of here in a few minutes, so stay switched on and get ready to burst out.'

Sergeant Robertson gave the ops room an instruction: 'Tell the pilot to approach from the north. We have gunmen out to the west, south and east in a horseshoe shape.'

Bravo heard shots from the area of the police station. They

assumed it was Iraqi police resisting the gunmen. 'Way to go,' said Sergeant Robertson. 'They're on our side for once.'

Corporal Miller was shot. It seems that he lost his balance in the area of the entrance to the police station, as his bloody hand print was found on the wall in this area when the building was later examined.

Corporal Miller was born in the North East in the early 1980s, a time of industrial decimation, high unemployment and low prospects. Raised in a proudly blue-collar family, he was one of those physically gifted boys for whom football offered alternative employment to the factories and docks. When he was released from Sunderland Football Club's School of Excellence, his father John shared his disappointment and drove him hundreds of miles up and down the country for trials with clubs such as Cambridge United. When his son reached school-leaving age, John Miller knew it was imperative he learned a trade. The army offered Corporal Miller a variety of skills options and the chance to follow in his father's footsteps.

He was joined in The Royal Military Police, but not in the Gulf, by his older brother. His letters home opened brightly with 'Hi Dudes', and he told his parents that sand was getting in places he did not think possible. His personal highlight was when he arrested three Ba'ath Party officials. He had handcuffed them and pulled sandbags over their heads – a practice outlawed after the death in British custody of Baha Mousa later that year but standard practice at the time. Corporal Miller was pumped with adrenalin as he ordered them to lie flat on their stomachs on the floor of his vehicle and pointed his 'shooter' at their heads. They were driven to the UK interrogation centre, where the shock of capture was maintained.

This had been a rare moment of excitement. Corporal Miller suggested that his parents were seeing more of the war on the television than he was on the ground. Their son had grown up fast in Iraq, and a philosophical strand emerged to his character. Living with the constant stress of operations and surrounded by hostile locals had made him realise how precious life was.

A trail of blood marked where Corporal Miller's fellow Red Caps must have dragged him inside. His field dressings were pulled from a webbing pouch and his uniform buttons undone. It had been a grave error on his commanders' part to withdraw morphine phials. The Royal Military Polices' phials sat in a box at Abu Naji. Dressings and bandages were wrapped tightly around Si's left shoulder, right arm, lower back and right thigh.

The sight of his colleague in such pain possibly flicked a switch inside Lance Corporal Keys. Sergeant Hamilton-Jewell directed Lance Corporal Keys to adopt a firing position on a diagonal axis from the main entrance.

The Chinook crew passed a message to Sergeant Robertson via the ops room that he should use his flares. He fired the trigger to send a stream of red smoke 12 metres into the air. As feared, the flare attracted unwanted attention. When Corporal Dolman whispered to Sergeant Robertson that he could see gunmen running towards the house, the platoon sergeant asked him to spare their soldiers the news.

Sergeant Robertson then shook his head as he observed the angle of approach. 'Wrong f***ing way. I said from the north.'

It was 1115.

As Wing Commander van den Berg steered the Chinook into position for a rear-end-first landing, Sergeant Rogers' men stood in the order of disembarkation. Private Phil Johnson, known as 'Tubs', was at the head of the queue. The ramp dropped down and a huge dust cloud rose from below. Locals engaged the helicopter with rocket-propelled grenades and small-arms fire, which tore through its skin. A warhead flashed metres from its rotor blades. When he saw tiny chinks of daylight in the fuselage, Sergeant Rogers thought that one of his soldiers had discharged his weapon negligently. A split second later, a round ripped through his inner thigh. The pilot steered his airframe away from another rocket-propelled grenade and low-hanging electricity cables. Royal Air Force medic Squadron Leader McCallum listened as the pitch of the rotors sharpened and sounded increasingly strained – as he described it, like car wheels gripping a mountain pass at speed. He looked down to see his lower right leg covered in blood. A round had cut through his calf.

Wounded paratroopers lay strewn on the floor and slumped

against seats, Sergeant Rogers among them. In spite of his wounds, he wanted the pilot to make a second attempt to land in order that the uninjured could deploy.

Private Johnson cried out, 'I'm hit, I'm hit.'

Private Chambers said that he was OK, but when he pulled his hand away, half his face collapsed. Private Mason sat apparently lifeless in his seat, his helmet holding his skull together. Private Johnson's colleagues undid his webbing and ripped open his uniform. They could not find a wound but lifted him to see a pool of blood on his seat. When Wing Commander van den Berg was updated on the casualties – seven wounded, including two head wounds – he knew he could not afford to risk attempting a second landing.

Sergeant Robertson watched in horror as his best chance of extraction faded into the blue sky. It is not known whether any of the Red Caps saw the Chinook fly away. Sergeant Hamilton-Jewell's men were not equipped with flares and were unable to signal their position to the pilot.

Sergeant Robertson turned to Corporal Dolman. 'What do I tell the boys now, John?'

Corporal Dolman did not reply, so Sergeant Robertson addressed his troops: 'Lads, remember we are paratroopers. It's backs-to-the-wall fighting now. We'll fight to the death. If a grenade comes over the wall into the yard, you will throw it back over. Keep Big Steve [Lance Corporal Oellerman] and Billy [Corporal Brown] supplied with ammo, but keep one round back for yourselves.' Sergeant Robertson thrust his forefinger up beneath his chin: 'That's where the last round goes, boys. Don't let them take you alive.'

'Sergeant Robertson.' It was Private Smith. 'They're coming through the south wall!'

'This is it, John,' Sergeant Robertson whispered to Corporal Dolman, who relayed a message from Gaz 1 that 200 gunmen were heading their way. Sergeant Robertson thought that their luck was out. He spoke to Captain Palmer: 'They're all honing in on us now. What's happened to the Chinook? We saw an RPG airburst close by but nothing else.'

'It took small-arms fire and has taken casualties.'

'What about the road move?'

An inevitable pause. What could Captain Palmer tell him but the truth? 'Another 20 minutes.'

'Twenty f***ing minutes! Is there anything else you can give me?'

'We're trying for some air cover.'

'Well, make it f***ing pronto.'

Sergeant Robertson slammed the phone down angrily. 'I don't want to talk to "Patsy" any more. He's winding me up.'

Major Tootal was updated. 'Focus on certainty,' he told himself again. With the Chinook inbound in five minutes, all medics were ordered to muster at the accident-and-emergency department. The doctor on board the helicopter gave a grave prognosis for one of the wounded paratroopers, who he feared might slip into a coma.

The unfolding crisis was by then the talk of divisional commanders in Basra; word also reached Permanent Joint Headquarters at Northwood, in Middlesex. 'Div' wanted updates in order to put a request to US commanders for air support – there was no offensive back-up available from The Royal Air Force. It was hoped that the Americans could provide Cobra helicopter gunships, or failing that a pair of US Navy F-15 jets. Just weeks after the death of Lance Corporal Matty Hull, and with British call-signs fighting in such close proximity to insurgents, the threat of another blue-on-blue loomed.

Questioned again by Major Tootal and Captain Todd, Warrant Officer Marley acknowledged that he was yet to hear from Sergeant Hamilton-Jewell and was no wiser as to his and C Section's whereabouts. The best he could do, which amounted to little, was to outline the measures he was taking. Even if the Red Caps had left Majar al-Kabir before the town erupted, there was no means of reporting their progress to Warrant Officer Marley: they were out of VHF and HF range, and the Maysan telephone network could only be used to call other local numbers. A vexed Warrant Officer Marley requested that a TACSAT (Tactical Satellite) message be sent to the Paras stationed at al-Uzayr. The instruction was for Sergeant Hamilton-Jewell to check in with the ops room at Abu Naji immediately upon his arrival.

As fellow Royal Military Policemen later confessed, the corps as a whole was guilty of negligence and complacency when it came to observing communications practices. One senior non-commissioned officer, a personal friend of Sergeant Hamilton-Jewell's who had served with him in the Balkans, said some Royal Military Policemen mocked those Red Caps who bothered with 'comms' as 'wimps'. They were supposed to be able to handle any situation without requiring the assistance of other units. Given the tepid relationship between the Red Caps and Paras, they would have wanted to exhaust all other options before requesting assistance. It was also said later that the isolation of Sergeant Hamilton-Jewell's section at the police station was a crisis only narrowly avoided on previous operational tours. As one serving Red Cap put it, it was 'macho to get yourself out of such a tight spot, without radios or calling in support. We're the RMP. We want to do our own thing.'

With the battle-group commander Lieutenant Colonel Tom Beckett on his way to Majar al-Kabir, Major Tootal remained in charge of the rescue mission. His biggest call at that moment was whether or not to deploy the female pilot's helicopter, which was now ready to lift off. The airspace over Majar al-Kabir was unsafe for air infiltration, and the second helicopter might be required to transport the most severely wounded to 202 Field Hospital at Basra, given the damage to the first Chinook. Wing Commander van den Berg's helicopter was stuttering back to base with approximately 100 holes in its fuselage. The second Chinook remained on the tarmac.

The road move came to a halt near the junction of Highway 6 and the road to Majar al-Kabir. Major Kemp was taken aback by the volume of gunfire. He ordered Scimitar armoured vehicles to be placed on either end of the vehicle column. When Lieutenant Phillips and Sergeant Turnbull looked at each other, both appeared frightened and shocked. So much for the one-off shooting they had been tasked to investigate. Sergeant Turnbull yearned for sleep, but the day was evidently going to be a long one. Neither he nor Lieutenant Phillips could get the radio to work. Major Kemp spoke to a Household Cavalry officer in command of the Scimitars: 'Will you advance?'

His reluctance was clear: 'Our vehicles are very vulnerable to rocket-propelled grenades. They're really not very well armoured. They will be destroyed.'

Sergeant Robertson spoke to Major Kemp shortly afterwards, by which time his company commander had established an incident-control point on the northern outskirts of the town: 'We're surrounded. Gunmen everywhere, particularly to our south and both flanks. What have you got? Can you help us out?'

'The Household Cavalry have got Scimitars.'

'Can you get them to me?'

'They don't like taking RPGs.'

'Oh, don't they? Do you think I do? It's getting hot to trot here.'

As an elderly Iraqi later told British investigators, he approached the police station to find gunmen with rocket-propelled grenades slung over their shoulders. When he asked where they were going, they replied that they were heading to the riverbank to attack British soldiers. The man was concerned to see a Land Rover ablaze and gunmen firing through the windows. They agreed to stop shooting.

The man said later that, as he went inside, he saw Lance Corporal Keys aiming his rifle at him. Sergeant Hamilton-Jewell spotted his progress around the perimeter of the courtyard and, seeing him unarmed, beckoned him forward. The Iraqi said that he saw Sergeant Hamilton-Jewell standing at the doorway of a storeroom with the other Red Caps sitting or lying behind him. Corporal Aston was wounded. Corporal Long was curled up in a foetal position, emitting noises of despair – the man identified Corporal Long from photographs. Corporal Miller was either drifting in and out of consciousness or already dead. Tables and cabinets were stacked in order to stop the door being opened once closed from the inside. Documents were scattered all over the floor. The elder agreed to act as Sergeant Hamilton-Jewell's mediator. However, gunmen were intent upon settling the blood feud with the white tribe in the traditional way; this was only a temporary ceasefire as far as they were concerned.

The crowd was smaller than before, and at around that time the crew of one of the helicopters tasked to observe the town suggested 'no untoward activity' in the vicinity of the police station, a report which gave those in the ops room some encouragement. However, the crew was equipped with primitive vision aids intended to aid observation at much lower altitudes than 5,000 feet. The crew could not distinguish someone carrying an AK-47 from one carrying a pistol, nor someone who was carrying neither.

The Chinook cargo hold was transformed into an airborne field hospital. Its walls were blood-stained and drilled with bullet holes. There was barely sufficient room, and one of the wounded was laid out across the ramp with his head cradled between a colleague's thighs as he squatted behind him. Adrenalin anaesthetised Squadron Leader McCallum from his own pain. His calf felt numb. Private Johnson told Lance Corporal Aspinall he was wounded in the leg. Yet when his trousers were cut away, there was no entry or exit wound. Only when they removed his body armour, webbing and shirt did they find the round that had entered his body close to his belly button and exited near his coccyx. One of his colleagues remarked, 'Your stomach looks more like an arsehole, mate.' As nausea overwhelmed him and he became less responsive, Private Johnson received morphine. Lance Corporal McMahon donated his phial – retained by virtue of his rank as a lance corporal. Many private soldiers had been ordered to return their supplies at the cessation of major combat operations.

At the moment of truth, Lance Corporal Aspinall forgot which end of the syringe was which. Did he prod Private Johnson with the yellow or the red nipple? Red nipple, yellow nipple, red nipple, yellow nipple. Red? Lance Corporal Aspinall injected morphine into his own thumb.

Medics and stretcher-bearers sprinted through the dust clouds towards the helicopter landing site. They were astonished by the interior of the Chinook. The cargo hold resembled the set of a horror movie: those who treated the wounded were as bloodied as those who had been shot. There was a cacophony of shouting as the victims were carried off, with one of the most severely injured howling in jubilation when it was confirmed the round had missed his penis and testicles. 'Thank f*** I've still got a cock,' he screamed. They were carried in single procession 250 metres to the hospital. Doctors were alerted in advance and prepared in anticipation of blood transfusions. Private Mason's condition was too grave to predict the outcome.

Lance Corporal Marsh and Lance Corporal McMahon sprinted away to join the last of those heading to the town. Seeing their blood-stained uniforms and thousand-yard stares, a senior non-commissioned officer questioned whether they should deploy. 'We're going back down, and that's non-negotiable,' they snapped back. This was a British blood feud, too.

The road move was incremental, with batches of soldiers departing Camp Abu Naji in convoys of open-top Land Rovers armed with Browning .50-calibre heavy machine guns and the lighter General Purpose Machine Guns as carried by infantry troops. The Land Rovers were barely armoured, and the troops were afforded scant protection compared to those waiting to advance in Scimitars. One group of vehicles was commanded by the enormous Colour Sergeant Cordell Luke, previously one of Lance Corporal Keys' instructors in 1 Para. When photographed together, Colour Sergeant Luke had appeared about three times Lance Corporal Keys' size. His men were itching to drive south in full knowledge that their vehicles would be targeted. There was no other way to aid Sergeant Robertson's extraction.

Major Kemp, at the incident-control point, received incoming shots from the sugar factory. Major Tootal heard gunfire when they spoke. 'Chris, it's Stuart. Are you in contact?'

'Everyone is in contact, Stuart,' Major Kemp replied.

Looking south, Major Kemp saw that the forces at his disposal were insufficient to fight through the crowds of gunmen. He grew impatient. He recalled thinking, 'This is taking too much time. We're taking too much time. I've got to get everyone together and make a plan. We've got to get this moving now.'

The day was approaching its hottest hour, the midday sun high and punishing all below. There was little Major Kemp could say to Colour Sergeant Luke as they parted: 'Just push down and do your best, working together. As soon as you've extracted Sergeant Robertson, get out.'

Sergeant Robertson issued a final order: 'John, I'll lead the Toms out. You bring up the rear.' Sergeant Robertson then turned and said, 'Lads, into your pairs. Fire and manoeuvre. Short bounds. We're going to marry up with the QRF. Buddy up. Go!'

Sergeant Robertson's men burst out onto the street and stared through the dust and haze. They dodged and weaved in pairs, hiding behind cars and telegraph poles as they sprinted towards the wasteland on the eastern riverbank, an area bisected by irrigation ditches. The force of Sergeant Robertson's personality and commitment to soldiering inspired the Paras. He was a source of undying hope.

Private Ellis found himself as Sergeant Robertson's buddy as he and his platoon sergeant ran over the uneven ground, covering each other's rapid, darting movements. Their ammunition stocks were almost as dry as their throats. Eyeing a crevasse, Sergeant Robertson pushed ahead, scanned left and right for gunmen, and then ordered Private Ellis on. The private soldier bounded forward and with the fearless enthusiasm of youth leaped the width of an irrigation ditch, full almost to its brim with stagnant green water. He landed with a thud on the far bank. He heard a splash behind him and turned to see Sergeant Robertson submerged. His platoon commander surfaced, his desert uniform glued to his muscular frame, clutching his satellite phone. Spitting a mouthful of fluid, he eyed the dripping handset at arm's length and shook it.

Private Ellis hunkered down on the sheltered side of the berm, awaiting Sergeant Robertson's next command. 'Comms are down,' said Sergeant Robertson. 'You're my comms now, Freddie.'

They could see Colour Sergeant Luke's vehicles in the distance, but how could Sergeant Robertson signal his position? The guns of the quick-reaction force were trained on targets 'danger close' to where Bravo were hiding. The threat of friendly fire returned as Joseph translated a gruesome chant. The gunmen were promising to castrate the paras when they captured them. Another man stood on the back of a pick-up truck, shouting through a megaphone. He encouraged everyone in the town to fight because the British were there to rape their women.

The quick-reaction force took a casualty. Private John Healy was shot while standing on a Land Rover providing suppressive fire. His mates carried him behind one of the vehicles. As his wound was dressed and bandaged, Private Healy was adamant that he keep his gun. 'Don't you dare take my weapon!' he screamed at one of his oppos.

At the police station, the crowd told the elder that if he wanted to be spared, he should leave immediately. Sergeant Hamilton-Jewell guarded the storeroom door, with his section, Lance Corporal Keys included, behind him. Faced by overwhelming odds, he took his passive stance to its limit. The gunmen sought to wring every last drop of suffering from the Red Caps and savour their agony. This was a ceremony. The British, closest cousins to the despised Americans, were at their mercy. Around this time, one of the Red Caps is thought to have show a photograph of his children to the gunmen, who were now effectively holding the six as hostages.

Sergeant Hamilton-Jewell had been looking forward to going home to a glorious English summer, to Katie and to his mother's bacon sandwiches. There would be plenty of time for nights in the pub, training, eating, joking, sharing amusing stories and photographs of Iraq, and taking Ollie to the park to see the ducks. He had joked with Katie that if he died she should put his foot on the mantelpiece. Life was to be treasured, 'gripped' as he put it, to be made the most of. His life was 'a small price to pay for peace'.

Sergeant Hamilton-Jewell was pushed back into the storeroom, and the torture began. The Red Caps were kicked and beaten, feet and rifle butts targeting their groins, as their post-mortem reports suggested. They were shot, most probably one by one, as each had his wounds dressed. Eventually, the deadly contents of rifles loaded to their brims were poured over them.

> Katie, if you receive this, then I am dead. I've got a few things I don't want left unsaid. You're on my mind every waking moment. I could happily have spent the rest of my life with you. I trust you. I feel happy and comfortable in your company.
>
> So what now? Have some adventures and live your life to the full. Make plans then make them happen. Don't let anyone treat you like shit, and don't take second best. Choose your mates well . . . Look after them. I ask you

think of me occasionally, and when you think of me, think good thoughts. Always smile.

I will watch over you . . .

Mum, don't be sad for me. I died doing a job I enjoyed. I had a good life. I valued right from wrong. I believed what I was doing was for the purpose of good.

There is nothing to regret in my passing . . . I fulfilled my ambitions. If there is a God, we will be reunited one day.

I did my duty . . . I hope you are proud of me . . .

Dr Firas Fasal, who was working at the hospital in the town, had heard that British servicemen were being held at the police station. He said later that he entered the building to see Sergeant Hamilton-Jewell in the doorway of the storeroom. He suggested that he thought the sergeant was trying to protect his colleagues.

Dr Fasal rushed out and jumped into an ambulance. At huge personal risk, he set off north up the main street towards where Major Kemp had established an incident-control point. He told Major Kemp that three or four men were being held hostage.

'Who works in a three or a four?' pondered Major Kemp. Perhaps the trio or quartet was a breakaway group forced to splinter off from Bravo. Captain Palmer also feared that Bravo had been overrun. The last he had heard from Sergeant Robertson before his satellite phone had failed was that he was low on ammunition and surrounded by enemy. Major Kemp cast a resigned glance towards the vehicle-mounted quick-reaction force. Until reinforcements arrived, his forces were too light to mount a meaningful thrust towards the police station without the risk of heavy losses. Nor was there any way Lieutenant Kennedy's men could make progress. His soldiers were lucky to be alive, and their weapons were almost dry.

Dr Fasal offered a solution: 'Do you want me to go back? See if I can bring them out?'

'Yes,' said a relieved Major Kemp. 'We do not have freedom of movement, and we're under fire from three flanks. We've only secured the rear. So please go back. Thank you.'

Two United States Navy F-15 Eagle fighter jets also sped

towards the town. Major Kemp assured the doctor that they would not drop any ordnance on him. It was decided, regretfully, in the ops room that as there were no 'Forward Air Controllers' on the ground – specialist trained troops who knew how to guide bombs onto targets – the lethal hardware must stay locked to the wings.

'Well, son,' the pilot Jet Jockey 1 told the watchkeeper Lieutenant Knighton, 'we have only got five minutes of fuel to loiter. I tell you what: how about we fly very low and fast? If we can't fire our cannons, we'll deliver chaff.'

While the two low-level passes did not send the mob fleeing, Sergeant Robertson was grateful for a brief respite as he planned his next move. He spent a couple of minutes sketching shapes and crosses onto a small pad: red crosses for enemy positions, blue crosses for friendly positions. Sergeant Robertson glowered across the scrubland towards the enemy positions and the main road. It was imperative that the quick-reaction-force vehicles advance. He put the finishing touches to his makeshift map. 'Well,' Sergeant Robertson exhaled, 'I've got nae comms with anyone now, Freddie, and I can't reach the QRF commander on my personal radio. You're going to have to get a message to him for me.' Sergeant Robertson's hand took on the shape of a spearhead angled in the direction of the British vehicles. 'Get your kit off, clean fatigues [remove superfluous items] and run over to where you see those Wimiks [Land Rovers].'

Private Ellis's eyes darted towards where Sergeant Robertson was pointing and back to meet his sergeant's stare. Nothing suggested that Sergeant Robertson was anything less than deadly serious. 'OK, buddy? Head down, arse up and when you speak to the quick-reaction-force commander – and speak only to him – give him this map. Show him where we are and tell him I want his vehicles to advance in order to provide a screen for us so we can extract behind his column. We'll cover you as you run.'

Private Ellis fumbled at the clasp to release his webbing belt and felt lighter for slipping off the string of pouches stuffed with magazine cases, emergency rations, an empty water bottle, a sandbag and the ubiquitous entrenching tool. When he placed his rifle on the ground, the reality of Sergeant Robertson's words sank in.

'Lads,' Sergeant Robertson boomed towards the other soldiers, 'get a magazine or two between youse and on my command put a burst down to support Ellis.' They nodded and smiled, relieved no doubt not to have been 'dicked' for such a task.

'OK?' Sergeant Robertson stared at Private Ellis. 'OK?'

'Yes, sergeant.'

'Good.' Sergeant Robertson nodded. 'Stand by. Go.'

To a chorus of his comrades' fire, Private Ellis darted across the uneven dusty ground. As he zig-zagged to avoid enemy rounds, all British and Iraqi eyes were upon him. The column of British vehicles seemed to jolt up and down as he leaped across hollows, ascending, descending, swerving left and swerving right. He made it to safety and delivered a report on the whereabouts of the other members of the Bravo multiple. This prompted the quick-reaction force to advance.

There was collective relief when news of Sergeant Robertson's extraction was reported back to the ops room. When Sergeant Robertson's multiple reached him, a confused Major Kemp demanded to know if he had all his soldiers.

'Yes, sir.'

'Count again,' Major Kemp responded sternly as Lieutenant Phillips looked on.

'Sir, I came in with 12 soldiers, and I've come out with 12 soldiers.'

'Well, whose are they [at the police station] then?'

Dr Fasal returned with grave news. He said that the British servicemen were dead and there were six of them. With all paratroopers accounted for, the deceased had to be the missing Red Caps. Major Kemp turned to Lieutenant Phillips and said, 'I think they might be your men. I assumed that they would have moved on before this happened . . . I am sorry.'

By this time, Lieutenant Colonel Beckett had joined Major Kemp. The commanding officer said, 'There is no need to go back in there if there are no British soldiers to rescue.'

Joseph spoke to Dr Fasal. 'Are you willing to go back and collect the bodies?'

'Yes, so long as you don't fire.'

'OK, they won't.' A chorus of 'cease fire' rang out.

Those who sat in the vicinity of The Royal Military Police desk searched for words to say to Warrant Officer Marley. His face puckered, his grief raw and intense. As he later suggested, he also felt guilt. To his great credit, he acknowledged a degree of responsibility. At the time of writing, he remains the only officer to do so.

Lieutenant Phillips and Sergeant Turnbull waited as the ambulance slowly drove towards the command post. It was 1255. Finally, the vehicle stopped, its rear doors swung open and white sunlight illuminated its shadowy interior. Sergeant Turnbull stared as bodies, half-dressed in bloody desert uniforms, were lifted onto stretchers and placed on the road. There was no sign of their webbing, rifles or helmets. When he walked closer to the corpses, he recognised Sergeant Simon Hamilton-Jewell, Corporal Russell Aston and Corporal Paul Long. 'I didn't even know they were there,' thought Sergeant Turnbull, scarcely able to comprehend the sight.

In his last letter home a fortnight before his death, Corporal Long had doubted his mother would recognise him, as he had lost so much weight; he gave the sweets she sent him to Iraqi children. He suggested a family picnic as part of his weight-gain strategy and included a joke that the reason women got married in white was because the dishwasher had to match the fridge and the cooker. He signed off with a reminder of how much he loved and missed her. On the day of her son's death, Pat Long ate fish and chips on the seafront at Cullercoats and looked forward to his upcoming birthday.

Dr Fasal returned, this time with Corporal Simon Miller, Lance Corporal Ben Hyde and Lance Corporal Tom Keys. It was 1308 hours. For a few minutes, the six bodies remained on the road as soldiers from other regiments peered over them, curious to see if they recognised them. Some were so severely wounded that only their drop-zone flashes, the square-shaped pieces of cloth stitched onto their upper right sleeves, revealed their identities.

'RMPs,' someone said. 'Hamilton-Jewell's patrol.'

Some took photographs of the Red Caps for their own personal collections; the faces were 'well shot up', as one remarked. The deceased were transferred to two British military ambulances for the journey to Camp Abu Naji, their bodies lifted onto bunks that lowered from the walls. A medic jumped down from the cabin and slammed the doors. The engine revved. The Red Caps began their journey home.

Lieutenant Colonel Beckett and the regimental sergeant major congratulated Sergeant Robertson for getting himself and his men out alive. Sergeant Robertson was recommended for, and received, the Conspicuous Gallantry Cross, the medal for valour second only to the Victoria Cross. The regimental sergeant major said, 'What you have done today, Sergeant Robertson, is amazing.' Lieutenant Kennedy and Corporal Dolman received Mentions in Dispatches.

Sergeant Robertson's citation read:

> Throughout this action, Sergeant Robertson displayed bravery and leadership of the highest order. He consistently placed himself in extreme danger with no concern for his personal safety. His cool-headedness and tactical skill were inspirational. Despite overwhelming odds and during a sustained firefight lasting over two hours in a built-up area, he managed to extract his entire multiple to safety without serious injury or loss of life.

Lieutenant Colonel Beckett had wanted to hand over a peaceful Maysan Province to the incoming battalion, The King's Own Scottish Borderers. Nobly, his main effort in the aftermath of the tragedy was to improve relations with elders and councillors. He visited the town to shake their hands and provide a personal pledge that the British wanted to forget the day and move forward. An Special Air Service raid to find the Red Caps' killers went ahead because Div and Downing Street demanded it. Corporal Miller's rifle was recovered from beneath a gunman's bed. Tests proved it had not been fired since it was last cleaned. Only his weapon was ever found.

The fact that no spent 5.56-millimetre rounds were found at the police station supported the conclusion that the Red Caps maintained their heroically passive stance to the bitter end, perhaps offering their weapons in a last bid for clemency. However, it cannot be entirely disproved that The Royal Military

Policemen responded aggressively at some point. While the BBC and media organisations visited the police station the following day, a few more days passed before the area was sealed off and Special Investigation Branch officers began to search for forensics.

When he returned to the police station a few days later, a local officer handed Sergeant Robertson a torn and partially burned photograph perhaps used by one of the Red Caps to plead for his life. Their killers had set light to the storeroom to cover their tracks.

Beneath a sinking orange sun, the tail of a transport aircraft cast a crucifix-shaped shadow across Basra International Airport. A breeze lifted a padre's purple stole as a bugler sounded the last post and the names of the six Red Caps were read out. Their coffins, draped in Union Jacks, were carried towards the steep metal cargo ramp. The aircraft hold was black but for its interior lights, which flickered like candles. As the Red Caps began another leg of their journey home, Lieutenant Colonel Eddie Foster-Knight paid tribute: 'Why did these men stand their ground at that police station in the face of such overwhelming odds? The truth is we shall probably never know, but there is a bond and a unique loyalty between soldiers, which is difficult to measure. Their duty was to re-establish law and order, and it is for that reason I believe they stayed there together. They conducted their duty in a brave and honourable manner. Tragically, they paid the ultimate sacrifice for their actions. We are fortunate as a nation to have such men, whose courage has allowed others to enjoy their liberty and freedom. We will always remember Simon Hamilton-Jewell, Russell Aston, Paul Long, Simon Miller, Thomas Keys and Ben Hyde.'

Family and friends of Lance Corporal Keys gathered on a windswept Welsh mountainside to pay tribute. Reg Keys dressed his son's body for his funeral and poured a last small tot of whisky onto Lance Corporal Keys' lips as he lay in his coffin. Lance Corporal Keys had died just days short of his 21st birthday. The postman delivered birthday cards and condolence cards to the cottage Reg built on the Cambrian slopes overlooking Bala. He told mourners, 'Five years ago, we gave the army a rather shy, introverted young sixteen-year-old boy. Sadly, what we see here before us today is not how we expected the army to return him to us. The day Lance Corporal Keys was killed along with his five brave friends, he was just four days short of his twenty-first birthday. Lance Corporal Keys' cards remain unopened. Wounds from the pain of the loss are still too raw to undertake such a task.'

In search of answers, Reg rang Major Bryn Parry-Jones, the commander of 156 Provost Company, who had returned to Britain just a fortnight before the tragedy. There was so much Reg could not understand about the practices that were in operation. His son's letters gave little away in terms of how the Red Caps were operating. Reg and Sally knew little about how vulnerable he was, how The Royal Military Police were taking their security for granted and how the breakdown of communication with other units, namely 1 Para, was putting their son's life in jeopardy. Major Parry-Jones explained that the de-scaling of ammunition happened routinely as tactical situations changed. Reg could not believe what he was hearing. 'The province had stabilised, Reg. The police force was coming together. Things looked rosy when we were leaving.'

'Things looked rosy? How can he say this?' thought Reg.

'It was not as if anyone went in expecting an angry mob,' Major Parry-Jones continued. 'They wouldn't have gone in if they thought it was dangerous. The ammunition scales were reduced because the situation was stable enough to allow this to happen. It's the old question of how much is enough? They had enough for self-defence. It was not as though they did not have any.'

Why enter the town so soon after the uprising on 22 June 2003? Better, surely, to leave the people be if that was what they wanted? That was Reg's view. The Royal Military Police officer responded, 'Majar al-Kabir had always been that section's responsibility. They knew it better than anybody. They had been there from the start. They knew the characters. They knew the police officers there. It was an area with which they were very familiar. The guys would not have followed orders blindly. There was no promise to the locals to stay out of the town. And to put it in context, there's no way of talking to these people unless you actually go and see them. You can't phone them up. You can't use a mobile phone because they didn't have any [at the time].

You couldn't write them a letter because there was no postal service, so the only way of communicating with them was to go and see them.'

Reg was unconvinced. He later said, 'It would appear to me that they sent these six young men into a police station to do a job in a hostile country with hostile elements with very, very little support around them. To think that they could get trapped with no immediate support to call upon is of some concern to me.'

He waited for nine months after his son's death for an army Board of Inquiry to publish its findings. The board, which sat in camera, concluded that the deaths were 'not preventable'.

To me, the facts suggest that the deaths were preventable and in my view they were the result of a blasé attitude towards security and communications by The Royal Military Police detachment at Camp Abu Naji and the attitude of the battle-group hierarchy towards units working in isolation but within the same area of operations. If Sergeant Hamilton-Jewell had taken with him an Iridium phone, as written battle-group orders insisted, he would have been able to call the ops room when the unrest began. Major Tootal would then have factored the presence of C Section being in the town into his rescue plan.

As Lieutenant Kennedy stated at the inquest in 2006, he would have gone to the police station that morning if he had known that the Red Caps were there. This would have made sense after the DAF was attacked and broke down on the crossroads, only 200 metres away. It was 1030, and the Red Caps were still alive – this is confirmed by the detailed statement provided by the interpreter. Alpha defended the police station on 22 June and could have done so on 24 June. That being the case, the Red Caps would have survived. Unfortunately, he received no such information when he checked out of the ops room at 0840 or subsequently.

Common sense suggests it is both practical and advisable that different British units are made aware of each other's presence when working in such close proximity, especially when the behaviour of one can have such a determining effect on the security of the other. Yet, according to Major Kemp and Major Tootal, it made no difference whether or not the Paras knew the Red Caps were in town, or vice versa.

The Board of Inquiry made 12 separate recommendations for changes to standard operational procedures. One proposal read: 'The board recommends that a review be conducted of Royal Military Police officer training to ensure that their young officers are better trained to command small, isolated detachments.'

It was regrettable that Lieutenant Phillips was unaware of such a critical battle-group order regarding the use of satellite phones. Major Parry-Jones should not have left Lieutenant Phillips behind to command The Royal Military Police detachment if he was too junior or too inexperienced to be abreast of key issues.

The inquest began at Oxford Old Assizes in March 2006. The families sat on two benches opposite the witnesses, as if they were a jury sitting in a criminal trial assessing the guilt of defendants. Coroner Nicholas Gardiner sat to their right behind a raised bench.

I find it difficult to accept Gardiner's conclusion that the deaths could not have been avoided. As previously stated, the most obvious opportunity to prevent the deaths came when Lieutenant Kennedy's men were only 200 metres from the station. Had he known that the Red Caps were there, he might have acted differently, as he told the inquest, 'We would most definitely have attempted to get to the police station.'

Gardiner suggested that neither the airborne reaction force nor the quick-reaction force could have offered assistance to the Red Caps, as the latter were already dead. Yet at 1200 Dr Fasal reported to Major Kemp that British soldiers were being held 'hostage' at the police station. As he surmised that the Red Caps were killed soon after the crowd converged upon the police station, it appears not to have mattered to Gardiner that Sergeant Hamilton-Jewell did not have an Iridium phone, nor that the Red Caps' whereabouts was a secondary issue in the planning and execution of the rescue mission.

After 24 June 2003, much was made of the failure to give the Red Caps suitable equipment. They were responsible for their own security and communication procedures and for ensuring that they had an Iridium phone. As the signals officer Captain Tony Bosley told the inquest, Iridium phones were scarce but available when requested. Representatives of 156 Provo Company who comprised the Stay-Behind Party did not request one.

Warrant Officer Marley had the dignity to admit at the inquest, 'I was within the chain of command, so I would have to say that I did have a responsibility.'

Gardiner halted Warrant Officer Marley's statement: 'This is a coroner's court, not a court of law. In simple terms, if you feel your answer is incriminating, then you are not obliged to answer.'

Lance Corporal Keys' father Reg never took his eyes off Lieutenant Phillips as he gave evidence. To Reg's dismay, he told the court that he 'could not recall' whether or not he attended the crucial battle-group 'morning prayers' meeting on 24 June, when each unit gave an overview of its operations. Given the significance of the events that followed, and how many times he must have recalled the day, it is surprising he could not recall whether or not he was there.

Asked by the barrister representing the Red Cap families if he requested a satellite phone, Lieutenant Phillips said, 'I don't recall asking for one. I was aware there was a limited number and none left for the RMP call-signs.'

He was pressed: 'Battle-group orders clearly stated that patrols were supposed to take satellite phones.'

Lieutenant Phillips replied, 'I was not aware ... I cannot recall.' He added, 'I was not aware the Paras were going into the town that day. I would not regularly go to commanders and ask where their soldiers were going. I knew where my men were ...'

Lieutenant Colonel Bryn Parry-Jones (he had been promoted) was another interested observer as Lieutenant Phillips provided testimony. He sat cross-legged behind the Ministry of Defence's barristers. When the coroner called a halt to Lieutenant Phillips' evidence and the court began to clear for lunch, a figure appeared in the corner of Lieutenant Colonel Parry-Jones's eye. He stiffened visibly as the man approached.

Reg Keys stopped about a yard from the lieutenant colonel. He shook his fist. Reg was on the cusp of that moment when anger turns to desperation. 'My son! My son!' Reg's voice broke. 'My son died, Bryn, because you ...' Reg opened his body to face Lieutenant Phillips, 'left that man in charge!' Reg began to shake. He was pulled away from Lieutenant Colonel Parry-Jones in tears.

As the inquest continued, Major Kemp was asked, 'You would have thought it was important to know that each patrol knew where others were at all times?'

'No,' he replied. 'Because the environment was benign and their functions were different, there was no requirement for mutual support. He [Sergeant Hamilton-Jewell] was not part of C Company. He had different tasks, set by the battle group, not C Company. The RMP had their own chain of command, and patrol and section commanders. I was not aware the RMP were in Majar al-Kabir, only that there was a possibility and that they could be at the police station. I knew that the RMP desk in the operations room had been unable to locate them or communicate with them. I thought they would already have moved on to Qalat Salih or al-Uzayr. Even if I knew for certain where the RMPs were and whether they were alive, I would not have been able to rescue them. I would have needed another manoeuvre group to open up a new path via the left. We were under heavy fire from the sugar factory. It was only when B Company arrived and the CO [commanding officer] that we would have been able to advance. But by then the situation had been resolved. Everyone, alive or dead, was accounted for.'

Major Tootal concurred: 'The two patrols did not need to know the other was there because the situation was benign. The threat to us was considered to be extremely low.'

However, Major Tootal did highlight that battle-group orders stated all call-signs should take Iridium phones on patrol: 'I would expect all commanders to extract the relevant information. Their people [RMP hierarchy] were not following exactly what they should have been doing. It was their responsibility to know. It was copied to them. They should have been carrying Iridium phones because it was in the orders. If you couldn't get a phone or a vehicle, you spoke to your immediate commander. His job is to get those resources for you.

'At the time this happened, I did not know they were going without equipment [Iridium phones]. If I received information about this, I would have taken remedial action. But with 1,500 people in the battle group, it was the responsibility of subordinate commanders to check these things. We trust them. It's fundamental to how the army works.

'I refute any accusation that we treated non-paratroopers any differently. I went to the memorial service for these men. I felt regret and anger. You have to understand the context of what was going on in the ops room at the time. This was a highly complex unfolding operation, conducted at long range. There were 30 to 40 people in the room who were doing their best to establish communications. I assumed the RMP had an Iridium phone. With all the things going on – rocket-propelled grenades destroying vehicles, seven casualties aboard a helicopter, twelve dismounted troops running out of ammunition – we had to focus on certainty.

'We would have risked our lives to save them, whether they were our cap badge or not. But in battle you must focus on certainty. That doesn't mean we were ignoring the RMP. Lieutenant Kennedy would have gone to the police station had he known they were there. He was under fire with a broken-down vehicle, yet still he would have gone. Sergeant Robertson's multiple were not in a position to help, and later on the helicopter reported no untoward activity at the police station. Perhaps that supported assumptions that they were not there. In chaos, someone has to make simple decisions.'

The thesis that the Red Caps' deaths were neither preventable nor avoidable is unconvincing. Adherence to battle-group procedures and more effective communication between different units sharing the same area of operations could have prevented this tragedy – and the Ministry of Defence and the coroner should have acknowledged as much.

List of the Fallen

Corporal Stephen Allbutt, 35 – Queen's Royal Lancers 41
Sapper Luke Allsopp, 24 – Royal Engineers 31
Corporal Russ Aston, 30 – Royal Military Police 72
Major Matthew Bacon, 34 – Intelligence Corps 158
Major Steve Ballard, 33 – Royal Marines 58
Private Craig Barber, 20 – Royal Welsh 249
Sergeant Duane Barwood, 41 – Royal Air Force 261
Major Nick Bateson, 49 – Royal Corps of Signals 227
Sergeant John Battersby, 31 – Special Air Service 255
Leading Aircraftman Martin Beard, 20 – Royal Air Force Regiment 250
Fusilier Russell Beeston, 26 – King's Own Scottish Borderers 90
Second Lieutenant Jonathan Bracho-Cooke, 24 – Duke of Lancaster's
    Regiment 209
Lance Corporal Alan Brackenbury, 21 – King's Royal Hussars 150
Lance Corporal Dennis Brady, 37 – Royal Army Medical Corps 191
Lance Corporal Shaun Brierley, 28 – Royal Corps of Signals 59
Corporal Jeremy Brookes, 28 – Rifles 231
Nicholas Brown (rank not disclosed), 34 – Special Air Service 262
Chief Technician Richard Brown, 40 – Royal Air Force 134
Lance Corporal James Cartwright, 21 – 2 Royal Tank Regiment 234
Lance Sergeant Chris Casey, 27 – Irish Guards 252
Senior Aircraftman Matthew Caulwell, 22 – Royal Air Force Regiment 245
Colour Sergeant John Cecil, 35 – Royal Marines 13
Lieutenant Commander Darren Chapman, 40 – Royal Navy 175
Trooper David Clarke, 19 – Queen's Royal Lancers 41
Rifleman Daniel Coffey, 21 – Rifles 213
Sergeant Eddie Collins (age not disclosed) – Special Air Service 253

Marine Paul Collins, 21 – Royal Marines 175
Sergeant Paul Connolly, 33 – Royal Electrical and Mechanical Engineers 129
Corporal Matthew Cornish, 29 – Light Infantry 186
Corporal John Cosby, 27 – Devonshire and Dorset Light Infantry 184
Wing Commander John Coxen, 46 – Royal Air Force 175
Lance Corporal Andrew Craw, 21 – Argyll and Sutherland Highlanders 101
Staff Sergeant Simon Cullingworth, 36 – Royal Engineers 31
Signaller Paul Didsbury, 18 – Royal Corps of Signals 152
Private Eleanor Dlugosz, 19 – Royal Army Medical Corps 219
Captain David Dobson, 27 – Army Air Corps 175
Private Mark Dobson, 41 – Green Howards 147
Rifleman Paul Donnachie, 18 – Rifles 226
Lance Corporal Allan Douglas, 21 – Highlanders 169
Senior Aircraftman Christopher Dunsmore, 29 – Royal Air Force
    Regiment 245
Second Lieutenant Joanna Dyer, 24 – Intelligence Corps 219
Corporal Steve Edwards, 35 – Royal Tank Regiment 249
Staff Sergeant Sharron Elliott, 34 – Intelligence Corps 195
Private Lee Ellis, 23 – Parachute Regiment 172
Lance Bombardier Llewellyn Evans, 24 – Royal Artillery 13
Lance Corporal Paul Farrelly, 27 – Queen's Dragoon Guards 183
Guardsman Stephen Ferguson, 31 – Scots Guards 256
Private Marc Ferns, 21 – Black Watch 118
Trooper Lee Fitzsimmons, 26 – Special Air Service 255
Lance Corporal Timothy Flowers, 25 – Royal Electrical and Mechanical
    Engineers 247
Lance Corporal Ryan Francis, 23 – Royal Regiment of Wales 244
Fusilier Gordon Gentle, 19 – Royal Highland Fusiliers 111
Flight Sergeant Mark Gibson, 34 – Royal Air Force 134
Flight Lieutenant Kristian Gover, 30 – Royal Air Force 112
Sergeant Stuart Gray, 31 – Black Watch 126
Kingsman Alexander Green, 21 – Duke of Lancaster's Regiment 207
Lieutenant Philip Green, 30 – Royal Navy 19
Captain Philip Guy, 29 – Royal Marines 13
Sergeant Simon Hamilton-Jewell, 41 – Royal Military Police 72
Kingsman Jamie Hancock, 19 – Duke of Lancaster's Regiment 194
Major Paul Harding, 48 – Rifles 235
Leonard Harvey, 55 – Defence Fire Service (Army) 71
Marine Sholto Hedenskog, 26 – Royal Marines 13
Sergeant Les Hehir, 34 – Royal Artillery 13
Sergeant Graham Hesketh, 35 – Duke of Lancaster's Regiment 201
Private Phillip Hewett, 21 – Staffordshire Regiment 153

Sergeant Christian Hickey, 30 – Coldstream Guards 161

Sergeant Jonathan Hollingsworth, CGC, QGM, 35 – Special Air Service 200

Captain Richard Holmes, 28 – Parachute Regiment 172

Lance Corporal Sarah Holmes, 26 – Postal Courier and Movement
  Regiment 255

Warrant Officer Class 2 Lee Hopkins, 35 – Royal Corps of Signals 195

Lance Corporal of Horse Matty Hull, 25 – Blues and Royals 48

Lance Corporal Benjamin Hyde, 23 – Royal Military Police 72

Marine Jason Hylton, 33 – Royal Marines 195

Corporal Richard Ivell, 29 – Royal Electrical and Mechanical Engineers 105

Kingsman Alan Jones, 20 – Duke of Lancaster's Regiment 226

Captain David Jones, 29 – Queen's Lancashire Regiment 81

Sergeant John Jones, 31 – Royal Regiment of Fusiliers 163

Fusilier Stephen Jones, 22 – Royal Welsh Fusiliers 120

Acting Lance Corporal Steven Jones, 25 – Royal Corps of Signals 134

Corporal Paul Joszko, 28 – Royal Welsh 239

Private Andrew Kelly, 18 – Parachute Regiment 68

Private Scott Kennedy, 20 – Black Watch 239

Private James Kerr, 20 – Black Watch 239

Lance Corporal Thomas Keys, 20 – Royal Military Police 72

Lieutenant Antony King MiD, 35 – Royal Navy 19

Gunner David Lawrence, 25 – Royal Horse Artillery 122

Lieutenant Marc Lawrence, 26 – Royal Navy 19

Corporal Ben Leaning, 24 – Queen's Royal Lancers 224

Private Joseva Lewaicei, 25 – Royal Anglian Regiment 181

Rifleman Aaron Lincoln, 18 – Rifles 218

Captain James Linton, 43 – Royal Artillery 76

Corporal Paul Long, 24 – Royal Military Police 72

Private Paul Lowe, 19 – Black Watch 126

Marine Christopher Maddison, 24 – Royal Marines 54

Flight Lieutenant Kevin Main, 35 – Royal Air Force 25

Lance Corporal Ian Malone, 28 – Irish Guards 63

Fusilier Stephen Manning, 22 – Royal Regiment of Fusiliers 157

Squadron Leader Patrick Marshall, 39 – Royal Air Force 134

Captain Ken Masters, 40 – Royal Military Police 160

Private Scott McArdle, 22 – Black Watch 126

Lance Corporal James McCue, 27 – Royal Electrical and Mechanical
  Engineers 66

Senior Aircraftman Peter McFerran, 24 – Royal Air Force Regiment 245

Private Kevin McHale, 27 – Black Watch 124

Sergeant Mark McLaren, 27 – Royal Air Force 222

Fusilier Donal Meade, 20 – Royal Regiment of Fusiliers 157

Lieutenant Tom Mildinhall, 26 – Queen's Dragoon Guards 183
Corporal Simon Miller, 21 – Royal Military Police 72
Private Adam Morris, 19 – Royal Anglian Regiment 181
Staff Sergeant Chris Muir, 32 – Royal Logistics Corps 61
Flight Lieutenant Sarah-Jayne Mulvihill, 32 – Royal Air Force 175
Piper Christopher Muzvuru, 21 – Irish Guards 63
Master Engineer Gary Nicholson, 42 – Royal Air Force 134
Sergeant John Nightingale, 32 – Royal Logistics Corps 91
Corporal Ben Nowak, 27 – Royal Marines 195
Private Lee O'Callaghan, 20 – Princess of Wales's Royal Regiment 115
Sergeant Robert O'Connor, 38 – Royal Air Force 134
Corporal Kris O'Neill, 27 – Royal Army Medical Corps 219
Lieutenant Richard Palmer, 27 – Royal Scots Dragoon Guards 174
Flight Lieutenant Paul Pardoel, 35 – Royal Air Force 134
Sergeant Norman Patterson, 28 – Special Air Service 99
Corporal Ian Plank, 31 – Special Boat Service 94
Colour Sergeant Mark Powell, 37 – Special Air Service 222
Corporal Dewi Pritchard, 35 – Royal Military Police 87
Gunner Duncan Pritchard, 22 – Royal Air Force Regiment 70
Corporal Gordon Pritchard, 31 – Royal Scots Dragoon Guards 169
Private Christopher Rayment, 22 – Princess of Wales's Royal Regiment 113
Corporal Christopher Read, 22 – Royal Military Police 242
Lance Corporal Kirk Redpath, 22 – Irish Guards 252
Sergeant Wayne Rees, 36 – Queen's Royal Lancers 205
Corporal John Rigby, 24 – Rifles 236
Sergeant Steven Roberts, 33 – Royal Tank Regiment 36
Staff Sergeant Denise Rose, 34 – Royal Military Police 125
Operator Mechanic Ian Seymour, 29 – Royal Navy 13
Lance Corporal Karl Shearer, 24 – Household Cavalry Regiment 62
Second Lieutenant Richard Shearer, 26 – Staffordshire Regiment 153
Corporal David Shepherd, 34 – Royal Air Force Police 70
Private Luke Simpson, 21 – Yorkshire Regiment 211
Kingsman Adam Smith, 19 – Duke of Lancaster's Regiment 219
Flight Lieutenant Andrew Smith, 25 – Royal Air Force 134
Trooper Carl Smith, 23 – Royal Lancers (Prince of Wales's) 172
Private Jason Smith, 32 – King's Own Scottish Borderers 77
Private Leon Spicer, 26 – Staffordshire Regiment 153
Sergeant Mark Stansfield, 32 – Royal Logistics Corps 254
Flight Lieutenant David Stead, 35 – Royal Air Force 134
Major James Stenner MC, 30 – Special Air Service 99
Lance Corporal Barry Stephen, MiD, 31 – Black Watch 35
Warrant Officer Class 2 Mark Stratford, 39 – Royal Marines 13

Lieutenant Tom Tanswell, 27 – Regiment Royal Artillery 192
Corporal Marc Taylor, 27 – Royal Electrical and Mechanical Engineers 122
Private Michael Tench, 18 – Light Infantry 208
Lance Corporal Paul Thomas, 29 – Light Infantry 119
Private Ryan Thomas, 18 – Royal Regiment of Wales 94
Private Kevin Thompson, 21 – Combat Service Support Battalion 229
Sapper Robert Thomson, 22 – Royal Engineers 104
Gunner Lee Thornton, 22 – Regiment Royal Artillery 189
Major Matthew Titchener, 32 – Royal Military Police 87
Private Pita Tukutukuwaqa, 27 – Black Watch 129
Fusilier Kelan Turrington, 18 – Royal Regiment of Fusiliers 65
Trooper Kristen Turton, 27 – Queen's Royal Lancers 224
Lieutenant Alexander Tweedie, 25 – Blues and Royals 62
Rifleman Edward Vakabua, 23 – Rifles 242
Gunner Samuela Vanua, 27 – Regiment Royal Artillery 188
Guardsman Anthony Wakefield, 24 – Coldstream Guards 149
Warrant Officer Class 2 Colin Wall, 34 – Royal Military Police 87
Major Jason Ward, 34 – Royal Marines 13
Lieutenant Philip West, 32 – Royal Navy 19
Flight Lieutenant David Williams, 37 – Royal Air Force 25
Corporal David Williams, 37 – Royal Air Force 134
Lieutenant James Williams, 28 – Royal Navy 19
Lieutenant Andrew Wilson, 36 – Royal Navy 19
Kingsman Danny Wilson, 28 – Duke of Lancaster's Regiment 216
Corporal Rodney Wilson, 30 – Rifles 232
Rifleman Vincent Windsor, 23 – Royal Green Jackets 103
Gunner Stephen Wright, 20 – Regiment Royal Artillery 188
Private Johnathon Wysoczan, 21 – Staffordshire Regiment 214